MADAM, MBA

Perry Gretton

Copyright (C) 2015, Perisys Pty Ltd

All rights reserved. Without limiting the rights under this copyright, no part of this publication may be reproduced, stored in a retrieval system or transmitted in any form or by any means, electronic, mechanical, photocopying, recording or otherwise, without prior permission of Perisys Pty Ltd.

First published 2015

ISBN: 978-0-9923647-1-7

This book is a work of fiction. All characters in this novel are fictitious. Any resemblance to actual events or persons, living or dead, is entirely coincidental.

Cover design by Perry Gretton.

Where an excess of power prevails, property of no sort is duly respected. No man is safe in his opinions, his person, his faculties, or his possessions.

—James Madison, fourth US president

I will tell you: he beat me grievously in the shape of a woman; for in the shape of man, Master Brook, I fear not Goliath with a weaver's beam; because I know also life is a shuttle.

—William Shakespeare,
The Merry Wives of Windsor, Act V

1. Over the threshold...

Maria Russo hauled down the roller door, locked it, and passed the car keys to Gina.

"Hang on to these, you'll need 'em."

"Not for long, I hope."

Gina dropped the keys into her handbag and smoothed down her skirt. She hadn't worn her navy blue business suit since she'd worked at the bank. Thankfully it still fitted after two years.

Her mother set off round the corner into Tolley Street and she started after her, before pausing to retrieve mirrored sunglasses and a headscarf from her bag.

When she caught up, they linked arms. Maria glanced at her and laughed.

"Are you that worried someone will recognise you?" Gina didn't answer. "You do still want to go through with this, don't you?"

"Ignore the cloak-and-dagger stuff, it just makes me feel more comfortable, that's all." She wasn't going to give her mother any excuse to put off her operation. However, there was no point in drawing attention to herself. She had her future career to think of. "It's only for a few days, I'm sure I'll manage."

She'd never walked along Tolley Street before. A typically quiet Surry Hills thoroughfare, it comprised a mixture of Victorian terrace houses—some well-maintained with ornate iron lace fences and balcony railings; others in obvious need of repair—interspersed with new apartment blocks. The traffic noise from busy Crown Street nearby hardly carried.

Despite her show of confidence, she became increasingly apprehensive with each step. She'd not forgotten her mother's words earlier: "These are tough women. It's not like the bank. You'll have your work cut out keeping them in line."

She recognised the challenge and intended to meet it. She'd been a manager before, and now she had an MBA, a prestigious one at that, to back her up. Besides, the staff would be obliged to respect her if only for her mother's sake.

As they drew closer to Casa Rosa, she said, "So I'm about to step into a nest of vipers."

"Don't dramatise. If you'd given me more time, I would have found someone to cover for me eventually."

Gina stopped suddenly. Her mother almost lost her balance, with her daughter's arm still linked to hers. "Eventually! It's not something you put off, Mama, it's too serious for that. The longer it's ignored, the worse it could get."

"It'll turn out to be nothing at all, you wait and see."

The two women continued on their way.

"You're in pain, Mama, so it's not nothing at all."

Maria pointed to a building across the street.

"We're there now."

She'd seen photos before, but this was the first time she'd been anywhere near the building. Casa Rosa comprised a pair of graceful, three-storey sandstone terraces situated between the offices of an accountant and an interior designer. The woodwork was freshly painted in dusky rose and black gloss. Two window boxes at ground level featured well-tended geraniums.

As they crossed the road, her mother called out, "Morning, Aldo" to a man entering the interior designer's office.

He gave her a friendly wave. "Morning, Maria." Gina wondered if he thought she was a staff member or, much worse, one of the escorts.

They approached the front door.

She held back while her mother pressed the bell. A moment passed before she heard the buzz of the electric lock being released. The door slowly opened. Glancing up and down the street, Gina hurriedly followed her mother over the threshold.

2. The campaign begins

Crispin Calloway, proprietor of the Monitor News Corporation, had a phone to his ear when Frank McAllister, features editor, and Larry Anderson, editor-in-chief and Frank's immediate superior, arrived at his ninth-floor office. He waved them to take a seat and continued talking for ten minutes. After the call was over, he stood and stretched his back.

"I've just had a chat with Koski, our esteemed Police Minister. Seems that now the Moral Australia Party controls the upper house, the government's under pressure to crack down on brothels. He's suggested we do an exposé on the industry, focusing on how illegal immigrants are being exploited, to get the public to see it's a real issue."

"And then they'll be covered in brownie points when they take action," Frank said.

"Of course." Calloway sketched a few ideas as he paced from one side of the office to the other, causing both men to turn their heads like fairground clowns to keep him in view.

"The Feds reckon there are five hundred illegals working in Sydney brothels."

He returned to his desk and stood behind his high-backed leather chair. He looked from Frank to

Larry and back again. "We need to move fast on this one."

Frank nodded his agreement. "It's been a while since we did a tom-bashing piece. If we get the story out before the police take action, it'll look as if we're setting the agenda."

"Good." Calloway eased himself into his chair and sat back, hands placed together as if in prayer. "Let's say two weeks, three at the outside."

Frank groaned inwardly. It would be a real struggle, but complaining was pointless. He turned to Larry. "All my people are tied up on other stuff and we still haven't wrapped up this week's stories. I'd put Isobel onto it—it's her territory—but she's on leave next week. Can you find me a couple of people to do some legwork?"

Frank knew he was understaffed everywhere, so whoever he nominated would be released under sufferance.

Larry mulled over the request. "Leave it with me—I'll see what I can do."

~~~

Larry provided Frank with two cadets: Lucy Lo, from the sports desk, and Daniel Bouvier, who worked for Andrea Kennedy, the Social Diary editor. They'd been on staff for eighteen months. Frank would have preferred more experienced reporters and said so.

"You're lucky to get them," Larry said. "Andrea is spitting chips. Reckons she'll be struggling without Daniel."

"What's so special about him?"

"His socialite mum. She moves in the right circles and so does he. He passes the juice on to Andrea. Even though I promised she'd have him back in a fortnight, she still gave me heaps. If you see her putting anything in my coffee, let me know."

"I'd better watch my coffee as well."

As Larry was leaving Frank's office, he said, "Oh and make sure he gets his hands dirty."

"Why?"

"His mother persuaded Calloway to take him on. Seems she used to work here one time."

"Bouvier...? Yes, I remember Yvonne. Great photographer. Classy lady, too."

"Maybe, but I don't like that kind of influence, so work his arse off."

~~~

Frank introduced the cadets at the kick-off meeting in his office.

Daniel looked relaxed and confident, which was reassuring. Whether he'd prove to be a help or a handicap remained to be seen. Seated alongside him, Lucy appeared small and slight. They contrasted in other ways—Lucy, bespectacled, pen poised, expression alert and watchful; Daniel, sandy-haired, half lounging in his chair, legs crossed at the ankle, an unopened writing pad placed on his lap.

Frank wondered what Isobel, sitting across from them, was thinking. She was his most experienced reporter and a first-class investigator, efficient to the point of cutting corners and disregarding rules when it suited her. Right now she was appraising Daniel, and judging by the way she touched her short blonde hair he passed muster.

He waited until he had their full attention. "Okay, two things to bear in mind." His eyes were on Daniel and Lucy as he spoke. "First, we don't want our opposition to find out what we're up to. Tell nobody, not even your closest friends, okay?" He waited for their acknowledgement. "Second, unlicensed brothels are run by nasty bastards who peddle drugs, run extortion rackets, exploit women, and god knows what else, so you don't want to get on their wrong side.

"Also, no-one will want to talk to us. Most illegals aren't allowed off the premises unless they're chaperoned by heavies. If you do talk to one, she'll clam up, because she won't want to be deported."

Lucy cleared her throat to catch his attention. "Would they be allowed to stay if they cooperated with the authorities?"

"That's the Immigration Department, and they deport them as soon as they're caught. That's the law."

"Can't the police do something?"

"They're understaffed and have bigger fish to fry. However, the Feds and the state police have just started an investigation, which is why we need to move immediately. Calloway wants it wrapped up in two weeks."

"I'm away next week," Isobel said.

"Then you're going to be busy this week." He turned back to Lucy and Daniel. "Any ideas on how we should proceed?"

Tentatively, Daniel said, "Maybe we could infiltrate an illegal brothel."

"And how would you go about doing that?"

Daniel shrugged.

Isobel said, "Seeing as these joints are mostly operated by Asians, the only one who'd stand half a chance would be Lucy." She regarded the girl through half-closed eyes. "How do you feel about working as a prossie, love?"

Lucy reared back. "Me?" Her face reddened as she shifted in her seat.

Frank moved quickly to pacify her. "Don't worry, Lucy, we'd never ask you to do anything like that." He gave Isobel a hard look.

"Sorry, Frank." She looked anything but remorseful.

"You need to do as much legwork as you can until you go on leave. Take Daniel with you. Meanwhile, Lucy, I want you to come up with a complete list of every brothel, licensed or otherwise, in the city. I want to know where they are located and who owns them."

~~~

Isobel and Daniel sat side by side at her desk. Daniel had his notepad open waiting for instructions, but the first thing she said was, "You friendly with Lucy?"

"Not particularly, why?"

"She was lucky to get the job, don't you think?"

"Really?" Lucy had always struck him as being bright and talented. In fact, if the truth were known, she was better qualified than he was.

"Yeah, we get plenty of candidates for cadetships and loads of Aussies apply."

Daniel glanced at Isobel and chose not to say anything.

"But it's positive discrimination. Give the job to a foreigner just because she's not white."

"Lucy was born in Strathfield, and has a first in Communications. I only managed a second."

Isobel sat up straight and became businesslike. "Okay, let's start. How are we going to infiltrate the triads?"

"Triads?"

She smiled. "Only joking. Believe me, we're going nowhere near those bastards." She pivoted in her chair so she faced him. "The first thing we do is chat with some of those street girls, but not when they're busy, and not when their pimps are around either. We'll probably need to pay them something, otherwise they'll tell us to piss off. I'll have a word with Frank about expenses."

"Do you reckon they know what's going on?"

"Some are bound to. That kind of thing is hard to hide at street level. Also, I know a few lowlifes who could give us leads. They've helped me in the past." She gave him a sly look. "Had any experience of prostitution before?"

"No," he said, and with more emphasis, "None at all."

"Good. In that case, you have a lot to learn. Should be fun."

He wasn't so sure about that, but he needed to look keen. "When do we start?"

Isobel grabbed her bag, pushed her chair away, and got to her feet. "Right now. We'll grab a bite to eat and then take a stroll round the Cross."

3. *Searching for aliens*

Isobel and Daniel spent two days patrolling the areas where the street girls hustled for business and approached as many as they could, but were given short shrift, the girls making it plain they wanted no media attention.

"These streets used to swarm with toms before they legalised brothels," Isobel said. "The ones you see now are druggies or just bad news. Not even the underground brothels will have a bar of them."

The few leads they did receive weren't substantial enough to follow up without corroboration, which wasn't forthcoming, so Isobel decided on a different approach. She knew people who owed her a favour, she said, and it was time she called one in.

~~~

They sat side by side in a coffee shop in Kings Cross, well back from the window, where they'd been waiting for half-an-hour to meet someone known only as Robbie. Daniel had grown tired of studying the no-frills decor. The place hadn't seen a fresh coat of paint since Federation. A sole waitress attended to the few customers.

"Great place to meet people," he said. Isobel gave him a dismissive look.

Although the coffee tasted like it had stewed since the previous day, he ordered another while Isobel called Robbie on her mobile phone for the third time.

"Where the hell are you? I can't sit around here all day, I've got a job to do...Well, get a move on...You're in the TAB, aren't you?...I can hear the race being called...For fuck's sake, Robbie!" She stabbed the end call button and dropped the mobile into her handbag. "You wouldn't read about it—the bastard has a bet on. Fuckin' gamblers..."

When she'd calmed down, she said, "So what made you want to be a journo?"

"It was my careers master's suggestion. I told him I didn't want to be stuck in an office all day. I was good at English and fancied being an investigative reporter—digging up the dirt on shonky politicians, uncovering fraud in high places—but I've been stuck on the Social Diary since I joined."

"If you think being an investigative reporter is glamorous, you've another think coming. It's hard yakka. You need your wits about you all the time. Ever see *All the President's Men*?"

He nodded.

"Thought so. Bet you see yourself as Bob Woodward."

"Maybe. I've seen the *Superman* movies, too."

"Uh-oh, I'm not playing Lois Lane to your Clark Kent." She became serious. "Close your eyes for a minute"

"What for?"

"Just close 'em. Now, keep your eyes shut and tell me how many customers are here besides us."

He remembered passing three men sitting at a table near the door when they arrived, and two young women who'd come in shortly after. Also a young man eyeing up the women as they sat down.

"Er...six?"

"Now open them and tell me again."

He looked around and realised he'd failed to account for an old man sitting at a table behind the open door. "Okay, seven."

"If you want to be a gun reporter, you need to be as sharp as a cop at a murder scene."

"Point taken. I thought you were checking my x-ray vision."

A minute later, a portly, middle-aged man bustled in and headed straight for Isobel's table. Panting with exertion, he flopped in the chair opposite and removed his cap to fan himself. "Sorry about that," he said, "but I was onto a sure thing."

"And was it?"

"Nah, came second. But I had it on each way." He gave her an apprehensive smile, which was not reciprocated, and wiped his forehead with the cap.

Isobel said, "Robbie, this is my colleague, Daniel. He's helping me research an article."

Robbie nodded towards Daniel and winked at Isobel, "Nice work if you can get it."

"Do your winnings cover the price of a coffee?"

Without waiting for an answer, she summoned the waitress, who took the order and gave the table a quick wipe with a damp cloth. Isobel waited until she'd left. "Robbie, you still work for those chinks in Darlo?"

"If you mean them Vietnamese blokes, no I don't. They use their own people now. But I still do a few favours for some others. Why d'you want to know?"

"We're doing an article on illegal brothels. We're getting nowhere at the moment. It's a closed shop, as you well know."

"And you think I can help?" He didn't look pleased at the prospect.

"You owe me one, Robbie."

He looked around the café before answering. "I might, but the people you're talking about don't sit around sewing quilts for refugees. If anybody dobs 'em in, well… it's goodbye, cruel world."

"I know, and of course I'll keep your name out of it, but could those joints you're working for be involved in any way?"

"Not as far as I know, and if they were, I wouldn't tell you, would I? I don't want a knife in me back. Anyway, a bloke's got to earn a living."

"Even if it supports sex slavery? That's what we're really on about here, isn't it? I can't believe a bloke like you wouldn't know a few addresses."

Robbie glanced around again before replying. "You know where Denfield Street is?" She nodded. "There's a place run by foreigners, not Asians though—might be Yugoslavs or Russians—they definitely have illegals."

"Asians?"

"Oh yes, all of 'em, I think."

"And you know for sure they're illegals?"

"No doubt about it."

"How can you be so sure?"

Robbie wiped his brow with his cap. "Let's just say I know, all right?"

"Don't fuck me about. I'm not letting you out of here until you tell me."

Daniel felt a twinge of sympathy for the man. Isobel had menace in her tone.

Though she continued to watch him intently, Robbie wouldn't answer.

"All right, if you're so sure, you're obviously involved in some way." When he still remained silent, she said, "Okay, who is she? One of the girls? Is that who you're screwing these days? Payment for services rendered, perhaps?"

"No, course not."

Isobel snorted contemptuously.

He sighed. "Okay, okay, it's my daughter. She works there as a receptionist."

"What number Denfield?"

"Seventeen. And if you hear it's going to be raided, let me know straightaway so I can get Wendy out of there."

~~~

After Robbie left, Daniel said, "Why did he owe you a favour?"

Isobel took her time before answering, as if unsure what to tell him. "In this business you get to hear a lot of things that don't make it into the papers for one reason or another—usually because we don't want to get slapped with a defamation writ. And some of what you hear, if you had a mind to, could be passed on to the right people and they'd pay you very well for it."

She lowered her voice. "Robbie nicked a briefcase belonging to perhaps the biggest crim in Sydney. He didn't know whose it was when he pinched it, of course, or he'd never have done it.

When he opened it and realised who it belonged to, he nearly shit himself. It contained a wad of money and some other material, which he thought I'd be interested in. But I wasn't going anywhere near it.

"I told him if he was fingered as the thief he wouldn't live to see Christmas. I also promised to keep schtum about it, as long as he returned the occasional favour."

"So what happened to the briefcase?"

"At the bottom of the harbour with some bricks in it, according to Robbie, minus the money I suspect."

"So what do we do now?"

"First, we stake out Denfield Street. We need to photograph everyone who goes in and out so we can decide who's the likely owner and who are staff."

"Then what?"

"Then you're going to pay them a visit."

"Me?"

"Of course. You're much better equipped to pass as a punter than I am."

He didn't know what to say. The thought had briefly crossed his mind, to be dismissed because he assumed his junior status would rule him out.

She smiled at his discomfort and patted him on the shoulder in mock sympathy. "I wish I could stick around to give you moral support, Superman, but I'm on leave all next week." She got to her feet. "Oh, and welcome to the world of investigative journalism."

~~~

Larry often dropped by Frank's office in the evening as he was about to head home. Frank looked forward to these sessions. They marked the winding down of the day's affairs, although he usually stayed on for another hour or so anyway. They would discuss the latest news, politics, and whatever was going on in the *Monitor*'s offices.

"Have you noticed," Larry said, "how Calloway seems more wound up these days?"

Frank scowled. "I could do without him taking so much interest in my area. Ever since the last election he's been on about resurrecting the old campaigns, like this brothels one." Calloway, an evangelical Christian, had built the *Daily Monitor's* circulation on similar crusades without sparing readers the salacious details.

"You think it's anything to do with the Moral Australia mob?"

"Odds on."

They, along with many commentators, had been surprised at the sudden rise of MAP. At the previous election, four years earlier, it hadn't won a single seat; now it had five in the upper house. As the two major parties had the same number of seats, MAP enjoyed the balance of power, and both parties needed to cosy up to them to gain support.

Frank said, "Calloway could easily be involved without it being obvious. I've been looking at MAP and their organisation structure is typically nebulous. Did you know they're set up as a private company?"

Larry shook his head. "Can they do that?"

"Presumably, or someone would have objected to it by now. Anyway, MAP has money coming in from the usual church groups but nowhere near enough to finance an election campaign. That points to one or two well-heeled donors hiding in the shadows...like our beloved leader, for example.

They're the kind of mob he'd run with. However, what's really bothering me is the Convinzi Trust."

"The what?"

"Exactly. I doubt anyone's heard of them, but they have a common director with MAP. They're also on the fringe of the fringe—like, for example, wanting to ban non-Christian religions from worshipping in public."

Larry nodded. "Muslims, in other words."

"And Jews."

After Larry left his office, Frank continued his research on the Internet. The more he uncovered, the more concerned he became. It wasn't too much of a stretch to believe the Convinzi Trust was using MAP as a respectable front for its own agenda.

4. On the job

Gina removed her sunglasses and looked around the foyer. Against the facing wall stood two half-moon mahogany tables supporting urns filled with gold, orange, and pink calla lilies. Gilt-edged mirrors and framed prints of elegant courtesans hung on the lavender-pink walls. Above her, a crystal chandelier cast a warm glow against the moulded ceiling. A wide, curved rosewood reception desk occupied almost an entire wall to her right.

The sound of passing traffic was barely noticeable, blocked by the heavily-curtained windows and solid front door. The lilies' fragrance added to an air of refinement.

So here was where her mother spent her days. For some reason she'd expected it to be more like a doctor's surgery with clients waiting on rows of seats. There wasn't a soul in sight except for a solidly-built woman of about forty sitting behind the desk. Seeing Gina she looked up and smiled.

Her mother introduced them. "You've heard me talk about Liz. She's been with us for nine years," she said proudly.

"And hated every minute of it," Liz replied, with feigned resentment.

"So why do you come in every day?"

Liz winked at Gina. "I have a rotten memory."

Maria asked if anyone was working.

"Juliet's in room three. Kelly has a ten-thirty booking, Chloe one at eleven. Baz's gone to fetch the milk."

As they moved away from the desk, Maria said, "It's our quiet time of day, so we just have one receptionist on. I'll give you a quick tour later, but first, coffee."

In the kitchen, Gina's attention was caught by a television showing a news update. Had the news presenter just mentioned something about brothels? She picked up the remote control and increased the volume.

"...determined to crack down on sex slavery in New South Wales. The Police Minister, Colin Koski, said today that a special task force had been set up to work with the Federal Police and the Department of Immigration to track down and prosecute the people responsible. In other news..."

She turned the volume back down. "Did you hear that, Ma?"

"Ignore it," Maria said, as she put the kettle on. "They're always saying what they're going to do, it's easier than actually doing it. Anyway, I'm running a legal business."

A young black man with a heavyweight boxer's physique arrived carrying four cartons of milk. He wore a red and green banded jersey stretched tight over his deep chest and a pair of khaki cargo pants. He flashed Gina a wide grin before saying to Maria, "Looks like I've timed it right—I could just go a cuppa."

"Gina, this is Barry Radebe, my gentle giant."

He gave her another big smile. "Your mum's always on about you."

"Baz drives the girls when they do outcalls," Maria said, "and does a few odd jobs and errands for me as well."

Baz's eyes were fixed on Gina. "Did you like America? My sister lives in San Francisco."

She detected traces of a foreign accent and recalled her mother saying he'd been born in South Africa. "I enjoyed it, but I didn't go to San Fran. All my time was spent in Boston."

"I'm hoping to visit my sister next year. We got split up when we were kids, see, and we've not seen each other since."

"But you keep in touch?"

"We write and sometimes talk on the phone."

His parents were killed when thieves broke into their house, she remembered. He'd been sent to live with an aunt in Sydney, who more or less left him to bring himself up.

As they sat at the table sipping their drinks, Maria said to Gina, "If you ever have trouble with clients, get Baz or Jock—our other driver—to come and help you. But don't call the police unless you really have to—I don't want to be charged with keeping a disorderly house and lose my licence."

Seeing the concerned look on Gina's face, Baz said, "Don't worry, it's not that bad. We haven't had trouble for a long time, have we, Maria?"

"Not since that sailor. He was an animal. Nearly bit Amber's ear off, and then he bashed her because she screamed."

"What happened to him?" Gina asked.

"Baz sorted him out"

"Goes against my principles, see, hitting people, but sometimes—" He clenched a fist and mocked throwing a punch, "—they need a little re-education."

Despite Baz's reassuring size, she remained apprehensive.

~~~

In her office, Maria explained her accounting system. Gina found it difficult to follow.

"It's time you bought a computer, Ma."

"I don't need one of those things? Alfred's perfectly happy with how I keep my books and he's an accountant."

"But it would be so much quicker and you could analyse how the business was going day by day and do cash flows and budgets and…I dunno, lots of things," Gina said.

"I'm used to doing things my way," Maria said in a tone that didn't invite further discussion. "Now, on the off-chance you have to take on a new girl, make sure they look and smell clean. Check for drug use, particularly heroin. Look at their arms, legs, buttocks, in between their fingers and toes, any place they can inject themselves, and if they refuse, tell 'em to bugger off. They're not shrinking violets. Don't be afraid to touch them either—some of them use makeup to cover the tracks."

This was getting too much for Gina. "I can't go touching their backsides!"

"It's simple enough. Just ask them to lift their skirts and take a close look. Nobody puts makeup on her bum unless she has something to hide."

Her head reeled as her mother continued to detail the recruitment procedure.

"...and then make sure they understand they're self-employed and must pay their own tax and insurance. All we do is rent our rooms to them. Finally—"

"Whoa, Ma, let me catch my breath. Is all this written down?" Gina wished she'd taken notes. She also wished she hadn't said the day before that managing the place couldn't be that hard.

Maria shook her head impatiently. "Of course not, why should it be? I already know what I'm doing. Also, don't forget to make them read the rule book—it's in that drawer over there—and sign a non-disclosure agreement."

"A what?" She knew what it was, but this was a brothel, not a corporation.

"We don't want them telling anybody what goes on in here. Discretion is the name of this game or we're out of business."

More than ever, Gina hoped her stint as a brothel manager would be short-lived.

~~~

That afternoon, after being shown where the supplies were kept, how to operate the equipment in the laundry, and sundry other tasks that Maria remembered at the last minute, Gina drove her mother to the hospital and stayed with her until she was allocated a room.

Maria placed her case on one of the two beds. "I hope I get the room to myself."

As she was speaking, a nurse came in bearing a clipboard and a hospital-issue backless gown. "You'll be lucky, my love. Now, if you wouldn't mind getting undressed and putting this on."

She received the gown in both hands as if it were an offering.

The nurse said, "You can hang your clothes in the wardrobe, and put your other things in the bedside locker." She gave Maria a reassuring smile. "They'll be quite safe."

Maria dropped the gown on the bed and turned to Gina. "Here…" She removed her necklace, earrings, and wristwatch. "Look after these for me."

Gina took the jewellery and briefly examined the necklace before dropping it in her handbag. She'd bought the chain and eagle-shaped pendant from a respected silversmiths in Martha's Vineyard.

The nurse went through the standard routine to confirm a patient's identity, concluding with, "And you're in for…?"

"They're going to look at my left kidney."

Gina shuddered at the thought.

The nurse made some notes and attached an identification tag to Maria's wrist. "Right, I'll be back in five minutes."

"They keep asking me the same questions," her mother said, after the nurse left.

"That's for your benefit, Ma. You don't want to have your leg amputated instead."

"Look, you might as well get back to work. Let them see you'll be in and out all the time. Keep 'em on their toes." She opened her handbag and took out a bunch of keys. "Before I forget, these are the keys to the building and the filing cabinet."

"Anything else?"

"I think that's it."

Gina gave her a hug. "Call me if you need anything, Mama. I'll be back in the morning to see how you're getting on."

"Stop worrying about me."

"Of course I worry about you—you're the only mother I have. And behave yourself—don't go bossing the nurses around."

She had good reason to worry. Her mother had been reluctant to seek treatment for her obvious pain, claiming it would clear up of its own accord. If Gina hadn't returned from the States when she did, her mother would still be in denial, and who knew where that might have led. It had been Gina's insistence she went for the MRI scan that revealed a growth. "Bossy boots," Maria had called her beforehand, which was rich coming from her.

As Gina headed for the door, Maria said, "One more thing. Keep an eye on Jock's timekeeping. He uses a calendar instead of a clock. I've warned him but he'll try to take advantage while I'm away. And make sure Mrs Danby waters the lilies each week. The poor old thing keeps forgetting."

"Mrs Danby?"

"The cleaner. She's seventy-four and can still touch her toes. I wish I could say the same."

~~~

Gina returned to Casa Rosa and found the place busier than when she'd left. A client sat staring at the wall-mounted TV in one of the waiting rooms. A red-haired girl in a short skirt that barely concealed her buttocks shepherded another client up the stairs.

In the reception area, a short, slim brunette dressed in a tight-fitting pink jumper sat next to Liz.

"This is Jos," Liz said.

"Hello, Gina." Jos had a high-pitched, little girl voice. She jumped up and came round the desk, setting her large silver hoop earrings swinging. She wore a skirt banded in primary colours, and pink stockings with silver ankle-length boots. "I've been dying to meet you. Your mum's always talking about you."

Her mother had said Jos could be "a bit scatty" at times but she looked at Gina in such a disarmingly bright and admiring way that Gina warmed to her immediately.

Liz said, "Jos's dressed down today. You should see her when she's feeling cheery."

"Oh, Liz, you know I'm always cheerful." She ran back to the desk as a call came through.

"I see you're busy," Gina said.

Liz said, "At this time of day, especially Saturdays, we get a bit of a rush on. Not all the girls have turned up yet, either."

So far, Gina hadn't met any of the girls, and it wasn't a prospect she was looking forward to. She went through to the office and removed her headscarf. Her first task was to examine the account books.

She spent half-an-hour flitting between pages of numbers before she had the hang of her mother's system. It wasn't conventional double-entry bookkeeping, more a hybrid journal and cash book. She couldn't imagine working with it all the time.

Feeling satisfied with her efforts, she strolled down the hallway to the kitchen to get herself a drink.

"Hi, you must be Gina."

The voice came from behind her. She turned to see an attractive Asian girl in an emerald silk cheongsam walking towards her down the hall.

"Liz said you were here. I'm Chloe." Her smile was warm and reassuring, revealing small, perfect teeth. "How's your mum?"

"She's okay. They're operating on her first thing in the morning."

"Is it serious?"

"I don't know. If it hadn't been for the specialist insisting she went in straightaway, I wouldn't be so worried."

"Your mum's as tough as teak, I'm sure she'll be all right."

As they entered the kitchen, Gina saw a blonde of about her own age sitting at the table reading a magazine. She wore a tight pink tee-shirt embossed with a yellow frangipani flower.

Chloe introduced her as Kellie.

Gina poured herself a coffee and sat at the table. She studied the two women. Neither met her expectation of what a prostitute looked or sounded like. They were too, for want of a better word, normal. The Asian girl could easily pass as a hostess for Singapore Airlines with her perfectly made-up face and demure appearance. By contrast, Kellie was a typical fresh-faced Aussie girl. Gina could imagine her tossing a surfboard into the ocean and paddling out to catch a wave.

She resisted the temptation to ask why they worked as escorts, not wanting to come across as judgemental. Sipping her coffee she listened as the girls chatted. Kellie glanced in her direction a few times, as if about to draw her into their conversation, but Liz came into the room and caught Chloe's eye. "Okay, princess, Mr Roberts is here to see you."

After Chloe left, Kellie said, "Beautiful, isn't she?"

"And so elegant."

Kellie looked at her expectantly. "I bet you're wondering why she's working here?"

Gina gave an apologetic smile. "Am I that obvious? I suppose it's the money."

"Well, she wouldn't do it for free. No, it's men. She hates 'em. It's her way of getting back at her husband. He was screwing around behind her back. Kept denying it, of course. Then one day she caught him shagging her best mate in their bedroom and threw him out. Says she'll never trust another bloke again for as long as she lives."

Gina smiled again briefly. She hadn't detected any bitterness in Chloe and the idea that someone who hated men would work so intimately with them made no sense to her. But what did she know?

"Most men aren't like that. How long was she married?"

"Four years. Still is—she's not given the maggot a divorce." Kellie chuckled. "She'll make him wait it out and in the meantime he's married to a hooker. How about that! Neat, eh?"

She studied Kellie. How did she manage to retain her vitality working in this industry? "What about you? Are you in it just for the money?"

"Well, it is pretty good, at least for someone like me. I'd rather do this than work for, like, fifteen bucks an hour in a milk bar."

"But considering how you earn it, is it really worth it?"

Kellie gave her an odd look and weighed the question before answering.

"I can only speak for myself. The hours don't bother me, and up to a point they're flexible. I don't mind the blokes either—most of them, anyway—and some of them are really, really nice, buying me presents and stuff. You wouldn't believe some of the things they give me—really expensive stuff sometimes, like Chanel No. 5. One bloke bought me a real pashmina scarf once. Said he bought it in Iran. I gave it to Mum." She smiled as a thought came to her. "Have you met Holly yet…"

Gina shook her head.

"She used to work in a shoe shop. Reckons she spent more time on her knees there than what she does here."

Gina couldn't help laughing. She became serious again. "Don't you worry about what people think of you?"

"Not much. I don't advertise it."

Her acceptance of sex work puzzled Gina. Surrendering her dignity and her body to the whims of a stranger—the thought repulsed her. She'd rather dig ditches.

"Supposing you couldn't do this sort of work, what would you do?"

Kellie twisted strands of her shoulder-length hair around her slender fingers as she thought the question over.

"One of the clubs, I guess. Topless or lap-dancing … something like that, but they might not take me on—there's this scar down my side…" She pointed to her left flank, "…where I was scalded when

I was a kid. One thing's for sure, there's no way I'd ever work in a shop or an office."

"But one day you'll be too old for this and then what?"

Kellie laughed. "I'll find some rich old bugger and talk him into marrying me. Then I'd keep feeding him loads of fatty food and shag him to death." She became serious again, pushing her hair back from her face with both hands. "I never think that far ahead, to be honest. I guess I'll take my chances when the time comes. I might even go back to uni and finish my degree. Your mum says you have one."

Gina didn't want to sound smug, but she couldn't resist answering, "Two, in fact."

Kellie's face broke into another grin as she indicated their surroundings with a wave of her hands. "Yeah, and look where they've landed you."

Gina recoiled as if slapped in the face. The remark had brought her fears to the surface again. She leaned over and hissed, "Yes, but they haven't landed me on my back with my legs open, have they?"

Seeing Kellie's smile dissolve into confusion, she jumped to her feet, grabbed her coffee mug and took it to the sink, where she slammed it onto the draining board.

As she marched out of the kitchen, she called out, "Make no mistake—as soon as my mother's back, I'm out of here."

5. Chloe

When she started at Casa Rosa it never occurred to Chloe that it might reflect badly on Bernie, her estranged husband. Kellie was the one who'd seen the poetic justice in the situation and brought it to her attention. She tried to set the record straight, but Kellie took no notice and continued to dramatise her life story.

She didn't despise men. For the most part, she'd grown indifferent to them, but she liked a few regular customers, and some she genuinely looked forward to, like Mr Roberts for instance. For the past year she'd been his first choice of companion. "You Asian girls know how to look after a man," he'd told her. "Not like Western girls, always needing to be told how wonderful they are." She could easily have disabused him of that notion but preferred to keep him on side.

Mr Roberts was a Londoner who'd lived most of his life in Australia. He was eighty-one: a tall, angular, and slightly stooped figure who, regardless of the time of year, dressed in a sports coat, cardigan, shirt and tie, and always removed his hat when he entered the building. He'd been coming to Casa Rosa for three years and everyone liked him.

She had no idea what his first name was; he was known to all as Mr Roberts and it seemed presumptuous to ask him. He once told her he'd started visiting Casa Rosa a few months after his wife died. His previous brothel experience had been in France at the end of the Second World War before he was married. "My wife was a very sexy lady," he said, "I had no need to play away from home."

Usually when she led him into the bedroom, he would start to tell her one of his many wartime tales. Sometimes he acted out the parts with such enthusiasm that he forgot the purpose of his visit until she found an opportunity to remind him. With little time left, he would settle for a kiss and depart only a little regretfully.

Today, he was subdued.

"Everything all right, Mr Roberts? You seem a bit quiet."

He squeezed her hand. "Sorry, Chloe. I nearly fell over on the way here. Slipped in the wet...tweaked a muscle, I think." He patted his right side. "Shook me up a bit."

"No worries. I'll massage it for you if you like."

He took off his jacket and with some difficulty lay face down on the bed, tugging his shirt and pullover out of the way to expose his midriff.

While she rubbed body lotion into his side, it occurred to her that a job as a masseuse could be worth considering for the future, once she'd saved enough to gain a degree of independence. She couldn't remain a sex worker for ever, even if she wanted to do, and she didn't.

She helped Mr Roberts to his feet and led him downstairs. He said he felt much better and kissed her on the cheek as she let him out of the building. She went back to the kitchen and found Kellie in earnest conversation with Holly.

"I like your hair," she said to Holly, whose spiky hair was newly dyed red.

"Yeah, thanks. You heard what Gina said to Kellie?"

"When?"

"Just now."

Unusual for her, Kellie looked chastened. She gave a brief account of her conversation with Gina. "And then she went fuckin' apeshit. Jumped right down my throat as though it was my fault she's working here. Then she swore at me and stormed out."

"Oh dear, Kell. I thought she'd be like her mum."

"If she's going to treat us like shit, she can get fucked. I can easily find somewhere else to work."

"Me too," said Holly.

Chloe didn't like the sound of that. Casa Rosa was one of the best houses in the business. Where would she find another place as comfortable and well run?

"Not fair on Maria, though, finding us all gone when she gets back."

"I'll come back when Maria comes back," Kellie said.

Holly looked from one to the other.

"*If* Maria comes back."

6. Caroline

"Being a madam sounds cool," Caroline Hogan said. She and Gina were sitting at a pavement café in Double Bay in the late afternoon sun, watching the locals parading toy dogs or hailing taxis to carry home their fashionable purchases. "I've often wondered what life in a brothel would be like."

Gina wasn't surprised by her reaction. Caroline's motto, which had frequently got her—and sometimes Gina—into trouble, was "Never die wondering." They'd first met in primary school, and had remained best friends since. She was also one of the few people who knew the true nature of the Russo's family business.

"Great, so you'll apply for the manager's job, then."

"Ah! I'd love to, but I think my boss would object, darl." Caroline worked as an associate for a Sydney-based law firm. "He's a dinosaur. Would you believe he told me last week my skirt was too short, and yesterday he said I answered back too much." She gave a throaty laugh. "He's quite sweet, really. I think I might be starting to grow on him."

It was the first time they'd seen each other for a year. Gina knew Caroline was keen to chat about her recent posting to Bangkok and share a little gossip, but Gina had problems she needed to discuss with someone she could trust.

She'd now had time to realise that, in rushing to help her mother, she'd not thought through the consequences. Perhaps if she'd been in less of a hurry they could have come up with a different strategy, one that didn't need her active involvement. But circumstances had conspired against her.

Pat, Casa Rosa's manager, had resigned and moved to Queensland just before Maria learned she needed exploratory surgery, an operation that couldn't be put off according to her doctor. Maria had advertised for a new manager but few people saw brothel management as a career choice. "Pat was with me for seven years. She was so efficient I never worried about a thing."

That was the core of the problem. Had Pat still been there, Gina would never have got involved. Instead, she'd be kick-starting her new career.

Caroline said, "So, how's your first day been? Met the girls yet?"

"Just a couple. They seem all right. I think boredom will be my main problem. There's not much to do apart from recording receipts and keeping the place clean."

"Sounds a breeze."

"But if anyone sees me there, I'm stuffed. My prospects will be cactus and I might as well toss my MBA in the bin. Two years of study down the drain. Who wants an ex-brothel madam as an exec?"

"You could disguise yourself," Caroline said with a sly grin. She rarely took anything seriously. "A blonde wig with wraparound sunglasses should do the trick."

"I'm relying on a headscarf and dark glasses at the moment."

She sipped her coffee and gazed at the people passing by.

"Anyway, that's not all that's on my mind."

"Uh-oh. What else is bothering you?"

"My mother, of course. She doesn't seem to realise how serious her condition might be. It's difficult not to think the worst. I'm just hoping it's easy to fix."

Caroline placed her hand on Gina's. "I'm sure it won't turn out as bad as you think."

"I hope you're right."

"Anything else?"

She let out a sigh. "Morgan."

Caroline finished her coffee and dragged her chair closer to Gina.

"Things not going so good between you two?"

"Things aren't going, full stop. I had to tell him about Mama and the business."

"Not good, uh?"

Despair washed over her as she recalled the parting moments with Morgan. The look on his face, the injured tone. She fought it off. She had to stay positive.

"Not one bit. If it hadn't been for that, I'd be flashing a diamond ring the size of a golf ball in your face instead of crying on your shoulder."

"If he loved you, he'd accept you for who you really are."

"You read too much Mills and Boon," Gina said. "His family's religious in that strict, old-fashioned way, and it's rubbed off on Morgan. It's all my fault. I should have told him right at the start, before I fell for the god-loving bastard, but I didn't want to risk having it blabbed around campus."

"Does your Mum know?"

"I told her we've split. Said it was because I didn't want to live in America and he didn't want to move here. I couldn't tell her the real reason. Even if she hadn't been ill, I wouldn't want to lay any more guilt on her."

Her mother had gone to a lot of trouble to keep Gina at arm's length from the business. All she'd ever wanted was for Gina to have a decent start in life without being tainted by association with prostitution. Until now she'd succeeded. Gina had got off to a good start at the Austral Merchant Bank before applying to Harvard.

She brightened. "I do have some good news." With all the events of the day, she'd almost forgotten. "I have an interview next week with McLeod & Loew. I wrote to them before I left the States." M & L was a leading Australian management consulting company—working for them would carry heaps of prestige.

"Excellent! I'll keep my fingers crossed for you. Just remember to remove your headscarf and sunnies when you turn up."

7. Slip of the veil

Gina was so busy checking the previous night's receipts, she forgot all about the time. When she eventually looked at her watch, she gave a start. She needed to get a move on or her mother would think she'd been abandoned. Pausing only to grab her handbag, she raced from the building.

As she rushed down the street, she heard someone call her name. She stopped, put a hand to her head and cursed. She'd left her headscarf behind. A tremor of fear ran through her body. Should she pretend she'd not heard? The voice sounded vaguely familiar. She couldn't hesitate any longer. Looking over her shoulder, she spotted Daniel Bouvier, an old friend from her university days, standing some distance away on the other side of the street.

She waved her hand in acknowledgement. "Sorry, Dan, can't stop. I'm running late."

She hurried to her mother's car parked on a meter nearby. If it hadn't been for the hospital visit, the car would have been in the lockup. She was relieved not to see a manila envelope stuck under the wiper.

It crossed her mind as she got into the car that Daniel could be a client of Casa Rosa. No, he wasn't the type. He must have another reason for being in Tolley Street.

With barely a backwards glance to check the traffic, she pulled away from the kerb.

~~~

Daniel watched the BMW accelerate down the narrow road. The brake lights glowed briefly as it approached Foveaux Street, before it turned left to disappear from view. After the car was out of sight, he continued to gaze down the road, trying to make sense of what he'd seen.

He put his hand in his pocket and drew out the sheet of paper Lucy had given him. It listed the addresses of all known and suspected brothels in the area. He scanned the page and then looked across the road at the number of the building from which Gina had emerged. No doubt about it: it was an established brothel.

What was Gina Russo doing there?

He crossed over and approached the house, one of a row of similar sandstone buildings occupied by various small businesses. The black lacquered front door set in a rose-coloured frame looked solid and impressive, with inlaid panels and polished brass fittings. To its right, a simple brass plaque had "Casa Rosa" engraved on it in copperplate writing; below that an ivory push button in a brass surround.

He composed himself and pressed the button.

He'd expected some feedback—a buzzing sound perhaps or the ringing of a bell—but he might as well have pressed the wall itself. Perhaps the button didn't work. Or maybe the place was unoccupied. No, it was too well maintained. Perhaps it wasn't open for business until later. He pressed the button again, then tried the knob, but the door didn't yield. He stepped back and looked around the doorway. Above the lintel a CCTV camera pointed in his direction. He gave it a polite smile.

A few seconds later he heard an electronic lock being disengaged. As he went to push the door open, it swung back under its own power. He stepped inside.

Whatever he'd been expecting, this wasn't it. He was standing in a softly lit foyer, the floor of which was laid with chequered black and white ceramic tiles. Soft classical music played in the background. To his right, behind a reception desk, two women sat talking on telephone headsets.

The door closed quietly behind him as he stepped slowly up to the desk. The larger of the women smiled and mimed she wouldn't be much longer. As he waited, he soaked up the restrained elegance of his surroundings, a welcome change to prowling the streets to familiarise himself with the area.

After finishing the call the woman removed her headset and came around the desk to greet him. He realised how tall she was when their eyes met at the same level.

"Welcome to Casa Rosa. This your first visit?"

To avoid confusion, he came straight to the point.

"Is Gina here, please? I'd like to speak to her."

"Gina? No, sorry, she's only just this minute left."

"Damn. Never mind, I'll call back later."

"I'm afraid she won't be back today. If you like, I could take a message for you."

"No, that's all right, it's not urgent. I'll drop by tomorrow."

The woman accompanied him to the door and saw him out.

He crossed the road and looked back at the building, wondering how anyone would guess it was a brothel unless it was specifically pointed out to them.

Back at the office, Daniel checked the business registration details for Casa Rosa on the Internet. He was surprised to learn that it was owned by Maria Russo, Gina's mother. Until that moment he'd been willing to believe her visit was in some consultative capacity, perhaps as an accountant or business adviser. As far as he could recall, she'd said her family was in property development.

When Isobel returned, he asked her if she knew anything about the brothel.

"Not much. They call it a bordello. It's supposed to be a cut above the others for what that's worth. A sort of boutique brothel, I suppose. Why do you ask?"

"Just curious. A mate of mine mentioned it. So it's respectable?"

She sighed. "We're talking about a brothel, Dan."

"You know what I mean."

"As far as I know it's never been in trouble. Who's the owner?"

"Maria Francesca Russo. Any idea who she is?"

"No."

"I Googled the name but all I could find in Sydney was a woman who sits on the boards of a couple of Catholic charities."

"I doubt it's her, then."

~~~

When Gina arrived at the hospital, she was told her mother had recently returned from the operating theatre and was still under anaesthetic. She spoke to a charge nurse, who said the surgeon had removed a growth from the left kidney. A section had been sent to Pathology to check for malignancy. More would be known the following day.

She wasn't sure what to make of the news. Her mother had said it was going to be an exploratory examination and yet they'd gone ahead and cut a tumour out. Maybe they wanted to avoid a second operation.

Because she'd been running late, she hadn't stopped to buy flowers. Then she remembered seeing a florist's shop inside the hospital's main entrance. After checking that her mother was still out to the world, she set off to find it.

On her return, bouquet in hand, she found her mother propped up with pillows.

"The nurse told me you were here," Maria said.

Gina handed over the flowers. "I had to queue. Hope you like them."

"They're beautiful. I love gerberas, but you shouldn't have gone to all that expense. I'm only in for an examination."

Gina took the bouquet and placed it on a chair. "I'll get you a vase in a minute. How are you feeling? Did the nurse say anything about the operation?"

"She said the doctor will be round soon to talk to me. I'm a bit groggy, that's all. Anyway, how are you getting on? Are they all being nice to you like I told them?"

"Don't worry, Mama. Everything's going smoothly."

"I keep thinking of all the things I forgot to tell you."

"Don't worry. Liz keeps me on my toes—she seems to know everything."

"She's a godsend that girl."

"Why didn't you make her manager?"

"I tried, but she doesn't want responsibility for other people. She said she'd done it before and it nearly made her a basket case."

Gina shook her head in bewilderment. "But she's so good at it. Everybody respects her."

When the doctor turned up, Maria told her to go home and not to worry about her.

~~~

Gina found Aunt Concetta sweeping the terrace when she arrived home. Concetta propped the broom against the wall and came over to where Gina stood in the doorway.

"How's your mama? I didn't get time to see her today because of the operation. I'll go round tonight."

She related what little she knew. "Would you believe she told me not to worry!"

"That's your mama."

The phone rang and Gina went to pick it up. A man's voice.

"Hi, it's Daniel...Daniel Bouvier."

"Oh...hi, Daniel..." At first she couldn't think why he would be calling, then remembered seeing him earlier. "Listen, sorry I couldn't stop to talk to you. I was running late for an appointment."

"That's okay. I'm just calling to see if we could get together for lunch. It's a while since we met."

She'd been holding her breath while he spoke. Now she let it out slowly. "Yes, that would be great, Dan. I'm a bit busy right now, though. Could I get back to you on that?"

"Yeah, sure." He cleared his throat. "By the way, I was a bit surprised to see you on Tolley Street." He paused, waiting for her to say something, but she had no idea what he was expecting. "You know...coming out of that brothel."

The phone almost slipped from her grasp as she took an involuntary step backwards. She gulped a deep breath to counter her rising panic, her thoughts racing. So he'd seen her coming out of Casa Rosa. What must he be thinking? She was a sex worker? Or brothel staff?

"You still there?"

"Sorry, Dan, I was distracted for a minute. Did you say a brothel?"

Oh god, she had a tremor in her voice.

"Yeah. It's called Casa Rosa."

What else did he know? Supposing he'd already mentioned it to someone else? If only she knew what he knew...

"Is that what it is, a brothel?" She laughed. "I wouldn't have known—I thought it was a doctor's consulting rooms. I had the wrong address. Right number, wrong street. That's why I was in such a hurry—I was running late."

"I hope you made your appointment."

"I did, thanks." And to discourage further questions: "Just a female thing."

She relaxed a little. She needed to end the conversation but didn't want to appear rude again. A thought came into came into her head.

"By the way, Dan, what were *you* doing outside a brothel?"

"I work for the *Daily Monitor*. We're doing an article about sex slavery. Apparently brothel owners are bringing in Asians illegally, using shonky contracts to keep them prisoner. I've been getting to know the territory and looking at some of the brothels we're suspicious about."

Was Casa Rosa on his list? She needed to choose her words carefully, get the tone right and not appear too interested. She took a deep breath and let it out before declaring, "Well, that makes a change for the *Monitor*. Normally all they want to do is close down brothels."

"Yeah, well, Calloway probably thinks it'll be another nail in their coffin."

"And why are you working for that pompous old god-botherer? Hardly your scene...unless you've joined the holy rollers, that is."

Six years earlier, when they'd been at university together, Gina had been to parties where Daniel had taken part in some of the more outrageous activities. She remembered one occasion when he'd passed out after drinking too much and a group of students, herself included, had stripped off all his clothes and left him overnight in Centennial Park. Early the next morning, he ran home naked and found his clothes neatly folded on the porch waiting for him. He'd taken it all in good part. She found it hard to believe he'd radically changed since.

Daniel said, "He's all right. Gives a lot of money to good causes. He's even set up a charitable foundation for mental health research."

"Both our mothers do charity work, but they don't shove their beliefs down other people's throats. Anyway, I never thought you'd be doing this sort of stuff. Last I heard, you were overseas doing aid work."

"You can only do that sort of thing for a while. Too demanding. I came back and scored a cadetship with the *Monitor*...ended up on the Social Diary. Now they've seconded me to Features. I guess they think I need to see another side of life. I don't mind, I've always wanted to be an investigative reporter."

All the while they'd been speaking she'd been trying unsuccessfully to devise a way to find out if Casa Rosa was one of the brothels he was checking on. She decided to come straight out with it. "That brothel you said you saw me coming out of, is that under suspicion?"

"Why do you ask?"

"Oh, you know, I might see my picture in the paper, that was all. You did have a camera with you."

"I'm surprised you noticed, you were in such a rush. Anyway, you're safe. The camera's intended to make me look like a tourist."

So she still didn't know if Casa Rosa was a target. She couldn't ask him any more questions without raising suspicion.

After mentioning her mother's illness and promising to let him know when she was available for lunch, she ended the call and mulled over what he knew and what he might discover if he kept hanging around Tolley Street. She had an uneasy feeling that her career prospects were already compromised.

~~~

Daniel was in a quandary. At university he'd been attracted to Gina, though she'd not reciprocated a romantic interest in him. At the time she was having an on-off relationship with her economics tutor, and during the off phase she hung out with a group that included him. They got on well together, sharing an interest in amateur dramatics: he as an actor, she as an occasional stage manager. Given her performance just now, perhaps they should have swapped roles.

His dilemma was that if he revealed he knew about her Casa Rosa association, she'd never speak to him again, which would be a pity, as seeing her again had rekindled his old feelings for her.

He was also mindful that she, or at least her mother, could provide him with useful information on illegal brothels, especially those like the one just around the corner in Denfield Street that he was keeping an eye on. It would not only help the investigation but gain him some kudos with the *Monitor* team as well.

At least he now knew why he'd seen her leaving Casa Rosa. She was managing it during her mother's illness.

He'd give her a week to call him, then he'd call again and repeat his offer of lunch.

~~~

Gina couldn't sleep. She kept replaying the conversation with Daniel, worrying that in some small way she'd disclosed her involvement in Casa

Rosa, or worse, that he might think she worked there as a prostitute. He was no fool and she couldn't shake off the feeling he wasn't convinced by her explanation.

When she wasn't analysing that conversation, she lay thinking about the potential outcomes for her mother. The possibility of cancer was real. If confirmed, its treatment would take some time, and that would mean putting off her career plans for a while longer.

Enough light streamed through the window for her to make out the painting of Morgan that Edith Chamberlain, Morgan's mother, had given her the previous Christmas. Edith's pictures hung in galleries in Boston, New York, and San Francisco, and now in this suburban bedroom in Sydney.

Morgan hadn't been happy about the portrait. His mother had painted it from photographs because he refused to sit for her. Gina didn't understand his reaction, considering how proud he was of his mother's success. Perhaps it was his father's influence. Little art was on display in their house. Despite his wealth and influence, George Chamberlain claimed to be a man with plain tastes living a simple life. The hypocrisy of keeping a luxury yacht moored at Edgartown didn't seem to occur to him.

She should take the picture down. Things weren't going to change between them, and it was too painful a reminder of her recent history, particularly those visits to Martha's Vineyard she'd so enjoyed until that last, calamitous occasion.

~~~

Travelling to Casa Rosa was now even more perilous with Daniel reconnoitring the area. She drove around the block twice to make sure he wasn't lurking about before parking the car.

After she'd recorded the cash receipts from the previous day, she took Baz along with her to the bank. When they returned, she found nothing to occupy her time, Liz having taken care of the laundry and checked out the rooms in Gina's absence. As it was approaching lunchtime, she decided to pay her mother an early visit.

She found Maria sitting up in bed, dabbing at her eyes with a tissue. Gina hurried to comfort her.

"Mama..."

Maria took a minute to compose herself. "The doctor says he has to do another operation. The tumour was malignant."

"Oh, no..."

"I have—" Maria paused while she recalled the name, "—renal cell carcinoma. He didn't think it was advanced but he'll have to take more of the kidney out."

"When?"

"Later today or tomorrow. He said my other organs might be affected."

Gina clasped her mother's hand in both of hers, trying to come to terms with the news. It made her so angry. Of all people why should her mother be struck down like this? She didn't deserve it. She was sensible, loving, selfless, someone who never set out to hurt anyone, who always put her family and her staff before her own interests. It was grossly unfair.

For her mother's sake she had to remain calm. "Mama, I know it sounds bad but you'll get better, I know you will. It's amazing what they can do these days."

"But you know what this means, don't you?"

Gina nodded. Overnight she'd weighed up the few options open to her if her mother was out of action for a long period. If the business couldn't be put on hold—a suggestion her mother refused to entertain—then Gina had little choice but to keep it going. That meant staying involved until her mother was fit enough to take back the reins. Her own plans would have to be shelved for the time being. She would cancel the appointment with McLeod & Leow.

She squeezed her mother's hand. "Don't worry, Mama. I'll keep the boat afloat. Relax, and try not to worry. Your health is more important than anything else."

8. Daniel in the den

Behind the rusted railings of a Victorian terrace, wind-blown litter congregated in a minuscule garden. Around the sash windows flaky green paintwork had partly worn away to reveal bleached woodwork. The front door fared no better. Daniel saw where the metal numerals had been removed and at some later stage '17' added in black paint by an untutored hand. No doorbell or knocker beckoned him; no camera scrutinised his features.

With some trepidation he tapped on the door with his knuckle. After a minute or so, he tried looking through the window, but the blind was down. He took a deep breath, grasped the doorknob, and turned it. The door eased open.

Visiting Casa Rosa had been a breeze. Its ambiance and legal status made it only marginally more confronting than visiting a doctor's surgery. Now he was about to spend time with a prostitute, a possibly underage illegal immigrant, on premises that the police could choose to raid at any time. It was a far cry from the Social Diary.

He stepped inside and closed the door quietly behind him.

No-one was around to greet him. He moved to the middle of the long, narrow room and coughed politely. As he waited, he ran his eye over the shabby decor. No fragrant lilies here. The place smelled of rising damp and stale cigarette smoke.

The furniture consisted of a coffee table with a few well-thumbed porn magazines lying on it, a row of four stackable chairs, and a frayed carpet. A television set mounted on a wall bracket faced the chairs, but it was switched off. At the end of the room a small desk stood next to a passage leading to the rest of the house. Apart from a mirror on the wall by the front door and a plain calendar hanging behind the desk, the place was devoid of decoration.

He could hear a subdued voice coming from another room and every now and then something bumped on the floor above; otherwise the place was surprisingly quiet.

With each passing minute, his resolve weakened. Whatever had made him agree to do this? Had he in fact agreed? Isobel had said he was doing it and he'd acquiesced. Could it seriously be considered part of his job description? If he left now, who could blame him? The worst that might happen would be the end of his secondment to Features; at least Andrea would be delighted to have him back.

As he sidled towards the door, he heard chair legs scrape on a wooden floor. Expecting to see Robbie's daughter, Wendy, he was surprised when a tall, dark-haired man emerged from the passage and walked towards him. He was unshaven and dressed in jeans and a white tee-shirt, the sleeves of which were stretched above muscled biceps. He had the hard, rugged look of someone who'd recently served in the armed forces or spent time in prison.

"Sorry, mate, I was on the phone. Can I help you?" He delivered the question in an offhand manner. Judging by the accent, English wasn't his first language.

Daniel fished a business card out of his anorak and handed it over. The cheaply printed card had been given to him by a taxi driver, who'd scribbled his own name on the back. Isobel had said most cabbies had cards issued to them by brothels—all he had to do was book a trip, tell the driver he'd heard of a good brothel in Denfield Street, and ask to be taken there.

After glancing at the card, the man said, "All our girls are Asian. You right with that?"

Daniel nodded.

"Take a seat and I'll see who's free."

He left the room.

Daniel wondered if the girls would have more than a cursory knowledge of English. If not, it would be a struggle to get any information out of them.

The man returned shortly with three girls tripping along in his wake. They were uniformly dressed in skimpy, see-through dresses and stiletto heels and paraded in front of Daniel without smiling. He would have to choose one, though he had no way of telling who was most suitable.

He cleared his throat and looked at each in turn. "I need someone who's experienced, someone who can help me to—"

The shortest of the girls pointed to herself. "Me. I've been here the longest." She stepped forward as if he'd already given his approval and stood next to him, placing a hand on the back of his neck. One small breast pressed against his shoulder and he detected the tang of inferior perfume as she stroked his head and rubbed her leg against his. He tried to contain his unease.

The man said, "Okay, you want Rosie here. Good choice—she's our best girl." He dismissed the other two with a wave of his hand. "How long do you want?"

He didn't know what was normal but decided to keep it short. "Half-an-hour?"

"That's $95, or $90 if you pay cash."

As he passed him his corporate credit card, he remembered it had the *Daily Monitor*'s logo on it. "Hold on a minute, I might have the cash." He took the card back and searched in his pocket for some money, but all he could come up with were four twenty-dollar notes. He handed the card back and prayed it wouldn't be scrutinised too closely. Why hadn't Isobel warned him about the credit card? The man disappeared into the back office and when he came back he asked Daniel to sign the receipt before returning the card.

So far, so good—now the serious fun was about to begin.

Rosie casually took his hand and led him upstairs to a room not much bigger than a child's bedroom. His eyes followed the frieze around the upper part of the walls. It confirmed his suspicion: the bedroom had been partitioned. Most of the space was taken up by a single bed with a purple cover and black satin pillows. The top of a small cabinet was littered with packets of condoms and uncapped bottles and tubes of lotion. On the floor beside the bed lay an open box of tissues. Recently sprayed air freshener failed to mask the smell of sex and sweat.

He hesitated before perching himself on the edge of the bed, hands pushed deep into the pockets of his coat as he stared at the floor. She sensed his nervousness.

"You not been here before?"

He shook his head.

"This your first time...in a place like this?"

Still staring at the floor, he nodded. When he looked up she was smiling. A hint of sympathy.

"Don't worry, I'll look after you."

When he'd asked for the most experienced girl, it had been to improve his chances of finding one who spoke English well enough to understand and answer his questions. Rosie's English seemed good enough.

Despite enjoying his discomfort, Isobel hadn't left him unprepared for the visit. She'd explained how most reporters traditionally avoided sex in such situations. "Tell them you're not ready yet. You'd rather talk for a while. The girls often get punters who are lonely and looking for a mother-substitute. Be careful how you ask questions though; don't make them suspicious."

The girl stood in front of him.

"We start by taking off our clothes."

As she started to undress, he said, as nervously as he could, "Do you mind if we talk first?"

She didn't answer until she appeared naked in front of him. "Okay?" She twirled around in front of him.

He looked—how could he not?—and noted the flawless skin, budlike breasts, and the slim hips of an adolescent's body. "You're beautiful, but can we please just talk until I'm ready? I need time to relax."

"Okay," she said, "it's your money. What you want to talk about?" She sat next to him and examined her long painted fingernails.

"I don't know." He pretended to search for a subject. "Maybe you can tell me if you like working here?"

She shrugged. "It's 'kay."

"Been here long?"

"Long enough. What about you? You like your job?" She casually ran her hand along the inside of his thigh.

"I do, but it's not like yours. You must get fed up doing what you do...you know, with strangers. I bet there are some real turn-offs."

She threw him a quizzical look. "It's just a job. You get used to it." She pressed her hand on his groin to check his state of arousal. "You wonder if you gay, right?"

He took her hand away. "No, course not, it's..." He paused for effect and hung his head a little.

"Yes?"

"I had a girlfriend. Her name was Jana. She lived with me for six months. Towards the end she began mocking me, saying I wasn't good enough in bed, and how I lacked imagination because I couldn't satisfy her. I'd get all worked up and then she'd jump out of bed and say she didn't feel like it any more. That sort of thing's not good for a bloke, you know, being humiliated like that. Shot my libido to pieces. Then she mocked me because I couldn't get it up. It was awful. In the end I told her to clear out, but she took her time leaving and that just made it worse."

He looked up to see her watching him sympathetically.

"Ever since she left, I've not been able to do anything…you know, physically. Not with anybody. It's so humiliating. I daren't ask anyone out any more." He paused for effect. "That's why I came here looking for someone like you, with lots of experience. I'm hoping you'll help me get my confidence back."

She laid a hand on his shoulder and said softly, "Of course I help you. I know lots of ways, but you have to take clothes off first."

He shrank back. "No, not yet. It's just…I'm sorry, I'm too nervous."

With one eye on the clock, he kept her talking, interweaving his imaginary problems with questions about her life, which she deftly deflected. He was pleased that she seemed genuinely interested in his sad little tale.

She pointed to the clock. "Your time is up. You want to stay longer?"

He shook his head. "I'll be back, maybe tomorrow or the day after. Will you be here?"

Her tone was flat. "I'm always here." She started dressing.

"I'm really, really glad I met you, Rosie."

She kissed him on the cheek as he got to his feet.

"Ask for me…Rosie. I make you real man again, promise."

~~~

Later that afternoon, Daniel sat with Frank and Lucy around the table in Frank's office and briefly described his visit to Denfield Street. He also explained how he and Isobel had previously taken photographs of people entering and leaving the premises and how he'd wired himself up to take more pictures inside.

"You got the prints?" asked Frank.

Daniel took the photographs out of a folder and spread them on the table. He pointed to one of them. "This is the bloke in reception. Nasty piece of work, I reckon." He separated two other pictures from the rest. "These are the girls they paraded in front of me." He pushed another two pictures towards Frank. "This is Rosie, with and without clothes."

"Looks like you had a good time," Frank said.

"It was nerve-racking. I kept my hands in my pockets most of the time so I could trigger the camera."

"She might be Thai or Cambodian," Lucy said, pointing at Rosie's picture.

"I never had chance to ask her," Daniel said. "She was cagey and I didn't want to make her suspicious."

"What's this bloke's name?" Frank said, picking up the photograph of the man in reception.

"I don't know. He had an accent—East European, I think. Here's a picture Isobel took of him outside, getting into a Merc."

Frank looked at the photograph closely. "Good old Isobel. She not only has the index number, but you can clearly see the name of the car dealer on the plate. Lucy, the Merc doesn't look that old so the dealer should still have a record of who he sold it to. If not, try Merc's head office in Melbourne—they keep good records."

Lucy said to Daniel, "Are you going back tomorrow?"

"Yes. I reckon it's going to take a few more visits before she'll trust me."

"She could easily suss what you're up to before then." Frank slid the two photos of Rosie over to Lucy. "How old do you reckon she is?"

She picked them up and studied each one carefully, concentrating mostly on the photograph where Rosie was unclothed. Shot from the knees upwards, it showed her pale, slim body with small breasts and a narrow tuft of black pubic hair. No scars or stretch marks were visible.

"To be honest, I can't say, but she's at least fourteen and maybe as old as twenty-one. Do you think she's under age?"

Frank nodded. "Could be. What was your impression, Daniel?"

"Her English was good and she seemed quite knowing. Like Lucy said, it's hard to tell just by looking at her."

"When you go back," Frank said, "make sure you pay cash this time and don't take your wallet in case they get suspicious and check you out. And that includes phones, cameras, and anything else that could give the game away."

Lucy looked worried. "Do be careful, Daniel."

~~~

When Daniel visited Denfield Street the following day, he was met by a young woman. She must be Wendy, he thought—Robbie's daughter. Unlike her father, she was slim and, despite a slight limp, quick in her movements. He asked for Rosie and after handing over the payment in cash was told to wait a few minutes. In fact, it was twenty minutes before Rosie appeared, with a man she led to the door and let out. Then, smiling politely, she came over to Daniel and invited him upstairs to the same room as before.

He sat on the bed, still warm from her previous encounter, and gazed up at her. Recognition showed on her face as he continued with the anxious manner of the day before.

"How are you?" she asked as she sat beside him. "Still nervous?"

"A bit." He looked down at his clasped hands and up again. "Do you mind if I ask you a personal question?"

She looked at him strangely.

"Do you have a boyfriend?"

"Why you want to know?"

"A girl like you, you know, so beautiful..."

She looked at him to see if he was mocking her. Realising he was serious, she said, "No."

"I was thinking about you last night, you know. I couldn't get you out of my mind."

She brushed aside the comment with a wave of her hand. "Don't think about me. Find a nice girl. Think about her instead."

Shyly, he said, "Supposing I were to ask you out?"

She laughed and shook her head. "No way. I cannot go out with you."

"Why not?"

She became businesslike. "You want to fuck?"

"I'd rather talk."

"What about?"

He wondered what subject would get her to reveal more about herself, but before he could speak, she said, "Tell me about Jana. Is she pretty?"

For a moment he was thrown, then he remembered Jana was his imaginary ex-girlfriend. He'd called her Jana because earlier he'd been reading about an athlete with that name.

Rather than answer, he looked into her eyes in what he hoped was an adoring fashion. This unsettled her even more.

"What's your name?"

"Daniel."

"Daniel, I don't want a boyfriend. I'm a working girl, 'kay?"

Aware he was overdoing it, he backed off. "Sorry, I didn't mean to upset you. But there must be a time when we could get together."

"We together now. Let's talk about something else or we have sex."

He made a show of being wounded by her remark. "I'm sorry, Rosie, I didn't mean to embarrass you. Let's talk a bit more."

"What about?"

"What would you do if you could do anything you wanted?"

She was silent for a moment. "I think I build a new house for my family back home and we all live there."

"Where's home?"

"Cambodia."

At last he was getting somewhere. "I was in Cambodia for a while. I was an English teacher."

Her face lit up. "Really? Where?"

"In the north. Siem Reap."

"We lived in Anlong Veng. Not far away."

She was silent for a moment.

He asked, "Did you come to Australia to earn money for your family?"

"Of course."

"Is it a big family?"

"Three sisters and two brothers. What about you?"

"Just me. I had a sister but she died of leukaemia when she was six." That was true. He'd been ten years old at the time.

She placed her small hand over his. "That's sad. My mother had a baby who died. He only lived for three days."

She slipped to the floor and looked under the bed. Reaching underneath, she pulled out a large shoulder bag. She rummaged through it and took out a postcard-size photograph.

"Is it safe to leave your bag under there?" Daniel said.

"We don't have place to keep things. I use this room most, so I leave it here."

She passed him the photograph. It showed three adults standing in the open doorway of a bamboo house raised on stilts. Immediately below them, six children sat on steps leading down to a paved yard.

"This is my family." She pointed to the tallest of the four girls. "That's me." Indicating the adults, she said, "That's my mother and father, and this my grandmother, just before she died."

"I'm sorry to hear that."

She stared at the photograph without speaking. When it seemed as if she were about to say something, she put the picture in her bag and shoved it back under the bed. When she looked at him again, she was fighting back tears.

"You must miss your family," he said.

"Can we talk about something else? You still have fifteen minutes."

He chatted aimlessly about his fictional activities for a few minutes and when he was confident she was off-guard again, said, "You know, I was serious about wanting to take you out. Can't we meet on your day off?"

"I don't have days off."

"Not even one?"

"No. Please don't ask again. In fact, it's not a good idea for you to see me in future. Try another girl or go another place."

"Okay, I suppose I'd better go."

She led him out of the door. "I'm sorry," she said softly.

~~~

Daniel waited another two days before going back to see Rosie. He was hoping it would have given her sufficient time to contemplate life outside the confines of the sordid brothel. However, the seed he'd sown was small and he had no idea if the ground on which it fell was fertile enough.

Again he was met by Wendy. After he'd handed over his money, she went off and returned with Rosie.

She looked startled and was about to say something, but stopped. Her mouth half open, she watched the dark-haired man Daniel had seen on his first visit walk into the reception area. He looked suspiciously at Rosie and then Daniel before going over to the desk.

Rosie regained her composure and led Daniel upstairs. As soon as the door was closed, she turned on him.

"I told you not to see me again."

"I know, but I want to be with you."

"You'll get me in trouble. I told you to ask for another girl or go somewhere else."

"Why?"

"Because we're not supposed to be so friendly with clients. It's against the rules."

"Rosie, are they keeping you here against your will?"

She turned away from him. "Don't be silly."

"Then why aren't you free to leave?"

When she didn't answer, Daniel sat on the bed, wondering what to say next. He remembered how the man in the lobby had affected her.

"Rosie, that man downstairs, is he the owner?" She nodded. "What's his name?"

"Ludo. Why?"

"I thought I'd ask him to let me take you out to dinner."

She looked incredulous. "You crazy? Don't you dare speak to him. You will get me into so much trouble."

"So I'm right. You're being held here against your will."

"Please, it's time you went. I'll find you another girl." She grabbed him by the sleeve and tried hauling him to his feet. "Come on. Now! And don't come see me again."

"Rosie, I can help to get you out of here."

She was pushing him towards the door.

"Rosie, listen to me. If you don't want me to speak to Ludo, you're going to have to tell me what's going on."

She stopped pushing. "What are you, a policeman?"

"Of course not."

"Then why do you keep asking me?"

"Because it's not fair. You should be free to do what you want."

She grabbed the door handle. "Come. I get you another girl."

"Rosie, what's stopping you?"

She tugged at his sleeve. "Please…"

"I'll go when you tell me what's stopping you from leaving." When she stayed silent, he added, "Okay, I'll go but I'll ask Ludo if I can take you out."

She seemed about to lose her temper, and then her face subsided into resignation. "Look, if I tell you, promise not to tell anyone?"

Should he lie to her? She was so close to telling him what he wanted to hear. "I can't promise anything, Rosie, except I won't put you at risk."

She picked at a loose stitch on the bodice of her dress. When she looked up, she said with a sigh, "I must pay back the travel money they lent me."

"How much?"

"Six thousand dollar."

"And how long will that take?"

"I don't know. I pay to live here, too. And taxes as well."

"So you're not sending money to your family after all?" She dropped her head and shook it. "Your mother and father must wonder what's happened to you. They must be worried. And all your brothers and sisters."

When she didn't look up, he dipped his head and saw a tear rolling down her cheek.

"Rosie, how long have you been in this place?"

She wiped away the tear and looked up. "Eight month, I think."

"How did they trap you like this?"

"I was student in Cambodia. I saw advert in the newspaper for girls to go to Australia to work in restaurant. The woman who fetch me from the airport brought me here instead. Ludo took my passport and ticket to go back home, and when I try to leave he beat me and lock me up."

She was weeping now, the grown-up veneer peeling away to reveal a frightened girl far from home.

"How old are you, Rosie?"

"Nineteen." She wiped her eyes on the hem of her dress.

Daniel put his hand on her shoulder. "You know you could leave if you wanted to. I can help. Will you let me? Please?" She didn't answer. "Do you sleep here as well?"

She moved to the bed and sat down. "No, they take us to another house where other girls like me and we sleep together."

"Can't you escape from there?"

"They lock doors and windows."

It wasn't going to be easy. "Rosie, you have to trust me. I have influence. I'll make sure you won't be sent back to Cambodia. Okay?"

God, he hoped Frank knew what to do in these situations.

A muffled sound came from the room next door and Rosie sprang to her feet. "Come on, you must go."

He lowered his voice and spoke urgently. "Trust me, Rosie. I promise I won't do anything unless you agree. Okay?"

She ignored him and opened the door. Not waiting to see if he was following, she tripped quickly down the stairs. He caught up with her as she reached the last tread.

Ludo still sat at the desk. In the mirror by the door, Daniel noticed him look up and check his watch as the two came into the lobby, surprised perhaps by the short duration of the visit.

As Rosie opened the front door, daylight exposed the fear in her face.

He was no sooner through the door than it closed behind him.

For the first time he realised the true gravity of what he'd undertaken to do and, more importantly, how his actions could be placing her at risk.

9. Mending fences

Ever since Kelly had touched a raw nerve, Gina had been intent on finding someone to take over the day-to-day operations so she didn't need to spend as much time on the premises. She'd almost given up hope when Simon Bradley's résumé came in from one of the agencies she'd contacted.

Simon was studying computer sciences part-time at the University of New South Wales, where Gina had obtained her first degree. In his mid-twenties, he was tall and lean, and wore narrow spectacles with thin black frames.

Before the interview, she'd prepared a list of questions, ones she remembered being asked herself when she'd applied to the Austral Merchant Bank.

"What sort of problems have you had in your current position?"

"The usual. Not all customers are reasonable, and sometimes people you rely on don't do what they're supposed to do."

"Do you get on all right with your manager?"

"Of course."

"And other staff?"

"No problems. They're a good lot."

"Then why are you leaving?"

He hesitated before answering. "We're being taken over."

"Why should that affect you?"

Again he hesitated. "They're much bigger than us. Everyone knows that when a firm gets taken over, the new owners bring their own people in."

"But why would they sack you? It's usually senior managers who get the push."

"I know, but I'll still be affected by the changes. They reckon there's a good chance we'll have to relocate to Epping—those they decide to keep on, that is. I can walk to the office now if I want to, but Epping's a half-hour train ride each way."

That sounded plausible. "What made you apply for this position?"

"You're a small business, not far from where I live, or from uni. And I'll be free of corporate witchcraft."

"Pardon?"

"The new owners are into all the management fads—you know, team building exercises, six sigma, quality circles..."

"So...?"

"You've obviously not come across them."

"I have an MBA. I'm well aware of those techniques. In fact, I've used some of them."

"You're an MBA?"

"So?"

"What the... I mean, since when did you need an MBA to run a brothel?"

She explained briefly how she came to be managing Casa Rosa, emphasising how determined she was to get back to the corporate world.

So far, he seemed to have what she needed. He was clearly intelligent and confident, possibly even too confident, but that could just be interview nerves. More importantly, having worked in an insurance broker's office for more than a year, he understood office routine and she could see no reason why he wouldn't settle in at Casa Rosa.

"Do you have a partner?" When he nodded, she added, "And she'll be okay with you working here?"

"She's a fitness instructor at Empire Gym—she gets propositioned all the time. We trust each other."

That wasn't what she'd asked, but no matter. After he'd answered a few more questions and she told him the salary, her mind was made up.

"Are you still interested in the job?"

"It sounds like it could be fun."

"I'll need to check your references before I can make a formal offer, but if they check out, can you start Monday?"

As she escorted him off the premises, she congratulated herself on being close to solving her major problem. A moment later, she realised he might find working in a brothel not quite what he expected and then she'd have the problem back again. She would need to make sure he was happy. She called the agency and asked them to follow up his references. If he checked out and turned up on the following Monday, she'd still need to stick around until he came up to speed. While Liz spent time training him she would need to lend a hand in reception, something she'd never intended to do in case a client recognised her.

As for talking to customers about their special needs, well, that was something she would have to learn to deal with. After all, to be a good manager, you had to get your hands dirty from time to time, metaphorically speaking of course.

Still, she was happier at the prospect of offloading the day-to-day management onto someone else's shoulders. It meant that at last she could get back to other activities, including catching up with her old pals. She'd be able to go to the gym as well, maybe even play netball again.

~~~

Feeling the need for a coffee, Gina wandered down the hall to the kitchen and found four girls sitting talking at the table. She recognised two of them, Kellie and Chloe, but she'd not met the other two before.

One of them, a stocky redhead with a chest rivalling Kellie's, held a lighted cigarette in her hand as she talked, occasionally tapping the ash into an empty coffee cup. Knowing her mother strictly forbade smoking in the house, Gina said, as she walked past the table, "If you want to smoke, please go outside and do it."

The woman looked up at Gina and back at the cigarette in her hand as if someone had surreptitiously placed it there. Without a word, she rose from the table and went out the back door, closely followed by Kellie.

As Gina filled her mug, Chloe said, "Juliette's boyfriend's giving her grief again."

Maria had told Gina about Juliette, who came from the English Midlands. Though she had more than her share of personal problems, she never let

Maria down. Unlike some of the girls, who refused to service certain racial groups or people with disabilities, Juliette discriminated against no-one and was game for anything.

"She knows it's against the law to smoke in a workplace."

Chloe shrugged. "She probably forgot where she was. By the way, have you met Tammi?"

Tammi, who was filing her nails, paused long enough to wave a manicured hand. "Hi, Gina. Nice to meet you."

Tammi was also Asian, and as slim and as svelte as Chloe. Where did her mother find these girls?

"Tammi's our newest girl," Chloe said. "She's only been with us a few weeks."

Gina said, "Ah, yes, Liz mentioned you."

Liz had said she'd been taken on after Maria dismissed a girl for misconduct. Although she'd never worked as an escort before, Tammi took to it straightaway. Her cheerful personality made her popular with clients, something Liz prized highly as it made her job easier when clients asked for a particular girl.

Gina took the coffee to her office and found Baz waiting for her.

"I've had some bad news, Gina. Linda, my sister—the one I told you lived in San Francisco—she's been in an accident. She's in intensive care with internal injuries."

"Oh, Baz, how awful. What happened?"

"She was crossing the road at the lights and a car came through on red and ploughed into her. They think her pelvis might be fractured. I need to be with her, she's my only family."

"Of course you do. You must go right away." But how was she going to manage without him? "Get down to the travel agents and see if they can get you on a flight as soon as possible."

"I'm sorry about this, Gina."

Gina checked her watch and saw it was five o'clock. "Don't be silly, it's not your fault. Go on, get a move on before they close. And tell them it's urgent."

No sooner had she solved one problem than she'd gained a new one.

~~~

When Gina arrived at Casa Rosa the next morning, Baz was waiting for her.

"Qantas has given me a compassionate passage. I'm flying out at twenty-five past one this arvo."

"Well done, Baz. I do hope your sister gets better quickly. Look after her for as long as you need to and don't worry about us. We'll cope."

She went with him to the front door and wished him a safe journey. At least he wasn't travelling to New Orleans. The news was still full of the devastation caused by Hurricane Katrina during the previous week.

On the way back to her office she passed Kellie, giving her a polite smile that went unacknowledged. Sitting at her desk she wondered what was bothering Kellie. Then she remembered.

When Kellie walked back past her doorway, Gina called out to her.

"Do you have a minute, Kellie?"

With some reluctance, Kellie stepped into the office and took the proffered seat. Today she wore a scarlet boob tube and white micro skirt. She crossed her legs and balanced a bottle of water on her knee.

Kellie waited for Gina to speak.

Gina cleared her throat. "I just want to say ... the other day ... I'm sorry for blowing up."

"It wasn't the other day, it was more than a week ago."

"Really? I've had so much on my mind lately I'm losing track of time. Anyway, I want to apologise for the way I acted. It was completely uncalled for."

Kellie gave a slight shrug. "I didn't realise it was such a sore subject, seeing as how your mum owns this place and you being her daughter."

"Yes, well..." What could she say? It wasn't easy to explain. "I suppose it does seem odd. My mother's always been discreet about this business. I didn't know about it till I was sixteen."

She remembered the shock when her mother told her. It was the day after her father's funeral. Laid low by grief, she'd stayed in bed, refusing to get up for meals. Her mother came and sat on the bed and told her how, when she was Gina's age, she'd first met her father and how they'd loved each other ever since. And then she described how they'd come to own a brothel. Gina was stunned by the revelation. As if her life couldn't get any worse, she was now a brothel owner's daughter. Humiliated and angry, she'd said awful things that she later regretted. Her Catholic school education had certainly not helped either. The nuns had drummed it into her that girls who were immodest or had impure thoughts would end up as prostitutes or worse.

Her mother waited for a few days, allowing Gina to grudgingly come to terms with her new reality, and then gave her a full explanation, one that made her realise just how much her mother had sacrificed for her.

"She was determined to do whatever it took to give me a good start in life so I never had to follow her example." She shrugged. "And now here I am."

Kellie seemed not to have heard a word. She fixed Gina with a challenging stare. "It's obvious you don't like it here. You don't like us much either, do you? Think we're all sluts."

Gina couldn't help thinking that if Kellie dressed the way she did, maybe she had only herself to blame. However, she'd not given much thought to whether she liked the staff or whether they liked her. Her closest contacts so far had been with Liz and Baz and she certainly liked them. Jos as well.

"You mean you and the other girls? It's not that I like or dislike you—I've only met you and a couple of the others—it's just ... I don't understand you, why you do what you do."

"Well, if I didn't want to do it, I wouldn't be here, would I? So what's the problem?" She waved the bottle about as she spoke. "I'm not taking risks. I'm on the pill, I practise safe sex, so what have I got to worry about? I mean, it's a joke, isn't it?"

"What's a joke?"

"I could pick up a bloke in a bar tonight, go to bed with him and it would be okay. That's what don't make sense. If it's free, it's okay; but paid for? Nah, that's wicked. See? It's a joke."

"But if you pick someone up, it's because you fancy him, it's your choice, and, who knows, it could be the start of a relationship, but here you don't know who you're having sex with. They could be serial killers for all you know."

"I get the final say. I don't take 'em all. And anyway every job's got some kind of risk. My mum got RSI from bashing a keyboard for years."

"Well, I couldn't do it. I guess you need to have the right personality or something."

Kellie rose from her chair and smoothed the creases from her tight skirt. "Don't worry about it. Soon as your mum comes back, you can buzz off to your new career and forget we ever existed."

"Thanks. Still, I'll try to be less touchy in future."

Kellie pointed to the calendar on the wall. "By the way, it's September."

"Oh, right."

After Kellie left, Gina ripped off the August page. She wondered how many more would be torn off before she was able to leave Casa Rosa.

Kellie's attitude puzzled her. The girl seemed to have no idea how much she devalued herself. She was bright, articulate, assertive: qualities that would help her make something of herself if she chose to. But then that was true of Chloe and Tammi and probably most of the rest of them. She would have to accept it was how they wanted to live and just mind her own business.

When she sat down again, her thoughts turned to Baz's absence. She must make more use of Jock. He'd already offered to work more hours if required, saying he needed the extra money for a European trip he was planning. However, Maria had warned her about his unreliability, and told her to use taxis when drivers weren't available. Gina had a better idea. Now Simon was on board, she would save money by driving the girls herself.

In the same spirit of efficiency, Gina decided Simon should focus on the front desk and not burden himself with bookkeeping. Instead, she'd buy a computer with a proper accounting system. Her mother could be out of action for weeks, possibly months—working on her peculiar manual system all that time was out of the question. She would show her mother how to use the computer when she returned.

Even so, now wasn't a good time to broach the subject with her—she'd only veto the purchase. After thinking it over some more, she resolved to go ahead and buy a desktop model and tell her mother about it later.

10. Further into the den

Daniel gave Frank and Lucy an account of his meetings with Rosie as they sat around the table in Frank's office. When he heard about her fear of being deported, Frank said, "She's not an illegal. She would have come in on a 457 temporary visa and it should still be current, so I can't see them sending her back if she was coerced."

"But if she's not an illegal," Lucy said, "why should we try to help her? Isn't our story about illegal immigrants and prostitution?"

"She was sponsored to work in a restaurant, not a brothel. What's more, it's an illegal brothel, and from what Daniel's telling us there are other girls working there too. Maybe some of them are under age. Also, it sounds like more than one brothel involved. We could get a good story out of this if we handle it right."

He turned to Daniel. "You say this girl is frightened. Do you reckon she'll stuff things up if we try to help her?"

"How do you mean?"

"Well, we can't go bursting in with all guns blazing to rescue her, can we? We need her cooperation and you haven't got that yet. And if she does agree to help, she could get cold feet when the moment arrives—or give the game away beforehand. I can't rely on someone we don't know, particularly if they're scared."

"Why don't I go back and talk to her then, get her cooperation, and tell her to sit tight while we get something sorted out?"

Frank shook his head. "I need to chat to the Feds first. They could be planning something themselves and I don't want to get them offside."

"But I could still go back and see her, Frank. She needs to be reassured." He had an uncomfortable feeling that procedural formalities were about to stuff up all the work he'd done to win over Rosie. The longer they left it, the more likely she'd think he'd just been big-noting himself.

"Leave it, Dan. Another day or two won't make much difference. Let's see what I can find out first."

~~~

Frank sat watching Calloway as Larry explained the situation in a tone tinged with apology. As expected, when Larry finished, Calloway turned to Frank and said, "Are you saying this is all we have to go on?"

"Afraid so. Isobel did have another informer lined up, but he had second thoughts and won't talk. This girl is our last real hope."

"Is she under age?"

"No, but she stays overnight with a group of similar girls and I reckon some could be under eighteen."

Calloway lowered himself into his chair. He looked to be turning the matter over in his mind. Frank knew he had lots of high-level contacts, so he wasn't surprised when Calloway leaned towards them and said, "Okay, I'll see what I can do to get the Feds on side."

~~~

Less than an hour later, Calloway phoned Frank and gave him a phone number. When Frank made the call he found he was talking to Superintendent Sam Chu of the Australian Federal Police. He'd not heard the name before. Chu was either a recent promotion or a transfer from a state police force. Frank would need to tread cautiously.

Chu said, "Those premises are under surveillance. We've seen your people hanging around, but weren't sure what they were up to. Any clue who the owner is?"

"The manager's name is Ludo, but we're following up on the rego of his car as well."

Chu's voice was muffled for a minute, as if he were consulting somebody, then it became clear again. "Okay, got it. That confirms what we know. Ludovic Gruban, a Serb. His partner is another Serb, Milan Ivandic. They own two other brothels that we know of."

"How come they're using Asian women?"

"Easy. Ivandic is married to a Cambodian woman. She brings them over on various pretexts."

Frank said, "Is there anything we can do together?"

"No, we can't have our investigation compromised or we'll end up raiding empty premises."

Frank bridled at the rebuke but kept his cool. "I just want to make sure we get a story. We've cultivated the girl and she'll give us something if we don't lose her."

"You might need treatment for it…"

Frank laughed half-heartedly. "Yeah, thanks. How long before you move on this?"

"Can't tell you that, but it won't be long."

"Within a week?"

"Maybe."

"Do you mind letting me know when the raids take place?"

"No can do, sorry. We're only interested in the sexual servitude aspects. You should have a chat with the local boys—they're handling most of this anyway."

"Who would that be?"

"Rod Farling—Chief Inspector Farling—is responsible for the operational side."

~~~

Over the years, Frank had watched Rod Farling rise through the ranks in the Kings Cross police station. They'd done each other a few favours during that time. Frank phoned him, giving more weight to the closeness of his contact with Sam Chu than was merited, hoping Farling would be impressed.

At the end of their discussion, Farling said he couldn't commit to giving Frank the nod when they were about to launch a raid, but if Frank were to keep calling him for updates… That was good enough for Frank. Now he had Farling's mobile number, he intended sticking close to him in the coming days.

He thought over what Chu had said about keeping well clear. If he didn't let Daniel return to the brothel, though, he'd have next to no story. On the other hand, if Daniel went back and compromised the investigation, Frank knew he could kiss goodbye to future cooperation from the police.

There was no point discussing this with Larry or Calloway—he knew what their answer would be.

He picked up the phone.

~~~

Ever since she'd seen him to the door on his last visit, Daniel had been unable to shake off the image of Rosie's anxious face. It had brought home to him how much of a responsibility he'd taken on and it weighed heavily on his mind. He was particularly keen to let her know he was organising to free her from the brothel and that she should remain calm in the meantime. However, he had no idea of how to do that discreetly without turning up at Denfield Street.

He'd considered asking Robbie to pass a message through Wendy, but then thought better of it. First he'd have to find Robbie, which wouldn't be easy unless he spent most of his time in the betting shop. Then he'd have to persuade Robbie to agree to go along with the idea. Finally, even if Robbie did agree, he couldn't be certain that Wendy would pass on the message. She might be too scared of Ludo to take that kind of risk.

He had no alternative but to see Rosie in person and wear the bollocking he'd most certainly get if Frank found out. And not only a bollocking—he could well find himself back on the Social Diary in very short order.

He was relieved when Frank phoned him.

~~~

Daniel turned up at Denfield Street wearing a white polo shirt, jeans, and trainers, and carrying two fifty-dollar notes in his pocket together with a handkerchief and nothing else.

Wendy was on duty. When he asked for Rosie, she said, "You were here the other day, weren't you?"

"Must be my fourth visit."

"I thought so. Take a seat. She'll be free soon."

After he sat down, he looked across at the desk and saw that Wendy had disappeared. A few minutes later, Ludo came into the reception area.

"You want Rosie?"

Daniel nodded.

"Okay, she should be free now. I'll take you up to her room."

Wondering why he hadn't been asked to pay up front as before—did they trust him now he was a regular?—Daniel followed Ludo upstairs. When they reached the door of the first room, Ludo opened it and beckoned Daniel to step inside.

The room seemed empty. Then a slight movement to one side of the door caught his eye. As he turned to look, a fist slammed into his face. His head snapped back and he staggered awkwardly.

As he tried to recover his balance, he was propelled forward by a shove in the back. He didn't see the outstretched foot. Arms flailing, he crashed into the wall opposite.

He twisted round to face the men, pleading with them to stop. In answer, Ludo's fist smashed into his temple. He blacked out and slid to the floor.

~~~

A barrage of kicks jolted him back to consciousness. He heard himself whimpering, still pleading for them to stop.

When the kicking ceased, he tried to get back to his feet. He was only half upright when one of the men grabbed his hair and thrust him face down on the floor, pinning him with a foot planted hard between his shoulder blades. A hand rifled through his pockets and extracted the two fifty-dollar notes.

Something was said in a foreign language. The other man replied with a snarl before giving Daniel a savage kick in the shoulder and another to his head. He raised his arms to shield his head, only to expose his flank to more blows.

When they grew tired of kicking him, more words were spoken, and then they grabbed him by the neck and arms and hauled him to his feet. He tried to say something, but his mouth was thick with blood. He could feel it dribbling down his chin.

The two men bundled him out of the room and forced him, stumbling, down the stairs. He thought they would throw him out the front entrance. Instead they pushed him along a corridor leading to the back door. From there he was half carried, half dragged through a gate and thrust into the service lane. He fell to his knees, breathing hoarsely, then collapsed completely. The gate clattered shut behind him.

For some time, he lay sprawled on the bitumen. He tried to make sense of what had happened, but every part of his body screamed with pain. He would collect his thoughts later. For now, he must focus on getting home.

He lifted his head to see if anyone was about. The narrow lane was empty.

A breeze picked up and blew dust into his eyes and mouth. He spat it out.

An attempt at raising himself proved too much and he lay down again. A minute or two passed. The pain was worse now. He had to move.

Summoning his remaining strength, he rose unsteadily to his feet and began a staggering, aching shuffle towards Tolley Street.

11. Out in the open

Gina finished entering the previous day's takings into the ledger, pleased to see that business remained steady. She'd hate for her mother to come back and find she'd lost custom.

Now it was time to visit the hospital.

As she stepped out of Casa Rosa, rummaging through her handbag for her car keys, she became aware of a man holding his head, groaning and stumbling around a few metres away. Drunk, probably, and in the middle of the day, too. She had little sympathy for people like that.

Finding the keys, she glanced in the man's direction, and was about to head off down the street when she realised who it was.

Her immediate impulse was to retreat into the building hoping she'd not been observed, but seeing blood on his hands and clothing she knew she couldn't ignore him. He chose that moment to take his hands from his face. Their eyes met. She rushed over to him.

"My god, Daniel, what happened?"

He leaned against a lamp standard, his hand pressed against his chest, wincing as he tried to speak through swollen lips.

"It's okay, Dan, tell me later."

"I was..." He paused, gasping. "...out of my depth."

"You'd better come with me." She took him gently by the arm and led him into Casa Rosa. As they walked through the foyer, she called out to Liz, "Fetch the first aid kit."

In her office she helped him to a chair. She stood back and examined his damaged features.

"My god, you have been in the wars. Wait while I get some water."

When she returned, Liz was waiting with the first aid kit. Gina took it from her and, seeing Liz's questioning look, said, "It's okay. I'll explain later."

Gina turned to Daniel. "I've brought you some ibuprofen to help with the pain."

He took the glass and swallowed the tablets.

Taking the glass from him, she said, "You must be in agony." She hoped the rest of him wasn't like his battered face. His right eye was so swollen it might close up completely.

Neither spoke as Gina treated his cuts and bruises. As she swabbed the blood from his face, she said, "You able to talk yet?"

Speaking with some difficulty, he gave her a brief rundown while she searched the first aid kit for antiseptic cream.

"You must go to the police—you're the victim of a serious assault."

"I need to talk to my boss first."

She finished tending his head injuries. "What about the rest of you?"

"They kicked me pretty hard, especially round here." He pointed to his chest and sides.

"Let's take your shirt off."

He raised his arms and Gina eased the shirt up over his head. She grimaced at the weals and bruises on his torso. The size of the swellings confirmed his account of the violent attack. When she touched his ribs, he yelped with pain.

"Daniel, if it hurts that much, you must go to the hospital. You need X-rays. I can take you—I'm going there anyway to visit my mother."

They fell silent again as she dabbed carefully at his injuries. It crossed her mind this was the most intimate moment she'd had with a man for months. Admittedly she'd been with Morgan at the beach when he wore his swimming trunks and she a bikini, but he'd always discouraged close contact. She couldn't recall touching his bare torso at all—in fact, she'd never laid a hand on any part of his unclothed body except his arms and face.

Daniel certainly wasn't reticent about displaying his body or being touched. He was a bit overweight, but less so than Morgan, and he wasn't pasty looking either.

She remembered trying to persuade Morgan to skinny-dip with her at night and he'd been seriously affronted—something she was sure wouldn't bother Daniel—and she wondered now if his concern was more about body image than any sense of propriety.

She brought her mind back to her current situation. After previously denying an association with Casa Rosa, she owed Daniel an explanation.

Gina said softly, "So now you know about this place and me..."

"I knew already."

She stepped back sharply to study his face. A frisson of dread ran through her body. "You knew?"

He reached out a hand to placate her. "It's okay, I've not told anyone."

"Really?" She let out a sigh of relief. "I don't want anybody to know I'm working here. You've no idea how important that is to me." She handed back his shirt. "They can fix up the rest of you at the hospital."

~~~

Daniel flinched as he touched the swelling on his face. He wanted to pull down the sun visor to see himself in the mirror, but Gina's driving bordered on the reckless and he didn't dare take his eyes off the road. For the same reason, he chose not to ask her about Casa Rosa—he needed her to focus on her driving.

Resentment welled up inside him, and not only towards his attackers. How had he let himself end up like this? Through his incompetence he'd blown a great opportunity. The *Monitor* would have exposed sex slavery and he'd have taken most of the credit. Now, Frank would transfer him back to Andrea and the boring cycle of PR events, promotions, and society parties. To make matters worse, he'd been beaten up by thugs who hadn't received the slightest scratch and would likely get away with it.

When he first started working at the *Monitor* he'd gone to the gym every second day. However, long hours with too much time spent at his desk, combined with excessive drinking, had turned him into an overweight shadow of his former self. If he'd kept up his exercise regimen then maybe he could have given a better account of himself.

"If ever I catch either of them on their own..."

Gina kept her eyes on the road. "Really?"

Her dismissive tone brought him back to earth. He should report the assault, but he wasn't sure how Frank might react to that. The police would be rightly pissed off knowing the *Monitor* had compromised their investigations, especially if the Denfield Street brothel was under observation.

As the Oxford Street traffic slowed to a crawl, Daniel gained enough confidence to take his eyes off the road and inspect his face in the visor's small mirror. His bruised nose looked to be slightly askew and he could see a distinct swelling under his right eye. The bruise extended into the socket.

Glancing his way, Gina said, "You'll have a real shiner in the morning."

He grunted his agreement. What were they going to say when he turned up at the office? He could expect a fair bit of teasing, especially from the older hands. That reminded him: he ought to call Frank.

"Do you have a mobile with you? I was told not to take anything with me to that brothel."

She pointed to her handbag wedged between the front seats. He retrieved the phone and made the call.

When Frank heard what had happened, he assured Daniel that the *Monitor* would take care of his medical expenses. "If you can't make it into the office on Monday morning, I'll conference you in to the project meeting. We'll need to come up with a new approach if we're going to get this story out on time."

"Frank, should I report this to the police?"

"That's your call, but if you're still in one piece, I'd treat it as on-the-job training. In any event, it'll be your word against theirs."

"I think I'll live, but I don't like the idea of them getting away with it."

"It goes with the job, mate, along with being sworn at, jostled, spat on, and all the other crap we journos put up with. I'll send a snapper over to get some pics of your war wounds. We can use them for the story."

They arrived at the outpatients' car park just as Daniel finished the call. Gina jumped out and went round to the passenger side to open the door for him.

"Thinking of a career change?" she asked.

"No, not at all. I'm having"—a stab of pain made him gasp as he twisted in his seat—"the time of my life."

She helped him to his feet and led him into Casualty. After he booked in, she left him in the waiting room, saying she'd be back in an hour to take him home.

The hour was almost up before a nurse came and directed him into a curtained-off cubicle. While being treated, he speculated on the cause of the attack. Could Rosie have had a change of heart? She was definitely scared of Ludo, having suffered at his hands before.

Perhaps Ludo had suspected something was going on? Maybe he'd overheard Rosie and Daniel talking. Those bedroom walls were like cardboard. Maybe he'd quizzed her, slapped the truth out of her.

Could Ludo have seen the logo on Daniel's corporate credit card and not attached any significance to it until he queried the frequent visits? According to Isobel, it was unusual for punters to visit brothels more than once a week. It cost too much. Maybe that was what had aroused Ludo's suspicions

The more he speculated about Rosie's fate, the more he was consumed by guilt. She would be punished, he was sure of it, even if she had told Ludo first. Given what had happened to him, He knew Ludo would have no compunction about bashing her. The man was a brute.

In his mind's eye a bleeding and bruised Rosie was locked in a room somewhere, cursing the day she'd stepped forward to nominate herself as the most experienced girl, and wondering if she'd ever be free to return home. All because of his reckless, amateurish attempt to rescue her. He groaned.

"Soon be finished," the nurse said, "and then I'll take you round to X-ray."

The best he could hope for now was that Ludo wouldn't want to compromise her earning potential. Either that or the police might act quickly and raid the brothel.

~~~

Daniel's X-rays revealed two fractured ribs on his left side. They would take three to six weeks to mend, providing he didn't do anything strenuous. The doctor gave him painkillers and recommended bed rest for a couple of days.

Gina drove him to his home in Double Bay. An empty wheelie bin standing on the nature strip reminded him that he'd fallen behind on his domestic chores.

"That's beautiful," she said, pointing to the orange bougainvillea that climbed a trellis next to the front door, "but it needs watering."

"Yeah, I keep forgetting."

She helped him in indoors.

"Isn't your mother home?"

"No, she's visiting my grandparents in France."

"You should call her."

He checked his watch. "Later. She's probably still asleep."

"I like your mum."

"I didn't know you knew her?"

"I was introduced to her when we graduated. Mama knows her because they're both on the Sacred Heart Halfway House committee." She led him to a sofa. "Right, sit down and I'll make you a drink. Coffee? Or something stronger?"

"Coffee's fine, thanks." He followed her into the untidy kitchen and showed her where the ingredients were before limping back into the living room and lowering himself gingerly into an armchair. A few minutes later, she returned with a mug of coffee and placed it on the table next to him.

"Aren't you having one?" he asked.

"No, I have to get back."

"Okay, but you still haven't explained about you and Casa Rosa."

Gina looked at her watch, wavered for a moment, then sat down next to him. "Okay, do you want the short version or the extended one?"

If the extended version meant she staying longer, that was the one he wanted to hear.

His injuries almost forgotten, he listened intently as she recounted the events leading up to her family's ownership of Casa Rosa.

"My mum says Papa was a charming rogue and a gambler, and mixed with some dodgy types."

Daniel interrupted to say, "Our paper calls them 'colourful Sydney identities'."

"I think these were lowlifes, to be honest. Anyway, when my mother met him she was only sixteen, not long out of school, and very unworldly. She fell for him big-time. They came from the same region of Italy, so they had something in common. He was devoted to her and they married when she turned eighteen. I was born the year after.

"Until then he'd been a fairly responsible husband, but not good at keeping a job. Then one day he won a lot of money at poker and used it to buy a big black Holden, so he could chauffeur those 'identities' about, as well as acting as a driver for various brothels. They were illegal then and Mum didn't like him doing it, but he said he was all right because he wasn't living off the earnings of prostitution—he was just a driver."

He said, "Still, I bet he didn't pay tax."

"All cash in hand, I expect. At some point he convinced himself that owning a brothel was the path to riches. Mama did her best to stop him, but he promised it would only be for a short while. Needless to say, he wasn't good at it, and when he was bashed up by one of the other brothel owners for stealing girls, he persuaded her to take over while he recovered.

"She didn't want to, but she had three mouths to feed so she had little choice. Luckily, my aunt Connie came to live with us.

"Mum was much better at running the place than he was. When he was well enough to go back she told him not to bother. For the first time in her married life she had a steady income and she intended keeping it.

"After a few years she decided to go up-market. She found new premises, called it Casa Rosa, and kept only the classiest girls from the old brothel. Casa Rosa went from strength to strength and finally she was able to buy our house in Vaucluse.

"Then my dad died."

It took a moment for Daniel to register her matter-of-fact statement. "Your father died? How old were you?"

"Sixteen."

"What did he die of?"

"He was stabbed to death. They never found out who did it."

She paused, as if collecting her thoughts.

"Anyway, a few days after the funeral two men turned up. They showed Mama a stack of IOUs. Gambling debts. She knew nothing about them because he was supposed to have stopped gambling. When she totted them all up she nearly had a seizure. The men said she must pay within a week or they'd torch the building. She knew they meant it."

"She must have been absolutely devastated," Daniel said. "First your dad and then that. I suppose she couldn't go to the police because the brothel was illegal."

"No, they'd been legalised the year before. She didn't go because she knew it was a waste of time. As they were leaving, one said, 'I hear you have a pretty daughter, Mrs Russo. Let's hope she stays that way.'"

"Shit, that would have scared her rigid."

She took her handbag from the coffee table and placed it on her lap. "It did. She went to the bank and remortgaged part of our house and most of the Casa Rosa premises. She paid up and kept going. Until now. I just hope she gets better quickly."

Daniel said, "I would never have guessed your background. I had you down as a rich kid."

"I never was, and if I can't keep the business going, I'll soon be busking in Pitt Street."

"So you're going to manage it for a while?"

"What choice do I have?" She looked at her watch and sprang to her feet. "I'd better go."

He rose from his chair with an effort and accompanied her to the front door. "Before you go, can I ask a favour? Would you be able to help in any way with our investigation?"

"I doubt it."

"What about your mum? One of your staff perhaps?"

"Maybe. What do you need to know?"

"Who's employing the illegals?"

"She's never had much to do with the other houses. She thinks she's a cut above them. Still, I'll see what I can find out." She patted him gently on the shoulder. "Call me if you need anything. I'll drop by tomorrow on my way to work to see how you're getting on, okay?"

"Okay. And maybe you could give me a lift to work?"

She said forcefully, "Stay home and rest. The *Monitor* can survive without you for a few days."

12. Charlene

Frank mulled over what Daniel had told him. Should he let the Feds know or take a chance that it wouldn't affect their operation? He decided to play safe and call Superintendent Chu.

After Frank told him what had happened, Chu said, "What did I tell you blokes? You should leave this sort of thing to the experts, not some office junior thinking he's Sir Galahad."

Frank felt like a schoolboy being hauled up before the principal. "Hold on, Sam. I doubt we've compromised your operation. They wouldn't have a clue what he was up to."

"How can you be so sure?"

"He never mentioned what job he did, and he carried nothing on him to identify who he was. They went through his pockets and stole the only thing he had, which was a hundred bucks."

Chu snorted his disdain for Frank's naivety. "Personally, that would make me suspicious. People normally carry some form of identification with them. Did he report it?"

"No. It's just his word against theirs."

"True. Most blokes won't own up to visiting a brothel anyway. Hopefully, they'll think he's a pest—

some religious nut wanting to save the girls. It happens."

"So you don't think we've compromised your operation?"

"We'll keep a closer eye on Denfield Street now and see if there's any change of activity. In the meantime, do me a favour and keep your people well out of our way."

~~~

An outgoing editor-in-chief had once told Frank he was the 'quintessential newspaperman'. He'd glowed inwardly at the praise, his self-perception validated, because that's how he viewed himself: a dedicated, twenty-four-hours-a-day pressman.

He played up to the stereotype: sleeves half rolled up, collar unbuttoned, tie loose—he even had a noticeable paunch to attest to being deskbound. He not only looked the part, he lived it as well, as testified by two failed marriages.

Getting a cracking story onto the front page was all he cared about, so when Calloway called him in to his office to say how disappointed he was with progress, Frank took it badly. The initial two weeks for preparing the story were nearly up. If Isobel hadn't gone on leave, or if he'd had another experienced reporter to call on, perhaps he'd have made a breakthrough, but Daniel had blown the one promising lead they had. It wasn't Dan's fault, of course. Frank shouldn't have sent a boy on a man's errand.

Nevertheless, he needed something worth printing.

The policy for campaigns of this nature was to make a big splash with the Saturday edition and then to publish related articles in the first two or three days of the following week. Right now he didn't have enough material even for the Saturday edition.

To make matters worse, until the police made their raids, he had no idea when that deadline would be.

~~~

Daniel arrived late for work on the Monday morning. He'd seen his doctor, who'd advised him to rest up for another day or two, but the prospect of watching hours of mindless daytime television was too dreadful to contemplate.

Isobel was sitting at her desk painting her fingernails when he arrived. She looked up and smiled. "Here comes the wounded warrior."

He responded with a rueful smile. "Want to see the bruises?"

"Depends where they are."

"In more places than I care to mention. How was your holiday?"

"Not long enough."

He sat down carefully in her visitor's chair. "Has Frank brought you up to date?"

"Yes, and he's not happy. He wants us to find a disgruntled prossie, or one who's no longer on the game, and write up a 'My Life as a Sex Worker' article with lots of lurid detail."

"How do we do that? Personal ad in the classifieds?"

"Hardly. Anyway, we don't have time for formalities. I'm calling on Robbie's services again. He says he knows a girl who'll talk to us if the price is right. We're seeing them this arvo."

They met in the same nondescript café as before. This time Robbie was waiting for them. Seated next to him, a dark-haired woman wearing a black leather coat watched them approach. He introduced her as Charlene. "But that's not me real name," she said, "just what I use for business."

"That's fine for the article," Isobel said, "but we need your real name as well, and your address." When Charlene gave her a suspicious look, she added, "Our auditors—they don't trust us where money's concerned."

"Orright, it's Cheryl Smith." She fished in her handbag and pulled out a driver's licence. She flicked it over to Isobel. "That shows I'm genuine. You can get me address from there as well."

Isobel pushed the licence towards Daniel, who copied the address as requested and made a note of her age: thirty-nine. He handed the licence back to Charlene, who gave him an encouraging smile. She would have been attractive but for her small, soulless eyes.

Isobel said, "So, you know what we're looking for?"

"You're digging up dirt on brothels, right? For that, er, newspaper of yours."

"More or less, but we don't want to hear about routine things. Our readers are aware of that. We need the more off-the-wall, kinky, weirdo stuff."

"Like what?"

"Like the wacky requests you get, the oddballs you work with—you know, the sort of stuff that'll make our readers choke on their cornflakes when they read it."

"Orright."

"Good." Isobel turned to Robbie. "Thanks, Robbie. I'll catch you later."

Robbie got to his feet. Looking down at Daniel, he said, "If I were you, I'd be more careful in future. You'll have worse than bruises next time."

He walked off before Daniel could think of a suitable reply.

Charlene watched Robbie leave the café before turning to Isobel. "So how much are you payin' me?"

~~~

Charlene talked for some time about life in the various brothels she'd worked in. From Isobel's expression it was clear she wasn't hearing anything new but Charlene rattled on. Daniel knew she sensed his discomfort at some of the things she was saying, though he did his best to put on a weary, man-of-the-world face, and she dwelled too long on particular incidents. So he wasn't surprised when Isobel interrupted her.

"You'd have come across some truly gross behaviour in your time, wouldn't you? Real sickos? Tell me about them."

"Yeah, you come across some weirdos in this business," Charlene said brightly, sitting more upright. She must have realised she wasn't delivering. "Like, I had this one bloke, all he wanted was to have the soles of me feet rubbed all over him, an' he was the one doing the rubbing. I lay there while he used my feet to jerk himself off. Then there was a pollie who put my underwear on and swanned around the room while I told him how gorgeous he looked. Another bloke—"

Isobel toyed with her mobile phone while she listened, turning and twisting it over as if she couldn't decide whether to keep it or throw it away. After more unsurprising disclosures, she interrupted Charlene again. "All right. Tell me about men who've treated you badly. You know, knocked you about or tried to get you to do things you didn't want to?"

"Yeah, well, you get them too, the ones who give you a smacking if you don't do what they want. Had a bloke pull a knife on me once, stuck it right in me throat"—she placed a finger on her neck where the blade had touched and jerked her head back for effect—"but I talked some sense into him and he calmed down. Nicked me, though. Trouble is, some of them are so pissed or on something, they can't perform, and then they blame you. Think you're a fuckin' miracle worker sometimes.

"Another one vomited in me face while he was on the job. Disgusting bastard! Seems he'd done it before. Some men are out and out grubs. One of 'em gave me HIV, I reckon."

"You're HIV?"

"Yeah, found out a few weeks ago."

"And you're still on the game?"

Charlene shrugged.

Isobel spoke sharply, "Is that a yes or a no?"

"I take precautions."

"Maybe, but you're still a serious risk. Where are you working now?"

"Nowhere special."

Isobel weighed the answer and then said, "All right, we need to move on. You ever worked with illegal migrants?"

"Dunno—they're not going to tell you, are they? I've worked with foreign students—Asians mainly. They're always bitching about being underpaid."

"Any names, places where they work?"

"Nah. They come and go too fast in this game."

Again Daniel saw that Charlene wasn't giving Isobel what she wanted. With a quick look to Isobel to make sure he wasn't acting out of line, he posed his own question. "Do some of the men insist on unprotected sex?"

"Bareback? Course they do. We're not supposed to, but then, you know..."

Isobel slipped her phone into her bag and clasped it shut. "But you let them anyway?"

"Yeah. They're paying after all and the owners don't like us turning business away."

Isobel became alert. "You mean the owners allow you to have unprotected sex?"

"Well, sort of. They don't tell you not to, like, but if a punter asks for his money back because you won't let 'em, well then the owners get real shitty with you, specially when business is slack."

"All of them?"

"Nah, just a few."

"Any names?"

The prostitute took her time preparing an answer, as if weighing up the wisdom of revealing the information. "There's one place. I worked there recently...called Casa Rosa."

"Casa Rosa? Are you serious?" He realised his mistake too late. Isobel looked intently at him for a second or two before slowly turning back to Charlene, who gave Isobel a quizzical look. He sensed his face redden and leaned back, hoping to keep out of Isobel's line of sight.

"We're talking about the place in Surry Hills that calls itself an up-market bordello?"

Charlene glanced at Daniel before answering, "Up-market? You coulda fooled me. Yeah, that's the one. Tolley Street."

"And did you know you had HIV when you worked there?"

"I found out just after I left."

"Who runs it?"

"Maria...Maria Russo."

~~~

Isobel quickly guided Charlene through other aspects of her working life—the unsocial hours, fear of disease, poor working conditions, lack of concern for her welfare by irrational and vindictive bosses—until she called a halt and switched off her recorder.

"I think I have enough to be going on with. Thanks for your time, Charlene."

"What about me money?"

"You'll be paid when the article gets published. That's how we normally operate."

After Charlene left, Isobel gave Daniel a long hard look. "Okay, so what's it with you and this Casa Rosa? You asked me about them before, didn't you?"

While he'd been expecting the question, he still hadn't made up his mind if he should tell the truth. He was torn between respecting Gina's confidences and yielding to his professional responsibility as a journalist. To make matters more difficult, he didn't trust Isobel well enough to keep a secret. Playing dumb seemed to be his best option.

"I was just curious, that was all."

"Why, you a client of theirs?"

He bridled at the suggestion. "Course not."

"Then why are you so curious?"

"No particular reason...just thought they were one of the better ones."

"I'll give you the benefit of the doubt...for now." From her expression it was clear she wasn't convinced.

He moved to change the subject. "Do you believe her?"

"About what?"

"Casa Rosa making their girls have unprotected sex?"

"Why not? Why would the owners care? It's more money for them."

He could hardly answer that question without revealing some knowledge of Casa Rosa's practices. Gina had been emphatic about their high standards of hygiene.

"But their clientele...they must be professional people, right? High flyers, like judges and politicians."

Isobel studied him in disbelief. "Why should that make a difference? They're men, aren't they?"

"I still can't imagine a place like that would risk its reputation."

She slowly shook her head and gave him a pitying look.

"Danny, mate, you've no idea, have you? Who's going to complain? Who's going to listen?" Before he could answer, she said, "At least *we* listened, and we're going to make it the centrepiece of the article. An HIV tom who doesn't use condoms and works in a legal brothel? Oh boy, Crispy's gonna love this."

~~~

When they returned to the office, Isobel gave Daniel the tape she'd recorded and asked him to write up the interview while she went to talk to Frank.

He was in a quandary. He was expected to type the transcript before he left for the day and yet he needed to talk to Gina. He'd left a message on her home answering machine asking her to call urgently, but she wouldn't have received it if she was still at work. He looked up Casa Rosa's number. When he called and asked to be put through to Gina Russo, he was told he must have the wrong number.

As soon as Isobel returned, he said, "Sorry about this, but something really important has come up. I'll come back later to finish the transcript."

Before she could object, he grabbed his jacket and took off.

13. Bearer of bad news

Chloe was farewelling a client when a taxi pulled up and a fair-haired young man with a bruised eye socket stepped out. She held the door open for him as he hurried in. He gave her a quick smile and thanked her before striding to the desk.

She wondered if he would be her next client. Business was quiet and he looked the type she liked: young, polite, friendly, and clean looking. They didn't get many of those.

As she started down the hallway to the kitchen, she heard him ask for Gina. Just her luck.

In the kitchen the television was showing a children's program. She turned it off, sat at the table and picked up a magazine. It was full of gossip and pictures of movie stars and pop idols. She tossed it to one side and cupped her chin in her hands. Working as an escort severely limited her social life. If it weren't for the occasional night out or clothes shopping with Kellie, Tammi, and the others, her life would be an endless cycle of work and sleep.

The idea of taking up remedial massage was becoming more attractive with the passing of each day. She knew it would be hard work but at least she could get back to something resembling a normal life. Kellie thought she was mad even to think about it, but then she'd been the one to introduce Chloe to Casa Rosa.

Chloe had been getting a handbag strap fixed in the Chatswood Chase shopping centre when she'd run into Kellie. The two women had met four years earlier on a three-night, under-35s cruise around the South-east Pacific. The hedonistic trip was also where she met Bernie, her now estranged and unlamented husband.

Kellie said she needed to rest her feet and suggested they go for a coffee and a chat. They found a table in the brasserie on the ground floor, where Kellie distributed her many shopping bags on the unoccupied chairs

She said, "Did you ever see that bloke again? The one who was all over you like a wet shower curtain?"

"Did I ever! I ended up marrying the mongrel."

"Uh-oh, bad move, eh?"

Chloe tried to keep the bitterness out of her voice as she explained how she'd caught Bernie in bed with her friend Lily.

"Your best mate?"

"Not any more. What a bitch!"

"God, a double whammy."

"I'm back at Mum's now. I couldn't afford to keep the flat on after I'd kicked him out, and then I was made redundant—not enough work. One thing after another, really."

"Yeah, life's a bitch sometimes. So what are you doing now?"

"I'm with two agencies but all I get are sales jobs. How about you?"

Kellie smiled. "I'm an escort."

"Escort?"

"You know, hostess, courtesan...hooker."

"A prostitute?"

"I prefer escort. Prostitutes are just druggies hanging around shop doorways giving it away to score. We escorts are a different breed altogether."

"But you still do the same thing." Chloe grimaced at the thought of having strangers pawing her body. "Better you than me is all I can say, even if it does pay well," she said, indicating the shopping bags. "What made you become a pros... an escort?"

"When I packed up uni, Mum and Dad didn't want to know me, so I moved in with a mate. I was broke and she kept hassling me for my share of the rent, so when I saw this ad in the local paper, I thought why not. Just do it for a little while till I got on my feet.

"Anyway, I turned up in trackies and trainers—I'd just been to the gym—no makeup on, no handbag. The manager took me on straightaway—they must have been desperate. You won't believe this. She leads me into the changing room, tells me to try on some spare clothes, empties her handbag, shoves some cab vouchers into it with a few condoms and lubes, and sends me out on my first job."

Kellie waited for her reaction. All she could manage was to shake her head in amazement and mutter, "You're unbelievable."

"Yeah? Well I went home that night with a thousand dollars stuffed down my knickers."

"A thousand?"

"Near enough. I've done better since."

"A thousand dollars... Jeez, Kell."

Kellie smiled. "Not bad, eh? You should give it a go."

"No way." She shivered. "All those strange men..."

"You get used to it. It's all an act. Some of them even turn me on, but most of them are like nervy kids. Anyway, the hours are flexible and the money's good—tell me how many jobs are like that?" Seeing Chloe wasn't convinced, she added, "It's a tough life for a woman on her own, you know—you can't be too precious if you want to survive."

"I'll manage somehow. Anyway, it would murder my love life...if I had one."

"Actually, I have a boyfriend—Dave. Been seeing him for a couple of months now."

"Does he know?"

"He doesn't need to. I told him I was a carer in an old people's home. Sort of true at times."

"What if he finds out?"

"Well, he'd have to turn up at Casa Rosa and see me there." She laughed. "He'd have a bit of explaining to do himself, then, wouldn't he?"

~~~

Daniel arrived at Casa Rosa by taxi and hurried through the front door being held open by an attractive Asian woman. As he entered, he noticed a young man sitting behind the reception desk, along with the woman who'd spoken to him on his first visit and who he now knew was called Liz. He approached the desk as she looked up and smiled.

"Hi, I need to speak to Gina, please. It's urgent. My name's Daniel Bouvier."

"I know. I'll see if she's busy." Liz phoned Gina and passed on the message. A moment later, Gina came into reception and immediately pointed to his face. "I said you'd have a shiner. How are you feeling?"

"Still a few aches and pains, but as you can see I'm back on my feet."

"You were supposed to stay home and rest."

"As long as I don't laugh or sneeze, I'll be okay."

She led him to her office. Once inside, she sat behind the desk and her tone became businesslike. "So what's so urgent that it couldn't wait until I arrived home?"

Daniel thought how lovely she looked in a white cotton blouse that accentuated her light olive skin and the straight dark hair that fell to her shoulders.

"One of your previous workers has told my paper that you—your mum, that is—encourages your girls not to bother with condoms if the clients don't like them. What's more, she's got HIV. You can imagine how that's going to look on the front page at the weekend."

Gina looked stunned. She remained completely still until, as the news sank in, her expression turned into one of outrage.

"That's ridiculous!" She was out of her seat and leaning so far over the desk that he instinctively swayed back in his chair. "Daniel, you know that's absolutely not true."

He stuck up his hands in mock defence. "I know, I know, but that's what she's told us."

Without taking her eyes off him, she resumed her seat. "Who told you this crap?"

"Her name's Charlene."

Gina jumped to her feet, stepped around the desk, and marched out of the office. A minute later she returned with a bemused Liz in tow. "Tell Liz who you said it was."

"She said her working name was Charlene, but her real name is Cheryl—"

"—Smith," finished Liz.

"So you know her?"

"Do we ever. She was a nightmare. Maria said taking her on was the worst decision she ever made."

"Why?"

"Maria's strict on house rules but Charlene managed to break most of them. We suspected her of stealing money from a client. When he complained Maria had to pay him out of her own pocket—he was in government, so she didn't want any trouble. Then Britney accused her of stealing her leather jacket. She denied that as well."

"What colour was the jacket?"

"Black, I think. Why?"

"She was wearing one like that when we interviewed her."

Liz threw up her hands. "See what a lying cow she is! Anyway, Maria gave her the push when we found out she was letting clients get away with unprotected sex."

"How did you find that out?"

She was away sick. A couple of her regulars tried to get the other girls to go bareback. They reckoned Charlene let them do anything they wanted—no condoms, no dams, nothing. The girls refused, of course, and told Maria. Then one of the men demanded his money back. I reminded him of our WorkCover obligations and he let it drop."

"She says she has HIV."

"What? Not while she was here she didn't. All the girls are checked every month, no exceptions. She's jerking you around."

Gina thanked Liz and after she left said, "Now you know the truth, what are you going to do about it?"

"I'm not sure there's much I can do."

"What about this Charlene woman? Surely you can make her retract her story?"

"She's getting paid for it. I don't like telling you this, but the onus is on you to refute the allegations, otherwise the *Monitor* will go ahead and print them."

She looked at him incredulously. "On me? Can't you take my word for it?"

"I do, but you know what tabloids are like—publish and be damned. Unless you jump in quick to stop them, they'll print it."

"If they do, I'll sue the bastards."

"Fine, but even if you win, the damage will have been done already."

She let out a sigh of despair.

"Mama's going to be devastated. I don't know if I should even tell her. This is absurd."

She grew angry again. "How you can work for that fucking rag, Dan? Can't you see you're tainted by it?"

When he didn't rise to the bait, she said, matter-of-factly, "Okay, you'd better tell me what I should do."

~~~

It was mid-evening by the time Daniel returned to the office. Isobel and most of the others had left for the day. On impulse he went over to Frank's office and stood in the doorway waiting to catch his eye. Frank was lost in concentration jotting down notes from his computer screen. It took him a minute before he realised Daniel was waiting to catch his attention.

"Sorry, mate, didn't see you there." He waved him to a chair in front of his desk.

"I didn't want to disturb you—you looked absorbed in what you were doing."

Frank smiled. "Extra-curricular activity. The Moral Australia Party has me intrigued. I'm trying to get a handle on them"

"I didn't vote for them."

"Me neither, nor am I likely to, but they're in a strong position to influence what we can and can't do. If they get their way, we'll end up losing the social advances that previous generations fought for, mine included."

"At least Calloway would be happy."

"Doubtful." Frank was looking at his monitor again. "He'd have no material for his paper and we'd be out of a job."

"I'm sure he'd find something else to campaign about."

Frank made another note on his writing pad. "Isobel tells me the two of you managed to bring in a good story today."

He still had one eye on the screen, only half listening as Daniel said, "We did, but...there's a big problem."

Frank didn't respond immediately, then he turned in his chair and gave Daniel his full attention. "I have a feeling I don't want to hear this."

"She's a liar—our informant, that is, not Isobel. She was sacked for not following the rules at the brothel she worked in. Nobody ever told her she shouldn't use condoms, and she never had HIV while she was there either. They're very insistent on sticking to WorkCover guidelines."

"How do you know that?"

"I know the owner of Casa Rosa. I went there and checked just now."

"Isobel never said."

"She doesn't know. I didn't want to let on. She can be…I'm not sure how to put this, but I reckon she'd try to exploit my relationship with the owner."

"Oh, it's London to a brick she would. That's why she's one of our best journos. By the way, how are you two getting on?"

"Okay, but she's making sure I know I'm a rookie."

"Well, you are."

"I know, but she likes to rub it in. I'm beginning to think she has a sadistic streak in her."

Frank laughed. "You should have seen her when she started here twelve years ago. Straight out of uni…thought she was going to get a byline in her first week. Needless to say, the old hands made her life a misery. But she's a tough cookie. She soon realised that if you can't beat 'em, you gotta join 'em."

He leaned back and studied Daniel. "You've given me a problem. If what you say is true—"

"It is, Frank."

"—then I don't have my main story for this week."

"I'm sorry…"

"Nothing to be sorry about. We're supposed to verify our stories as best we can. Isobel knows that, but where prostitution's concerned it's not so easy." He looked Daniel straight in the eye. "Are you certain this brothel is okay?"

"I trust them, Frank. They sacked the girl in question and they're willing to swear on a stack of Bibles she's a liar. I think you'll be getting a solicitor's letter fairly soon."

"Okay, I'll talk to Isobel first thing tomorrow and see if she can come up with another lead—Calloway wants something juicy for the weekend and it's my balls on the line."

He expected Frank to turn back to his monitor but instead he sat watching Daniel long enough for him to feel uncomfortable. "Larry reckons you snagged this job because your mum's friendly with Calloway. Is that right?"

He would have preferred not to answer. His mother had wangled the cadetship without his prior knowledge and he'd felt guilty about it, even though his heart was set on becoming a journalist. The favour was supposed to be kept secret—the last thing he wanted was for his colleagues to think he was receiving special treatment. Isobel, for one, would give him heaps. Now it appeared Calloway had mentioned it to Larry.

"I'd rather it wasn't common knowledge. I'm serious about this job. I've wanted to be a journalist since I was a kid. I'd hate it if people thought I couldn't succeed on the same terms as everyone else."

"That's good to hear, mate. However, I can't guarantee it won't get around the office. In fact, if I were you, I'd take it for granted it'll be common knowledge sooner than you think. You can't keep a secret in a place like this. For my part, though, I won't say anything—I won't even confirm it to Larry." He gave Daniel a reassuring smile.

"Thanks, I appreciate that."

"However,"—Frank paused for effect—"you're going to have to put in the hard yards if you want to be taken on merit."

As Daniel was about to leave, Frank said, "One other thing—how come you didn't tell us you were good mates with a brothel owner?"

"Actually, it's her daughter. Mrs Russo's just had an operation for cancer and her daughter's standing in for her while she's recovering."

"I'll do what I can to keep her name out of the paper, but the way things are going, Dan, all I can say is she'll be lucky not to get sprung."

14. Ace reporter

When Daniel walked into the office the following morning, Isobel shot up from her workstation and marched straight at him. As they converged at his desk, she said, "What the fuck you playing at, Daniel?"

Those nearest to them turned to see what the fuss was about. Daniel grabbed her arm. "Not here! We need a meeting room."

"Let go of me!" She shook his hand off but followed him as he set off down the corridor to look for an unoccupied room.

Finding one free didn't look promising, and he was about to suggest going down to the foyer when a meeting room door opened and out trooped its occupants. He shepherded Isobel inside. As soon as he closed the door, she came up close, eyes burning.

"You went behind my back and blew my story right out of the water. Thanks a lot, pal! You and I are supposed to be a team, right? You're supposed to be helping me, learning from me. Instead, you fucking ran off to your brothel friends to warn them!"

Before he could reply, she said, "And what's more, you've made me look a right fucking dill, like I don't know what the fuck I'm doing."

"Hold on, hold on... Look, I'm sorry I didn't tell you, but if I had, you wouldn't have let me go. I didn't trust that woman, and I was right."

She prodded his chest with a forefinger, causing him to wince. "Who gives a flying fuck if she's telling the truth? For fuck's sake, Daniel, they're prostitutes, scumbags, the dregs of society—nobody gives a shit about them. They don't have morals—they're in it for the money, first and last."

He stepped back to avoid further finger stabbing and stumbled into a chair. He took the opportunity to sit down.

"What about your morals? You don't give a stuff if you destroy the lives of law-abiding people. You'd rather print lies than check the facts. That brothel's a legal business—it pays taxes like we do, same as casinos and pubs and a stack of other businesses you might think immoral."

Isobel looked at him incredulously. "You're working for the *Monitor*!" She moved to take the seat opposite him. "All right, let's have it. You're obviously friendly with the Casa Rosa people. You a customer or what?"

"The owners are friends of mine, okay? Respectable people. They don't deserve to be bundled in with all the slimeballs and lowlifes like the one in Denfield Street. This is the last thing they need—their business is barely keeping its head above water."

"Don't give me that shit. You should have told me all this before. You're covering up for them, aren't you? Charlene was telling the truth and you don't like what she said."

"Trust me, she's a champion bullshitter."

"Trust you! That's a joke." Her tone changed. "You're not cut out for this type of work. I'm going to ask Frank to take you off the story. I'm better off on my own."

He shuddered with fear on hearing that declaration. If he was taken off the story, he'd never get another shot at this kind of journalism, the kind he'd dreamt of for years. He'd be confined to reporting on charity balls and celebrity book launches and eventually end up writing horoscopes. He tried to think of a way to get her to change her mind. There had to be something he could do that she couldn't.

"Supposing I went back to Casa Rosa to see if they can give us some leads on the illegals? I'm sure they must hear things, know people we could talk to. Customers, even. Word must get around. It's worth a shot."

She got to her feet and went to the door. As she opened it, she said, "Just remember, if you don't find us a story quick smart, you'll be back working for Amanda and it'll be your friends making the headlines on Saturday."

~~~

Gina couldn't believe how late it was when she woke. The clock said eight-thirty.

She cast her mind back to the previous night. She'd gone to bed at a quarter to one and lain awake chewing over Charlene's allegations. She must have dozed off around one-thirty. Now she was groggy, as if she'd drank heavily the night before, when all she'd had was a single glass of wine.

She slipped on her dressing gown and went downstairs to find her aunt cleaning the living room.

"I didn't want to disturb you," Concetta said, switching off the vacuum cleaner. "I looked in your room and you seemed so peaceful, like a baby. I thought I'd let you sleep a little longer. You deserve it, working so late."

"Thanks, Connie, but I shouldn't have slept in." Her self-discipline was slipping. Usually she slept for no more than six hours at a stretch.

Concetta said, "Would you like breakfast? Fried egg, ham, tomato?"

"I'll just have muesli, but thanks all the same. I wouldn't mind a coffee, though."

Gina put muesli and milk into a bowl and took it out to the terrace. The sun was warm and a slight breeze rustled the palms.

She'd forgotten how beautiful Sydney could be. The sky always appeared higher and larger than anywhere else; everything seemed more vivid in outline and colour. Currawongs and magpies called to each other around the bay; below the terrace rosellas chattered and squabbled among the banksias and grevilleas.

It brought back a memory of when she'd taken Morgan to see an Australian film in Boston. The carolling of Australian magpies on the soundtrack had made her unexpectedly homesick, much to his surprise.

She wondered what he would make of this panorama. She imagined his father's yacht at anchor in the bay below, Morgan on deck waving to her.

No, that was never going to happen. She must learn to push him out of her mind and move on.

When her aunt came out with the coffee, she brought the telephone as well.

"Someone for you."

Her first, irrational, thought was she'd somehow summoned up Morgan, but it turned out to be Daniel. "Oh," was all she managed to say when he announced himself.

"Gee, am I that unpopular?"

"Sorry, I was expecting someone else."

"Are you still pissed off at me because of Charlene? I was trying to help you. I thought you knew me better than that."

She wasn't altogether sure why she bore him a grudge. She liked him well enough, but she was uncomfortable about his job at the *Monitor*—it was bound to bring them into conflict sooner or later. The *Monitor* would always find a reason to put sex on the front page to sell its grubby newspapers. "Sorry, Dan. I'm not pissed off at you. Look, there's a lot going on in my life at the moment and..."

"That's okay."

She softened her tone. "I spoke to our solicitor like you suggested and he's coming round this morning to speak to Liz. He's also agreed to visit my mother and get her to sign a statutory declaration as well. He said he'll send a letter and the stat decs to the *Monitor* by courier."

"You know, if I hadn't seen you that time, I'd never have known about you and Casa Rosa and so I wouldn't have been able to warn you."

He had a point, she couldn't deny that. She was shooting the messenger.

"I really do appreciate you coming to see me yesterday."

"That's what friends are for. Think no more of it."

"I owe you one."

Daniel cleared his throat. "There is something you can help me with. Remember I asked you to find out about illegals...?"

~~~

Three of the Casa Rosa girls were at her mother's bedside when Gina arrived with the solicitor. Although she told them she would only stay for a minute, they made their excuses and left.

The solicitor took Maria through the deposition, and after she signed it he left.

Maria grabbed Gina's hand. "Hey, good news—I'm going home tomorrow."

"Excellent! You'll be able to rest up properly now."

"I hope I won't be a burden on Connie."

"You know she loves looking after you."

Concetta chose that moment to arrive.

Gina said, "I'll leave you two to chat for a bit. By the way, Mama, do you mind if I bring a friend back with me? He's trying to get some information for a newspaper article he's writing."

Her mother was by herself when Gina returned an hour later.

"Mama, this is Daniel Bouvier."

Maria stared at him. "You're Yvonne's boy, aren't you? I haven't seen her for ages."

"She's doing a lot of work overseas, so I don't see much of her either."

Maria pointed to his face. "You look as if you've been ten rounds with Mike Tyson."

Gina couldn't help herself. "If he had, he wouldn't have lasted more than ten seconds."

He gave her a disappointed look. "I'm afraid Gina has a low regard for my abilities, Mrs Russo. I'm a reporter. Being attacked is part of my job description, apparently."

Maria said, "There's far too much violence these days."

"I'm getting over it. Anyway, I'm trying to find out about women working in brothels who shouldn't be. Illegals. I was hoping you might know where this sort of thing is going on."

She considered the question. "I know it goes on, but I don't have anything to do with it. All my girls are legal and I do everything by the book. I'm sorry, I wish I could help you." She turned to Gina. "Have a word with Liz. She'll know if anyone does, but Pat was the one who had her ear to the ground."

Gina said, for Daniel's benefit, "Pat was the manager who left recently."

Maria said, "Liz will have Pat's number."

~~~

Daniel returned with Gina to Casa Rosa just as Liz arrived. Gina asked her to talk to him about the illegal brothels.

"Use my office," she said. "I'll cover the desk for you."

He said to Liz, "What we're interested in are those who bring in girls from overseas."

"They're mostly out west, but I don't know any names. Pat might. I can call her if you like."

She reached Pat without difficulty. Daniel wished he could hear both sides of the conversation, especially as Liz's tone varied so much as they swapped news. One moment she was expressing surprise, the next uttering subdued responses. They chatted for so long he wondered if she'd forgotten the reason for the call. He gave her a meaningful look, but she barely glanced at him as she continued to be engrossed in whatever Pat was telling her.

Finally, she mentioned why she'd phoned and the conversation became businesslike in tone. For the next five minutes, she jotted down names and addresses and explanatory notes.

She put the phone down. "There's a few possibilities, but don't get your hopes up. It's mostly rumour and it could be out of date. Those places are forever being closed down and then sprouting up somewhere else."

He wished she'd be a bit more upbeat. Isobel was expecting him to come up with something meaty to get stuck into, not hearsay and gossip.

"I'm more than grateful for what you've given me."

"Okay," Liz said, "but don't let on where you got this information from. There are some ugly bastards out there and we don't want this place torched."

15. On the job

Early evening and already the reception desk was overloaded with appointments. Gina didn't understand why.

"There's an international insurance agents' conference at Darling Harbour," Liz said, "and the Swans' game at the SCG. And to top it off, Jock's not turned up yet, so I've had to book cabs for Holly and Amber."

"Where's Jock?"

"I don't know, but you need to speak to him. He's too unreliable. Oh, and the taxis are running late. I'll need another one for Sheri if he doesn't turn up in a minute."

She'd been warned about Jock's timekeeping. She would need to get on top of that before further chaos ensued. Meanwhile, she had the immediate problem of making sure Sheri got to her appointment. She was still using her mother's BMW. She'd need to buy her own car when her mother came back.

"Don't bother. I'll take her in my car. And I'll have a word with Jock when I get back. He knows damn well we're short-handed."

~~~

Chloe knelt over her client's supine body. He said his name was John. How many of those did she meet? He looked to be in his mid-thirties. His pale, flabby body, still damp from the shower, told her he was in definite need of the workout she was about to give him. She smelled alcohol on his breath, but he didn't seem drunk. If he had been, he wouldn't have made it past Reception. Casa Rosa was strict about that.

She had a good memory for faces and she couldn't recollect seeing him before. As with all her customers, she'd chatted to him for a few minutes to help him relax before suggesting they remove their clothes. He was reluctant to talk, although that wasn't unusual. His mood alternated between distraction and alertness.

"Something bothering you? Is it your first time?" she asked.

He shook his head but didn't meet her gaze. "I'm okay. Got a lot on my mind, that's all."

At her request he stretched out on the bed. He closed his eyes while she brought him fully erect with dexterous use of her fingers. With her lips and teeth she manoeuvred the condom over his penis and eased it down with her fingers. She was surprised he didn't show any emotion while she was doing this—most clients enjoyed the experience. He remained motionless as she smeared gel on the tip of the condom.

Placing her hands for support on his corpulent belly, she eased herself onto him. He moaned quietly in time with her rhythm. She watched his face for signs of increasing arousal, but he seemed content to let her continue at a regular pace. She knew if she rushed him, he might feel cheated. Some customers were particular about using their allotted time to the maximum; others focused on getting relief and didn't care. As this was her first time with him, she had no idea which category he fitted in. After ten minutes of steadily bobbing up and down in his lap and receiving no noticeable response, she decided he belonged in the first category.

Her thoughts drifted. The day before, she'd tried on an electric blue sheath dress in a Pitt Street fashion store. It fitted her to perfection and she'd almost bought it, even though it was more than she normally paid for a dress, but then she'd realised it would hang in her wardrobe waiting for the special evening out that was unlikely to happen. Since starting at Casa Rosa, her life consisted of little more than work and the occasional outing with Kellie or Tammi to the shops and pub.

John opened his eyes. "Okay, doggie style now."

Chloe dismounted and crouched down on her hands and knees. He climbed back on the bed and knelt behind her. She put a hand between her legs to help guide him in.

She was happier in this position as it was less tiring. His movements were machine-like, steady and even, and she wondered if he was one of those men who could maintain an erection for hours without being able to reach a climax. She hoped not. A long session would leave her sore.

He withdrew. As she turned to see what he wanted to do next, he grabbed her hips firmly and prodded her anus with the tip of his penis.

"No, not that." She spoke firmly but without alarm. It wasn't unusual for a client to try something they hadn't agreed to, especially when aroused, and usually they would stop when told to. John ignored her and tried once more to penetrate her.

"I said no! Let's try something else."

Before she had a chance to turn round to face him, he shoved her face into the soft pillow and straddled her back. Pinned down by his weight and fighting to breathe, she struggled to get out from under him, but he grasped her arms and yanked them behind her back. Holding them together by the wrists with one hand, he shuffled backwards.

Now was her chance. She lifted her head to shout for help. Before she could let out a cry, his other hand slammed into the back of her head, forcing it further into the pillow.

Writhing and squirming, she hoped to dislodge him by sheer persistence, but no way could she match his strength. She gave up and laid still.

Once more his penis probed between her clenched buttocks. Determined to thwart his efforts, she crossed her ankles. Now he'd have to use one hand to force her legs apart, and that would give her an opportunity to try something different.

He must have realised this too, because he stretched his body over hers. Able now to free one hand, he placed his head sideways on hers to keep it pressed down.

Now he was using his legs to prise hers apart, his hand squeezing between her thighs and into the cleft of her buttocks.

She couldn't breathe. Panic welled up inside her. She was suffocating.

If only she could reach the alarm button. It was so close.

His penis, pressing hard against her, couldn't overcome her resistance. He moved his hand to the side of her head. He must be about to use it to replace the pressure of his head when he lifted it.

She had to do it now—the moment he shifted his head she must scream as loud as she could.

His weight eased. Now! With a supreme effort she forced her head up from the pillow. His hand smacked it down immediately, her muffled scream absorbed by the fabric. She wept a mixture of rage and self-pity as she realised the hopelessness of her situation.

No-one would have heard her.

~~~

After dropping Sheri off, Gina drove down George Street to the Hilton to pick up Holly. She'd been hoping to find her standing alone on the pavement. Instead, a crowd milled around, and it was impossible to make out who was waiting for her. To make matters worse, she couldn't find a parking space.

Repeated flashing in her rear view mirror alerted her to a bus bearing down, asserting its right of way. She drove on, turning left at the lights into Park Street.

She turned left again at the next street. As she approached Market Street her phone rang. When the lights changed to red, she snatched the phone from her bag and pressed it to her ear.

Liz. "Holly's called to say you drove right past her. What's the problem?"

"I had a bus up my arse—I couldn't stop."

"Don't let that bother you—you'll only be stopped for a few seconds. Didn't you see her? She said you had enough time to pick her up."

"Lots of people were around. Besides...I can't remember what she looks like."

"Haven't you met her yet?" Liz sounded exasperated. "Short, spiky hair. Bright red. A punk. You'd better get back quick—she's booked for an in-house in ten minutes."

Gina had seen her. On the edge of the crowd, walking towards the kerb. Dressed in black leather with a nose ring. It hadn't occurred to her she might be one of her girls.

"Shut up, bitch!" The shout and the slap across Chloe's shoulder revealed his increasing frustration. He pushed into her more brutally than before.

Her sobbing must have relaxed her sphincter, because his penis was easing into her. She tensed up again, forcing him out. His response was to drive down with such determination she was afraid he'd injure her.

Sobbing uncontrollably, and in utter despair, she yielded.

And then it stopped.

No pain, no pressure on her head.

His weight rolled off her. Dazed, she heard voices as she lifted her head. She looked round in time to see a startled look on his face as two hands squeezed hard around his neck hauled him backwards. He fell clumsily to the floor by the side of the bed.

Liz stood over him.

"Get dressed and get the fuck out of here, you scumbag." She snatched his clothes from the chair and threw them at him.

Chloe gazed at Liz in relief and admiration. "Oh Liz, am I glad to see you. That bastard was trying to greek me."

A slight movement in the open doorway caught her eye. Simon, wide-eyed, stood watching her, his face distressed and fearful. No sooner had their eyes met than he disappeared.

Liz said, "Kellie's downstairs. I'll send her up once I've thrown this piece of cat shit off the premises."

The man had managed to pull on his trousers and shirt and was picking up his socks when Liz said, "Don't bother with them. Just get downstairs and fuck off."

Head bowed, cradling his shoes and socks in his arms, he scurried out the door, Liz following close behind.

~~~

Chloe sat on the bed with Kellie's arm round her shoulders. She'd wrapped herself in a Casa Rosa bathrobe and sat with her legs drawn up, head resting on her knees. Her hair had come loose and shrouded her face but her appearance was the last thing on her mind.

"Is this the first time someone's tried that on you?" Kellie said.

Chloe nodded.

"What a bastard! I wish Baz had been here. He'd have sorted him out."

Chloe lifted her head and looked at her friend. "Why did he do it? Why didn't he just say that's what he wanted in the first place? He could have had one of the others. Juliette's on tonight, so's Candy. They both do greek."

"Because he wanted to hurt you, Chlo, that's why. Some men are like that. It's a power trip. They can't perform otherwise." When Chloe didn't answer, she said softly, "Did he hurt you?"

"A bit."

"Are you bleeding?"

"No, but I can still feel him in there. I wouldn't even let my husband do that, and that's when I loved the two-timing bastard." She shuddered. "My wrists hurt." She held them out for inspection. Kellie took each hand and gently turned it over. Bruises were evident on both wrists.

"My shoulder hurts, too. He was so strong. I don't know how Liz managed to pull him off."

"Liz's a gym junkie. He must have realised how strong she was when she dragged him off you. Besides, he knew he'd be in deeper shit if he played up."

"I didn't think anybody would hear me. He shoved my head into the pillow and I couldn't breathe."

"Lucky for you Tammi was finishing up in the next room. She thought she heard you call out, and then she heard the man shouting."

Chloe felt drained. "I hope I never meet another one like him."

"Simon should never have let him in. Liz wouldn't have. Take the rest of the night off. Go home and have a good soak in the bath."

"I'll be all right—give me time to pull myself together. I'll be fine."

If she didn't get to see at least one other client that night, it would be her last day at Casa Rosa.

~~~

Driving back with Holly, Gina had received a brief call from Liz warning her there'd been some trouble, but she was still unprepared for the sight of two police officers waiting in Reception.

Eyes trained on Liz, she approached the desk. Liz immediately looked sideways at Simon, who bore the expression of someone who'd prefer to be anywhere but right there at that moment.

Keeping her voice low, she asked, "What are the cops doing here?"

"Sorry, Simon called them." She gave a quick rundown of what had taken place.

The senior of the two officers approached Gina. "Are you the manager?"

"Yes, I am. But before we go any further, we're not making a complaint against anyone. As far as I'm concerned"—she stole a look at Simon—"the matter has been dealt with to my satisfaction."

"That may be so, madam, but an incident was reported and we need to take down some details."

She sighed. "Okay, if you must. Please come down to my office." She nodded to Liz, who left the desk and followed her down the hall.

~~~

After the police left, Gina and Liz returned to the reception desk where Simon, sitting with his headset draped round his shoulders, gave them a reproachful look. "Well?"

"Listen," Gina said, "I thought I made it crystal clear when you started that you were only to call the police as a last resort."

"But Chloe was being raped. Isn't that serious enough?"

"It is, but not enough to warrant you making unilateral decisions. Why didn't you speak to Liz first?"

"She was upstairs."

Liz said, "But you could have waited till I came back down. I wasn't gone that long."

Simon fussed with the headset. "I didn't want the bastard to get away with it."

The two women looked at him thoughtfully. Gina itched to reprimand him further, but it was his first transgression and, though she didn't care to admit it, if she was too hard on him, he could leave and then she'd have to repeat the tiresome process of finding another manager.

"In future," she said, "don't call the police unless al-Qaeda has taken over the building and are about to blow it up, okay?"

Simon looked deflated. "I honestly thought I was doing the right thing in the circumstances."

Liz said, "Anywhere else, you might have, but not in this business. Mark it down to experience."

"Experience? Some experience. Left to me, that bastard would have been arrested. Rape *is* rape, you know."

"Unfortunately, Simon, when it comes to sex workers, the courts don't believe there's such a thing as rape. When did you last hear of one winning a sexual assault case?"

He jammed his headset over his ears as an incoming call flashed on the switchboard.

16. Moving along

It was past midnight when Gina arrived home after an exhausting evening. Ferrying the girls to and from their appointments had proved more demanding than she'd expected. Dropping the girls off hadn't been a problem. Going back to pick them up was another matter. If she arrived early, finding a parking spot close by was a challenge. If she was late, the girls wandered from the agreed rendezvous, causing her to drive round the block until she found them.

Jock had eventually phoned in to say he had a migraine. Fortunately, Liz stayed back late to keep track of the appointments, otherwise Gina would have ended up in total confusion.

She tried to catch up with Chloe to see how she was, but Kellie said she'd gone home early. She wondered if Chloe would be deterred by her encounter with the rapist. Of the girls she'd met so far, she liked her the most. She was also the most popular with clients. Kellie said she'd bounce back soon enough but Chloe wasn't Kellie. The two women were different in many ways.

Gina kicked off her shoes and padded into the kitchen. She found an open bottle of Cabernet Shiraz in the kitchen, poured herself a full glass, and took it into the living room. Sprawled on the sofa, she looked out towards the silent harbour, its foreshore picked out by the lights of dwellings and moored boats. Normally she would have found this scene restful, but the day's events continued to play on her mind.

Her situation was starting to look hopeless. First it was Daniel's discovery of her role, then the *Daily Monitor* had Casa Rosa in its sights, and now her name was on record as a brothel manager with the police. How long would it be before word got out that she was a madam? What would she do then? Most of her friends would probably disown her, and she could kiss goodbye to her career prospects in Australia. Maybe she would go back to the States—as long as she stayed well clear of Boston and Morgan.

It occurred to her that if Jock had turned up as he was supposed to, she wouldn't have been off the premises when Chloe was assaulted and the police wouldn't have become involved. His timekeeping was unacceptable. She needed reliable people around her. Tomorrow she'd let him know that if he didn't shape up he was out of a job.

Added to her woes, she must explain to her mother, already skeptical of her daughter's management skills, what had happened that night.

She downed the rest of the glass in one go and headed for the comfort of her bed.

~~~

When she arrived home, Chloe bolted the door and switched on all the lights. She flopped on the sofa and stared at the wall, her mind consumed with the attempted rape. She hadn't seen another client. She should have, like climbing back onto a horse straight after you've fallen off, but she couldn't shake off the memory of nearly being smothered to death. What if Tammi hadn't heard the man shouting? Would he have strangled her to keep her quiet? It didn't bear thinking about.

It was the first time she'd needed to use the panic button and she'd been unable to reach it. Some brothels issued their girls with alarm switches that hung around their necks but Maria didn't like them. She'd heard of a woman in America who'd been strangled by the cord. When Maria came back from hospital, Chloe would ask her to change her mind.

She had to go back. Perhaps in the morning it wouldn't seem so bad. Everyone said how rare it was to be attacked, though Tammi said in her second week she'd nearly had her ear bitten off. She was lucky it was still intact. Chloe had seen the scar.

She had to go back because she needed the money. Though she was a couple of months in front on the plan, the loan payments for the flat were high. She couldn't be without a job for long.

Before Casa Rosa she's been waitressing. The pay had been pitiful. It hadn't taken her long to realise the restaurant was permanently understaffed. Along with the other women, she'd been rushed from start to finish of her five-hour shifts. It wasn't surprising that she kept thinking of Kellie. A thousand dollars a night! When the job got to be too much, she jacked it in. The next day she met Kellie for lunch.

She recalled that meeting almost word for word.

"What's holding me back," she told Kellie, "are the blokes. They could be all sorts. Smelly, dirty, ignorant—you know what I mean."

"It's not that bad. Some of them treat you like they were handling carcasses in an abattoir, but they're in a minority. We make them take a shower and check them out before we get started, so at least we know they're reasonably clean. And of course they have to use protection."

"I'm sure I'd get a six foot sumo wrestler who'd suffocate me." Chloe shivered at the image.

"Right from the start you let them know you're in charge, and you never let them take control, no matter how much they sweet talk you."

"You make it sound easy."

"It's not. It's like any job—it takes time to learn the ropes, but I've managed and I'm sure you would, too."

"What are they like?"

"The nervous ones are the easy ones. A few think you must do everything they want without question. Some just lie on the bed and expect you to get on with it. Most, though, are respectful."

Chloe had started at Casa Rosa the following week and her first client was much as Kellie had promised.

She recalled how she'd started the shower running and called his name. He strolled nonchalantly into the bathroom, surprising her with his golden brown skin, except for his feet and buttocks, which were alabaster white. He would have to be an outdoor worker.

She watched as he stepped under the shower. When she was confident he was washing himself properly, she returned to the bedroom and removed her clothes. Sitting on the bed, she wondered who was more nervous: her or John.

He returned from the bathroom, towel wrapped around his middle, and sat next to her.

"This your first time?" she asked.

He shook his head. "No, I come here every couple of weeks."

"Okay, so what would you like to do?"

His answer was unexpected.

"Do you mind if we kiss?"
"Mouth-to-mouth?"
"Yes."
She smiled. "Sorry, I don't do that."
"Oh…"
"But we can kiss everywhere else, just not on the mouth. Okay?"
"All right, but I want you to act like you're my girlfriend. I don't want the porn star treatment."

And so they lay together and she caressed him like he was her boyfriend and eventually they made love in a conventional manner.

Afterwards, Kellie asked her how it went. Chloe admitted it had been, if not pleasant, at least not unpleasant.

"Was he nice looking?"
"Not bad. Beautiful body, though. Tanned and quite muscular."
"Hung like a horse?" asked Kellie, with a mischievous grin.
"More like its jockey, but he was a damn sight more considerate than Bernie ever was. If the rest are like him, I won't have much to complain about."

~~~

Gina was late up again the next morning. She skipped breakfast and was on her way out the front door when the phone rang.

"Gina? It's Jos…Jocelyn…in reception. There's a bloke here waiting for you with a computer. Says you asked him to deliver it this morning at nine o'clock."

Twenty-five minutes later, she found a young Chinese sitting in one of the waiting rooms with two large cartons and looking agitated. "I don't think he realised what sort of business we're in," Jos said, with a laugh.

The man had a different concern. "I'm on a one-hour limit and I've only got five minutes left."

"Don't worry," Gina said. "They don't come round here that often."

He wasted no time in unpacking the equipment and setting it up on the desk. "Is that the only phone outlet?" He pointed to the single socket on the wall.

"I've no idea." She had a quick look around the room. "Could be. I'll see if anyone knows."

Jos told her all calls came through the switchboard and a separate line into Maria's office didn't exist. The man said in that case he couldn't do any more, as the modem wouldn't work through a switchboard—she would need another line installed.

Access to the Internet and e-mail wasn't vital. It could wait until she found a good time to discuss the computer with her mother. Another problem to add to a growing list.

Thinking of her mother, Gina remembered she was supposed to pick her up from the hospital and take her home. She looked at her watch: ten-thirty. She should have left half-an-hour ago.

~~~

Daniel hadn't been confident about the information Liz had given him. She'd made it sound too speculative. Presenting it to Isobel the day before, he'd noticed she didn't look convinced either, just thoughtful as she scanned the notes he put in front of her.

This morning she had a different attitude. Walking over to his desk, she waved the notes in her hand. "Remember that stuff Charlene told us about the

Asians? Something about them not getting a fair share of their earnings because they were students?"

"Isn't that because their visas don't allow them to work more than twenty hours a week during term time?"

"And she said she didn't know which brothels they were working at. We might have the answer here. Your friend's given us two addresses where she reckons foreign students are employed full-time and they're both legal houses."

"Uh-oh, I'm not visiting any more brothels. I still have the bruises from the last one."

Isobel smiled. "But look on the bright side, Daniel—you got free S & M."

"No, they stole a hundred dollars off me."

"I hope you've put it on expenses."

She was on her way back to her desk when she stopped and turned back. "Before we can get started, Frank has to check those addresses with the Feds. If we get the green light, we'll call on Charlene again. I'm sure she'll open a few doors for us if we pay enough."

He grimaced at the thought of another meeting with Charlene.

"I hope she proves more reliable this time."

~~~

After driving her mother home from the hospital and leaving her in Concetta's care, Gina returned to Casa Rosa.

Simon called out to her as she passed through reception. "Remember that bloke who attacked Chloe last night? Take a look at this."

He handed her a picture of a man being shoved towards the front door by Liz.

"Where did that come from?"

"I took it with my phone camera. It's not very sharp but he's recognisable."

"What do you want me to do with it?"

"I thought you could copy it and circulate it round the other houses."

"Good idea. I'll ask Liz to see to it." Simon was trying to make amends for the previous night. He didn't need to. "By the way, I'm sorry I was a bit hard on you last night. I know you meant well."

He smiled shyly. "It's okay, I'm still learning the ropes. This business has its own set of rules, it seems."

17. *Persona non grata*

Frank had left two messages that morning on Chief Inspector Rod Farling's voicemail asking him to phone back. It was now mid-afternoon and so far no call. He would have phoned him at his office but Farling had asked him not to do that. Frustrated by the lack of a response, he went over to Larry's office, only to find he was out for the rest of the day. He returned to his desk and placed another call to Farling. After four rings he was again put through to voicemail. It was pointless leaving another message and he dropped the handset back on its base.

He contemplated phoning Sam Chu, then thought better of it. Chu already considered him a pain in the arse.

As he pondered his options, Isobel walked past with a sheaf of papers in her hand. He called her in.

"You're looking worried, Frank. What's up?"

"Nothing, that's the problem. I can't get hold of Farling—he seems to have gone walkabout."

She took a seat opposite him. "Maybe things are hotting up. They could be getting ready to carry out the raids."

"If so and nobody bothers to tell us, we'll be up shit creek."

She rolled the papers into a tube and tapped it rhythmically on her knee. "Sorry, just a thought. There could be other reasons. He might be sick or at a conference, or even tied up on another case."

"Then why hasn't he let me know?" When she shrugged, he said, "Sorry, I'm a bit twitchy. I don't exactly have a lot to go on."

"I spoke to that prossie, Charlene, again. I ran the two addresses past her. She said they had foreign students working full-time."

"We can't move until we hear from Farling. Did she have anything else to say?"

"Nothing of interest. She likes to big-note herself, but she's getting past her use-by date. She's still holding to her story about Casa Rosa."

"That's to be expected, seeing as she's waiting to be paid for it. Anyway, as things stand, I have one story featuring Daniel and a possible second on Rosie, provided we find her in time. I've asked Lucy to do a backgrounder on prostitution in Sydney with as many stats as she can find. She's also preparing a map showing where all the known brothels are. That's about it. Not much to show for all the effort we've put in."

She laid the rolled-up papers on the edge of his desk and tried unsuccessfully to straighten them out. "I know, but we'll have the police raids if all goes well."

Frank wished he could be more confident of the outcome. He looked at the solicitor's letter and the affidavits in his in-tray and rued Daniel's interference, however justified. Perhaps some aspects of Charlene's story could be used as filler for Lucy's article on prostitution.

One thing was certain: this story wasn't going to be an eight-page hard-hitting exposé.

Isobel said, "Isn't printing the brothel locations a bit like advertising them?"

"No, we won't give actual addresses—we'll only highlight how many there are. People might be surprised. Calloway hopes so."

~~~

Next morning the police announced that a media conference would be held at 10 o'clock.

Frank let rip with a string of oaths when Larry handed him the fax. The subject line said, "Police Raids Uncover Sex Slavery". He'd missed the action and his exclusive.

Larry said, "I think we'd better go and see the old man."

~~~

Calloway stood looking out of his office window—a clear sign he was unhappy. He'd heard Larry's description of the meagre content of the weekend's edition in silence.

He came away from the window and walked around the backs of the seated men.

"What went wrong, Frank? I thought I'd set it all up for you."

Frank chose his words carefully. Calloway didn't condone the use of strong language.

"The contact you gave me—Sam Chu—wouldn't agree to give me the nod when the raids were about to take place, but the bloke running the local operation, Rod Farling, said he would—unofficially. I couldn't contact him yesterday to find out the latest and this morning I learned he'd been rushed to hospital the day before with appendicitis. Needless to say, he hadn't mentioned to anyone that we should be tipped off."

Calloway went to his desk and stood behind his high-backed chair on which he rested his hands. He gave each man an accusatory stare. "And all we have to work with is what they'll hand out at the media briefing? Is that it?"

"More or less. I've sent Isobel along. She might tease something out of somebody."

"So that's our exclusive down the toilet. Do we have enough material for a four-page spread?"

"Not really—just Daniel's story about being beaten up and a backgrounder."

Larry said, "What about the brothel you said was flouting the safe sex regulations?"

"No go. Their solicitors issued a denial. They reckon our informant was a liar."

Calloway gave Frank a sharp look. "What's all this about?"

"Isobel's been talking to a woman who used to work at a brothel in Surry Hills, where she reckons they told her she didn't need to use protection. When the brothel heard about it, they said she was a liar and a thief and sooled their lawyer onto us."

"How did they find out?"

Frank loosened his tie a bit further. "It's a small industry. Word gets around fast."

Calloway looked from one to the other in astonishment. "Why the hell aren't we running this? We have an example of serious health risks to the community—wives catching syphilis and AIDS from their cheating husbands—and you're just ignoring it?"

"But the brothel strenuously denies it. They've given us stat decs."

"So? We'll say they denied it. No-one's going to believe them anyway."

Larry said, "If we go ahead, they could sue us."

"Let them. We have deeper pockets. They'll soon chuck in the towel."

When Frank and Larry didn't say anything, Calloway continued, "Okay, run it past Legal and then go to town on it. If you can get pictures of the owners or managers, all the better. And let me see the draft editorial, Larry, this afternoon. Play up the health risks—I want the shock jocks raging about this."

~~~

Frank called Isobel into his office and asked her to shut the door before he explained what was happening.

"It's vital we don't let Daniel know we're going to print the brothel story in case he tips off the owner and she injuncts us. Can you get him off the premises until tomorrow?"

"I gave him the material I brought back from the media conference. He can write that up—it won't take long." She paused. "I suppose he could visit the parents of the girl who was murdered on the train yesterday. They're in Canberra. I could have him fly down there this afternoon and make sure he stays overnight."

"That would be ideal. I'll let the Canberra office know he's coming and ask them to organise a time early tomorrow morning with the girl's parents." He made a note on his pad. "Now, we need a snapper to take a picture of the brothel, preferably with someone going in, and another one of whoever's running it."

She pursed her lips. "Daniel's the only one who knows who that is."

"What about that prossie you spoke to? She should know, shouldn't she?"

"You're right. I'll get onto her."

As she got up to leave, Frank said, "Get Daniel out of the office as soon as you can. I don't want any more complications."

18. *The moment of truth*

As Gina drove to Casa Rosa on Saturday morning—in her newly acquired secondhand red Golf GTI—it crossed her mind that, unlike her mother, she was working seven days a week. Maria managed to take at least one day off each week, usually two.

She'd like to do the same, but didn't feel able to leave Simon in charge for more than a few hours, even with Liz on hand. It wasn't his fault he wasn't able to take full control. He'd taken time off for his exams, and she'd neglected to spend enough time with him when he was free. She would make it her highest priority to train him in the administrative work.

When she arrived at the bordello, Gina was surprised to find an angry Liz standing in the foyer.

"What's up?"

Liz thrust a newspaper into Gina's hands. "See for yourself."

Gina stared at the front page of the *Monitor*. One-third of the way down, below a lead-in story about a rugby league player accused of rape, was the bold heading: 'Shame!'. Below that, a picture captioned 'Maria Russo leaving her Casa Rosa brothel' showed a woman stepping out of the front door. Gina looked up.

"This is you, Liz."

"Don't I know it. What's my family going to say when they see this? They don't know I work here. God, I'll kill that bastard!"

Gina barely heard her. The full import of the article was sinking in and her mind was a confusion of thoughts. "How could they?" She looked up to see Liz watching her. "He's betrayed me. I can't believe it. He's supposed to be my friend." She was beginning to tremble. "What are we going to do, Liz? This'll ruin us."

"I don't know. You'd better read the rest."

She glanced at the second page, where two pictures of a bruised and battered Daniel appeared next to the story he'd written, and at the third, featuring the story about Casa Rosa. There were shots of the back of a client being let into the premises and another of a woman identified only as 'Charlene, a former prostitute'.

"I'll sue that cow!"

"They've mentioned your mum's name."

She flicked to the next page, which showed a map of Sydney brothels. The article was headlined, 'Map of shame'. Below that was a straightforward account of the police raids carried out two days before.

Turning back to the previous page, she read the article featuring Charlene. When she finished, she closed her eyes and breathed deeply. She needed to keep a cool head.

When she opened her eyes, she realised Liz was still staring at her. Gina shook her head. "I don't know what to say, I really don't. I can't get my mind round any of it. Why would they do this to me? To Mama? To you?"

Instead of answer, Liz, her face grim, went to sit behind the desk.

Gina walked down the hall to her office. Seated at her desk, she stared at the monitor's blank screen, unable to bring herself to switch on the computer. Why bother? There wouldn't be any business today. For a time she didn't move.

As the initial shock wore off, she tried to piece together the events that had led to this moment. For some reason, Casa Rosa had been singled out for the *Monitor*'s attention. The only link with that paper was Daniel. He'd sat in her office while she tended his wounds. She'd taken him to the hospital, run him home, worried about him, called him to make sure he was okay, and this was how he chose to repay her: by carrying on the deceit of being her friend while he was using her to get a story for his paper. Hadn't he said he'd always wanted be an investigative reporter? The depths to which some people would descend to further their ambitions...

Profound dismay tinged with dread engulfed her. He'd betrayed her and the worst of her fears had now been realised. She struggled to comprehend what it would mean, not only for herself but for her mother and Casa Rosa.

The effect on turnover concerned her most. Regular clients would run for cover and it could take many months before the business got back to its current level. If the business wasn't profitable, her mother would lose almost everything she'd worked for.

She had to do something, but what? She hadn't a clue—she'd never faced anything like this before. She needed to talk to her mother. She would know what to do—after all, she'd battled to build the business up from nothing. But first she must be told about the article before she heard it from someone else.

As she passed through reception, she said, "I'm off home to break the bad news. Do you mind if I take the paper with me?"

Liz handed the *Monitor* over. "Can I make a suggestion?"

"Sure, go ahead."

"We should place a printed statement in the waiting rooms giving our side of the story."

Gina hesitated, anxious to leave. "Okay, that makes sense, but can it wait until I've spoken to my mother?"

"Supposing I draft something while you're out? You can dress it up when you get back?"

"Thanks, Liz."

As she left the building it occurred to her that the family business extended beyond the Russos.

~~~

Gina gave her mother a summary of the article before handing her Liz's copy of the newspaper. All the while Gina was speaking, Maria stared at her in disbelief, not saying a word. Now, her reading glasses poised on the end of her nose, she read the front cover. When she turned the page and saw how much remained to be read, she passed it back. "You read it to me—I can't see much through these glasses."

"That's because you were supposed to have your eyes tested ages ago—before I went to America, in fact. You really must stop neglecting yourself." She turned to the Casa Rosa article and read it aloud. When she mentioned Charlene's allegations, her mother snorted. "*Madonna mia*! The lying bitch! All she ever did was rob me and my girls. How dare she, the cow!"

Gina finished reading the article and put down the paper. She waited for her mother's reaction, but her face showed little expression as she gazed out the bedroom window. She'd become increasingly morose since her operation, especially after starting chemotherapy, which made her nauseous and listless.

After a pensive moment or two, her mother said, still looking out the window, "When we started in this business, your papa told me we'd make so much money we'd retire after five years and live like royalty. That must have been fifteen years ago. Instead he passed away and I'm no closer to retirement than I ever was." She sighed and looked at Gina. "Things never work out like they're supposed to."

"As I'm finding out. I can't believe what's happened. To think that less than two months ago I was planning a new career. Instead—"

"You have started a new career."

With a touch of bitterness, Gina said, "Being a madam is hardly what I had in mind." They were silent for a few moments. "What are we going to do, Mama?"

"I don't know. I'm not sure I care anymore. It all seems so pointless."

"Don't say that. Course it's not pointless. You've worked hard all your life—you deserve better than this."

"I started with nothing, I can end up with nothing. I'll survive one way or another."

"How? You still owe the bank. You're not well enough to work and you won't be for a while yet."

"I can sell this house and find something cheaper, outside the city."

Gina shook her head. Her mother was clearly depressed.

"It's not going to happen, Ma. I won't let it. And I'm not going to have them ride roughshod over us like this—we must be able to do something."

Her mother gave her a challenging look. "Right, Miss MBA, you're the business expert, you're running things, why don't you tell me what *you* want to do?"

What did she really want to do? She'd like to throttle Daniel and do the same to Charlene, but that wouldn't wind the clock back. Yet returning to the status quo in double quick time was the only way they could move forward, or the business would be sunk. It was all on her shoulders.

"I'll go and make a cup of coffee while I think about it."

Leaning against the kitchen bench, waiting for the coffee to percolate, Gina wondered if her mother blamed her for what had happened. All these years without any bother and the moment it was handed to Gina for safekeeping, Casa Rosa hit the headlines and was in danger of closing down. First the cancer and then this; her mother must be asking herself what she'd done to deserve such bad luck.

Gina suffered her own loss of self-esteem. Her management skills had been well regarded at the bank where she used to work. It was on that basis she'd applied to the Harvard Business School for admission to its renowned MBA program. The day she received the letter of acceptance ranked as one of the happiest in her life.

She retraced in her mind the events leading up to this moment since arriving home from the States but could find nothing that pointed to bad judgement on her part.

On the other hand, her judgement regarding Morgan had been appalling. She could hardly blame his reaction when she told him what her mother did for a living. What made her think he'd overlook her family running a brothel? And what possessed her to think she could conceal it for so long? She'd expected far too much of a man with his background.

Whether it was the contrast between the two men that brought him to mind or that she'd avoided thinking about him until now, her thoughts turned to Daniel and his treachery. Her anger rose as she remembered how he'd insinuated himself into Casa Rosa and gained her trust. She couldn't fathom what had driven him to betray her. It couldn't be ruthless ambition—he was far less of a go-getter than she was—nor could she think of anything she'd done to offend him. Why would he sacrifice their friendship after all this time? Her inability to understand his actions only made her more furious.

As she poured coffee into two mugs and placed them on a tray to take upstairs, she asked herself how she would tackle an issue like this if she were the CEO of a big company. Her training told her she would need to formulate a strategy: have a clear objective, assess the feasibility of different options, select one, develop a plan of action, and then implement it. A PR program would help too, but she could hardly try that.

She knew the objective well enough: survival. So what options did she have? The first was obvious: she could do nothing and wait until the storm blew itself out. The business would run at a loss until one day, if it didn't go broke in the meantime, it would again make a profit. At some point, when her mother was fit enough to resume control, Gina would restart her career and hope that people had forgotten her connection with Casa Rosa. She called this the 'low-profile, low-risk option': keep your head down and wait a while—maybe a few months, maybe a year—before popping your head back up to sniff the air like a meerkat and carry on as if nothing much had happened. Most people would agree that it was a safe and sensible option, but then she wasn't most people.

She took a clean plate from the dishwasher and emptied a packet of chocolate cream biscuits onto it.

The second approach she called 'high-profile, high-risk': crash through or crash and burn; put your life on the line and take no prisoners; go down in a blaze of glory or break through in triumph. She'd never been afraid to take risks. As Papa used to say, there's no thrill in gambling if you can afford to lose.

Doing nothing would eat away at her self-regard. Besides, nobody should be allowed to walk over her and her mother and get away with it. She would meet the enemy head on.

Satisfied with her decision, she mounted the stairs to brief her mother on her plan.

19. Another moment of truth

Daniel spent the morning in Canberra interviewing the parents of an eighteen-year old student who'd been stabbed to death on a Sydney suburban train.

He hadn't relished the prospect of intruding on a family's grief, but the parents were cooperative and provided him with three photographs, which he promised to return as soon as he'd copied them. They showed him her school reports and the academic prizes she'd won. They allowed him into her bedroom. It was a typical teenage girl's room, pink and lilac, with soft toys and posters of Eminem, 50 Cent, and Justin Timberlake. When he learned she'd been a promising pianist and active in the university's drama society, he sensed a connection with the dead girl. For her parents, though, he felt nothing but sorrow.

By the time he left, he had enough material for a full-page article, which he intended to draft on the return flight.

He'd been surprised he was chosen to do the interview. Surely the *Monitor* used freelance reporters when they were short-handed? He had no experience in dealing with bereaved relatives either, nor had he worked on a crime-related story before. All Isobel had said to him was that it would be valuable experience, but wasn't he supposed to be on secondment for the brothel story?

He wondered what Andrea, his previous boss, would say when she found out he'd been given another story to work on. Could this mean he was now permanently in Frank's department? That thought cheered him. He wouldn't care if they sent him to Bourke and back—working on features was much more interesting than swanning around society events picking up gossip. Still, Andrea would hit the roof if he didn't go back to her section as promised.

~~~

He finished the story in longhand as the plane approached Mascot airport and passengers were told to prepare for landing. While he was packing the notebook into his briefcase, he noticed a copy of the *Monitor* stuffed into the seat pocket in front of him. Remembering the exposé was due to be published that day, he unfolded it to the front page.

The picture of Liz emerging from Casa Rosa jolted him. He flicked to the inside pages, hastily scanning the article about Charlene and Casa Rosa as the plane touched down on the runway.

A cold fury enveloped him. He'd been made a fool of, sent out of town so they could publish a story libelling an innocent party, a story for which Gina would hold him accountable.

He'd been betrayed.

~~~

His heart thumping from exertion and repressed rage, Daniel charged into the *Monitor* building. Still clutching the newspaper he'd picked up on the plane, he barged into Frank's office and tossed it on his desk.

Frank affected not to be aware of his presence. He signed an expense form, placed it on a pile of similar forms, and selected another to look at. Daniel moved to stand directly in front of him, willing him to look up, but his boss still ignored him.

He snatched up the newspaper and dropped it on top of the forms. Frank casually swept the paper to one side with a hairy hand and continued to ignore the intrusion.

No longer able to contain himself, Daniel grabbed the newspaper and waved it in front of his boss. "Come on, Frank, for fuck's sake look at it! You got me out of the way so you could print this crap and now you're too ashamed to look at your handiwork."

He wanted to smack him around the head with the paper. Instead, he took a deep breath and lowered his voice. "I told you it was all lies, didn't I? An innocent woman, a woman with cancer, a widow woman is having her business ruined just so you can have your front page story. You should be fucking ashamed of yourself—no wonder you can't look at me."

Frank dropped his pen and leaned back in his chair. The look he gave Daniel was defiant, but it contained more than a hint of guilt, even resignation.

"Okay, I hear you. You're angry at me. I don't blame you. I'm not happy about it either, but I had no choice. We didn't have another story ready. We had little to work with, so Calloway wanted it printed, and we did as we were told. We also printed the brothel's denial."

"I can't believe this. Don't you have a conscience?"

"Listen, Dan—like it or not, we're in the business of selling newspapers. We need a supply of good stories, even if we don't personally agree with them, or we're out of business. And don't forget we helped to get Rosie out of that brothel. It was what you wanted, wasn't it?"

Struggling to keep his anger in check, Daniel leaned over the desk and pointed a finger at Frank. "That's cynical rationalising and you know it. If you hadn't felt so guilty, you wouldn't have got me out of the way." When Frank didn't answer, Daniel straightened up and said, "Okay, carry on fooling yourself, but you're never making a fuckwit out of me again. I'm out of here."

Tossing the newspaper into the waste paper bin, he marched out of the office.

20. Career change

Gina arrived at Caroline's Rose Bay apartment with a bunch of mixed flowers, a bottle of chilled Semillon, and a fresh copy of the previous day's *Monitor*. She was so eager to discuss the article, she nearly handed Caroline the newspaper first, curbing her impatience at the last moment to proffer the wine and flowers instead.

Watching Caroline put the bouquet into a vase, she could hold back no longer and blurted out what had happened. Caroline listened patiently, carefully arranging the flowers in the vase until she was happy with the display. When she took the newspaper she said, "You'd better fix yourself a drink and take a seat while I read this chip wrapper."

Gina poured herself a glass of wine and sat at the table on the small balcony. The apartment overlooked the greens of the Royal Sydney Golf Club, close enough to be hit by a poorly struck ball. She tried watching the golfers but found herself repeatedly glancing at Caroline, who was engrossed in the articles.

Eventually Caroline put the paper down and whistled in surprise. "Oh my, you are in the poo! I suppose you want to sue the bastards for every last cent and then some."

"If only…"

"I know—not a snowball's, darl."

Caroline came to the table with entrées of smoked salmon, cream cheese, capers, and rings of red onion. She sat down and gave Gina a sympathetic smile.

"First, you should know defamation isn't my area. You need a specialist lawyer. I know one or two people who might help you, but they don't work for us—we don't do defo. I'll talk to them if you like and see what they have to say but I'll warn you now—they're expensive, and they won't take you on unless you can afford to pay for the court case."

Gina's spirits dropped. "How expensive?"

"Very. However, let me think about it. I'm confident you can sue those dropkicks for libel, but what you can expect by way of damages isn't straightforward, and won't be anywhere near as much as you think you deserve. Also, you need to have the jury on your side and, let's face it, your business doesn't exactly evoke sympathy."

"But that's ridiculous, Caro. They've accused us of exploiting our girls, when we've always been strict about safe sex. We never compromise on hygiene. Christ, when we take the girls on we even give them a handout based on the Occupational Health and Safety Act."

"I know that, but a jury won't, and it might not make much difference even if they do. To a lot of people prostitution is immoral. So—and this could be tricky—you'll need affidavits from your girls and some of your clients. You must show the allegations were false and the *Monitor* was advised of this before they published. Like I say, defamation's not my speciality…but if ever you want help merging with another brothel, I'm definitely up for it."

"Gee, thanks. I'm trying to get out of this business, not further into it."

"One more thing—you'll need to show that the business has nosedived because of the article, and that might not be easy. It'll take time to show you've lost customers and, anyway, you're expected to take reasonable steps to mitigate the effects."

Gina moved the onion rings to the side of her plate and sampled the smoked salmon.

"How do you mean?"

"You can't let the business slide. You have to do something to save it, otherwise the other side will say the business went downhill because you didn't know how to manage it. And seeing as how you've only just taken over..."

"Oh my god, this is getting worse. If I make it more profitable, I undermine my own case. That's ludicrous!" She paused to give herself time to calm down. "So, do I have to wait to see how things turn out before I can sue?"

"No. The sooner you start, the sooner it'll go to trial. You do realise though that most of these cases get settled out of court?"

"You mean they'll pay up?"

"Depends. If the litigant doesn't pull out, the lawyers usually negotiate and try to agree a figure that's acceptable to both sides. If it's not, that's when it goes to court. Most payouts don't come anywhere near the damages claimed. And if you lose, the lawyers' fees will probably bankrupt you anyway. Even if you win, they'll still take most of what you get."

"I know. The system's geared in favour of the big end of town. But I don't see why little people should cop all the shit. Mama's worked hard all her life and the *Monitor* can put her out of business and be totally unaffected by it, just so they can sell their shitty papers."

They ate in silence while Gina considered Caroline's advice. It wasn't going to be easy. She didn't relish the thought of paying lawyers' fees either, but she'd stand no chance without an expert by her side.

Caroline broke the silence. "Let's see what I can find out. It's good you did your best to warn them not to publish. A good trial judge will make sure the jury understands that."

"It'll be even better if he's one of our clients."

Caroline laughed. She stood up to take the plates away and Gina followed her into the kitchen.

Caroline said, "You're really in the wars, aren't you?"

"I can't believe Daniel did this. Why? What harm have I done him?"

"I don't know. Maybe after all this time he's become career-conscious. Still, that doesn't sound like him, does it? Maybe he's into a serious relationship and getting ready to settle down. Does he have anyone?"

"Not as far as I know."

"Pity he's dropped you in the poo, then. I used to see him at the gym and, to be honest, thought he wasn't a bad sort. Quite fanciable, in fact."

"If I get my hands on him, there won't be anything left for you to fancy."

As Caroline put the coffee on to percolate, she said, "By the way, did Morgan ever get in touch with you?"

"No, or I would have to tell him I was running a brothel now instead of just being a brothel owner's daughter. I can imagine how he'd feel about that."

Caroline chuckled. "At least you could promise him a good time."

"That's the last thing he'd want."

"Don't you be so sure. He's a man, isn't he? By the way, do you still have that painting his mum gave you?"

"On my bedroom wall. Connie dusts it every time she cleans my room. She looks at it for ages. I think she's fallen in love with Morgan."

"I'm surprised you haven't taken it down."

"I've thought about it. It's the symbolism, I suppose."

"I don't want to disappoint you, darl, but it's been over a month. I think he's licked his wounds by now and found someone else. Isn't his mum a famous painter?"

"I don't know about famous, but she's certainly successful—Morgan said her pictures sell for thousands of dollars."

"In that case, why don't you flog the painting and put the proceeds towards the costs of the libel action? You'll need every penny you can get."

~~~

After leaving Frank's office, Daniel went to his desk and filled a plastic bag with his few personal belongings. As he left, he dropped the Canberra article on Isobel's desk. No-one noticed as he slipped out of the building and headed up George Street.

He walked rapidly, his mind broiling with the events of the previous twenty-four hours. Reaching Park Street, he turned right and headed to Hyde Park. His anger was abating. He needed to sit down to think things over.

The park was busier than usual. The mild, sunny day had lured people away from the shops. They strolled around, or sat or lay in the shade of a tree. Most benches were occupied. Not wanting to share a seat, he sat on the grass to watch the activity around him.

By now his feelings about Frank's behaviour were under control, so he turned his thoughts to some remaining issues. The first was to let his mother know he'd resigned. She'd be annoyed, possibly very annoyed given her efforts to land him the job. On the other hand, she had strong principles and, he hoped, could understand why he wouldn't work for an unscrupulous organisation. Besides, he'd never let her down before—that had to be in his favour. Even so, he wasn't looking forward to giving her the news.

The second issue was his employment prospects. Walking out of a job wouldn't endear him to his next employer, no matter how noble his reasons.

He knew also that if he stayed with the *Monitor*, Frank would have sent him back to work with Andrea, but working on the Social Diary had lost whatever appeal it originally had, not that he'd ever been that struck on it anyway.

He was thinking journalism might not be his true vocation, though it had been his career objective ever since he'd won a school prize for English. Other jobs needing good writing skills. Perhaps he should try something different, something that capitalised on his strength as a communicator and offered a worthwhile challenge.

He had a close friend who worked in public relations, but he wasn't sure if that was ethical enough for his peace of mind. He had another friend in advertising. Maybe that would suit him better. It couldn't be too hard to make the grade as a copywriter. Working in a creative environment would be fun, too.

Both of them would be at cricket practice in the morning. He'd sound them out then.

Finally, Gina. The moment he'd read the stories, he knew she would hold him accountable. Somehow he had to let her know he'd been deliberately misled and sidelined.

He reached in his pocket for his phone. It belonged to the company but it was unlikely they'd cancel it so quickly. He selected Gina's home number and listened to the dial tone. Just when he thought it would ring out, Maria answered the call.

"Hello, Mrs Russo. Sorry to trouble you, but can I speak to Gina, please?"

"Sorry, she's not here. Who's it calling?"

"Daniel Bouvier—remember me?"

A pause. "Leave her alone, you've caused enough trouble as it is." She cut the call before he could say another word.

He didn't have Gina's mobile phone number and couldn't think of another way of talking to her without being unduly intrusive. He'd wait a couple of days and try again.

~~~

As soon as Gina arrived home, she went to her room and stood in front of the painting of her and Morgan. His eyes met hers and for a fleeting moment she thought his image had come alive. Her heart skipped a beat. She must have drunk too much.

She unhooked the picture and propped it near the door, face to the wall.

Next morning she went to the storeroom and gathered a large piece of bubble wrap, two pieces of stout cardboard, a ball of string, and some wrapping paper. She laid the painting face up on the desk in the study and used kitchen scissors to cut the cardboard to size. She took a last look at the scene of Morgan and herself standing on the wide front steps of the Martha's Vineyard house. Edith had cleverly captured the essence of Morgan: the confident exterior not quite masking the reserved, uncertain man within. He hadn't been keen on having the photo taken that formed the basis for the picture. His reluctance to have his likeness portrayed was something she'd never been able to fathom.

She placed a piece of cardboard over the image. When she'd made a secure parcel, she went to the study to compose a letter. As she wrote, she imagined Edith reading it in her sunny conservatory. The vision encouraged her to describe her experiences since returning to Australia. She apologised for misleading the Chamberlains, remembering how she'd told them her family was in property management, a universally respectable occupation.

When she finished, she put the parcel near the front door. If there'd been a courier office open on Sundays, she'd have sent it straightaway to avoid time for second thoughts. It would have to wait until the morning—she'd take it into the office and have it picked up from there.

~~~

The *Daily Monitor* was published every day except Sunday, when it appeared as the *Sunday Monitor* in a slightly different format.

A *Sunday Monitor* reporter had been given the task of tracking down Rosie, the girl Daniel had hoped to rescue from the Denfield Street brothel. He'd been successful and the *Sunday Monitor* now had Rosie's story.

In the article she described her working conditions and how she couldn't leave until she'd paid her "taxes". Daniel's notes had been used for the account of his attempt to get her out, but his name wasn't mentioned—he was simply "a *Monitor* reporter".

He was pleased to learn that Rosie wouldn't be deported. She must have agreed to testify against the two Serbs. Her travel documents and passport had been recovered and now she worked as a waitress in a Thai restaurant in Newtown.

~~~

When Daniel failed to turn up for work on Monday and then Tuesday, Frank began to worry he'd gone for good. He called Daniel's mobile phone.

"So what's the story, Dan? You coming back to work or what?"

"I thought I made my position clear last Saturday."

"I was hoping you'd had time to cool down and think it over."

"Sorry, but I meant what I said."

Daniel's intransigence surprised him. He should have come to his senses by now. "Are you seriously going to walk away from a job that others would lop off sundry body parts to get?"

"Absolutely."

It was spoken with such finality that Frank saw no point wasting any more words. "In that case, you'd better come into the office to complete the termination formalities."

"I'm never stepping inside that building again."

"You need to finish up properly, Dan. Just stop by for five minutes and get it over and done with."

"Sorry, Frank, I'm not going in there."

Frank mulled over his refusal.

"Okay, if you don't want to come into the office, why don't you meet me in the Civic at lunchtime? Ten minutes—that's all I'm asking."

Daniel took his time to answer. "All right. Ten minutes—that's all."

~~~

The Civic Hotel, on the corner of Pitt and Goulburn Streets, was a classic example of art deco architecture.

For a while it had fallen into disuse, but since its refurbishment in the late nineties it had been Frank's favoured watering hole. He arrived at the main bar at twelve-thirty. Daniel had yet to appear.

Frank ordered a schooner of beer and looked around for a vacant table. The only one available was further from the street door than he wanted. He took his beer over and sat down and hoped Daniel would find him among the crowd.

While he waited, he removed the exit interview forms from his pocket and spread them on the table.

He could easily have filled them out himself. Daniel had made it abundantly clear why he'd resigned. "Reason for leaving?": *Treachery*. "Would you consider working for the Monitor Group again?": *Not in a million years*.

Frank doubted he would ever find himself answering those questions. He was too old and set in his ways to want to change employers. But if he did, what reason would he give? Would he say he needed to regain his personal integrity, assuming it could be resurrected?

He remembered starting at the *Monitor* as a cadet intent on becoming a star reporter like Carl Bernstein, the *Washington Post* journalist famous for exposing Watergate. It hadn't taken him long to compromise his ideals working for the Old Man, as Crispin Calloway's father was known. Calloway Senior didn't tolerate anyone who challenged his credo, best summarised as "we do whatever it takes to sell newspapers".

Maybe Daniel was right to get out while he was still young, before becoming jaded and cynical like Isobel and so many others.

"G'day. Sorry I'm late."

He looked up to see Daniel approaching the table. "Hi. Sit down while I fetch you a drink. What will you have?"

"A middy of light, thanks."

"You can take a squiz at the paperwork while I'm gone."

When he returned from the bar, it was obvious Daniel had ignored the forms. He pulled his glasses out of his pocket, put them on, and picked up the papers. After briefly scrutinising them, he looked up to say, "By the way, you know you can come back and work for Andrea—she's been angling to get you back ever since Larry abducted you."

Daniel half smiled and shook his head. "No, I'm through with the *Monitor*."

"Worth a try..." Indicating the papers, he said, "We have to go through these formalities when people leave, but it's also a formality to give a month's notice." He looked over the top of his glasses for a reaction. Daniel shrugged and said nothing. He put the papers down and removed his glasses. "Look, this crap isn't important—nobody looks at it anyway. Actually, I wanted a quiet word with you. If I thought it possible, I'd try to get you to change your mind, but I doubt you would anyway—you're too much like your mum."

"You know my mother?"

"Yeah, we worked together when she started with the *Monitor*. She didn't stay long. Classy lady, though. Good photographer, as you know."

"She doesn't talk much about her time at the *Monitor*."

"No? It was a long time ago. Damned good journo, too. She could be very persistent when she wanted a story. I remember once, there was this prisoner who said the police had bashed him senseless and they wouldn't let anyone near him. Somehow she slipped into the hospital where he was being treated and snapped him lying in bed with all his stitches and bruises on show. Superb picture. Calloway was editor-in-chief in those days and slapped it on the front page. Caused an uproar in Parliament. He treated her like a princess after that. She couldn't put a foot wrong. We even speculated they might have been, you know, having an affair." He looked at Daniel for confirmation.

"I've no idea, Frank. It would have been before I was born."

"Of course, before your mum met your dad, I think. How's he getting on?"

"Still in London. Bought himself a partnership into a marine legal practice. They're still married, by the way. Neither of them seems interested in divorce. I guess if one of them wanted to remarry that might change, although Mum says she'll never marry again. She likes things the way they are."

Frank knocked back his drink. "Fancy another?"

"No thanks, I'll be off in a minute."

Frank peered into his empty glass seeking inspiration. If only he could get this young man to see sense. All he saw were the last drops of his beer.

"Before you go, I want you to know I think you have the makings of a fine journalist. I saw the story you did on the parents of that poor girl who was murdered last week. Very moving. We ran it yesterday and had a lot of positive feedback."

"Thanks. I'm glad something good came out of my trip to Canberra."

"I know, I'm sorry about that."

"I promised to send the photos back to the Ashtons…"

"No worries, I'll take care of it."

They sat in awkward silence until Frank, giving Daniel an odd look, said, "By the way, did something go off between you and Isobel?"

"Go off? How do you mean?"

"She was mighty pissed when you left. I thought maybe you two had been cosying up to each other."

Daniel shook his head. "She's not my type. She was dirty with me about tipping off Casa Rosa. That's probably all it is."

"Fair enough. So, have you thought about what you're going to do now?"

"I'm not sure. I might try copywriting or PR." Daniel finished his drink. "Sorry, Frank, but I have to go."

"Okay, but before you leave, can I have your corporate card and the mobile phone. I can get away with not filling in the paperwork but Larry will crucify me if you don't give me those."

~~~

Frank's question about his mother started Daniel thinking. He knew she'd worked for Calloway and that sometimes they met for lunch. He'd seen pictures of them together on the social pages, but she'd been photographed with lots of other men, too.

At the moment, she was away on a *Time* magazine photo shoot in Eastern Europe. He'd have to wait until she came home in a week's time before he could find out if Frank's suspicions had any substance, which he doubted.

Meeting his ex-boss had been stressful, but not as much as he'd expected. Despite their disagreement, he had a high regard for Frank's professionalism. The risk of being persuaded to go back to the *Monitor* had prevented him staying longer at the pub. Now that he no longer had the mobile phone and corporate card, his ties with the company were severed and he was free to do as he pleased.

One issue remained unresolved and seemed likely to stay that way. He hadn't managed to tell his side of the story to Gina. On the one occasion she'd answered the phone, she chewed him out so loudly his ear ached afterwards. Her parting words were, "And don't call again." If that was her attitude, writing to her would be pointless. He ought to accept her rebuff as one of life's little injustices, but being unable to tell her his version of events gave him a sense of grievance.

She'd cast him in the role of Judas Iscariot and the unfounded accusation rankled every time he thought of her.

21. Girding her loins

Feeling the need for exercise and to breathe fresh air, Gina left Casa Rosa to go for a walk, her thoughts preoccupied with the events of the past few days. The exposé had brought home to her how much she was a prisoner of her past. No matter how she tried, she couldn't shake off the fact she was a brothel owner's daughter. Even in America, thousands of miles from where she lived, it had still affected her.

Her intention had been to turn back when she reached Oxford Street, but striding away from the bordello was liberating and she carried on walking. A light breeze kept her from becoming too warm.

While she was crossing Elizabeth Street, her phone rang.

"Hiya, darl!"

"Hey, Caro."

"You're outdoors. Where are you?"

She looked around and realised how far she'd walked. "On Park Street. I'm stretching my legs and clearing my mind."

"Good. Keep walking and we'll meet at Town Hall. I'll be ten minutes. I need to chat to you about the defo."

Twenty minutes later, standing on the Town Hall steps, Gina caught sight of her friend and waved to her.

As they sat down, Caroline said, "I spoke to one of the defo guys I mentioned last Saturday. It's pretty much what I thought."

"Which is…?"

"He said the other side will mount a vigorous defence because they pay hefty indemnity premiums and don't want them going up any further."

Gina pulled a face. "Bully for them. Did he think I had a strong case?"

"Morally, yes. Legally, maybe. There are no certainties when you enter a court, especially if it's a jury trial."

"How did he rate my chances?"

"He said you're up against a powerful media group. It'll be like getting into the ring with Mike Tyson." She mimed an uppercut.

"I'd rather he said it was like David and Goliath. At least David won that one."

Caroline studied Gina's face carefully. "His advice is to save your money. Only rich people can afford libel actions."

The rebuff deflated her. She sat wondering at the inequity of it all, the sheer one-sidedness favouring the privileged. She wanted to cry, to scream, but Caroline was watching her, waiting for her acquiescence, her acceptance of reality.

Gina shook her head. "In other words I'm stuffed. Just because I can't afford to take the *Monitor* on, they can do what they bloody well like." She sprang to her feet and looked down at Caroline. "It's totally, friggin' unfair. I can't sit back and let them get away with it. Who knows what they'll do to us next? I'm going ahead."

"But you can't afford it. You won't be allowed to take them to court if you can't pay the costs if you lose." She tugged at Gina's skirt and in a phoney Bronx accent said, "Siddown, kiddo, it ain't over till the lawyer lady says so."

She sat down. "What else is there to say?"

"I spoke to the defo bloke on Monday. Afterwards, I got to thinking about how I could help you. Then I had an idea. I may not be able to represent you officially—my firm wouldn't let me do it even at mates' rates—but I can still help. My idea is that I advise you as best I can—you have to know I'm not an expert in this sort of thing—and my dad will process the paperwork through his firm. He said he doesn't mind."

"But he's a suburban solicitor—won't it look odd if he takes on a libel case?"

"They handle a variety of work. Anyway, the only costs will be court fees and the like and I can do the rest."

"Are you sure? It's a lot to take on."

"Of course I'm sure. When did I ever do something I didn't want to? Besides, I've become too comfortable lately. I need to learn something new. But there is a proviso. If the other side doesn't yield during settlement, you must pull out, because from there on it gets too expensive. The *Monitor* can afford the best barristers in Sydney and I won't let you bankrupt yourself."

"Caro, I don't know what to say. Can you really find time for all this?"

"I'll give it my best shot. Let me start the ball rolling and see what happens when they receive the writ, but bear in mind these cases take years to come to court."

"Why? It's not that complicated."

"Partly procedural stuff—you can't avoid the settlement process—but the *Monitor* will delay and try to wear you down. That's why you need to be certain it's what you want to do."

Without hesitation, Gina said, "I'm definitely going ahead. That sanctimonious arsehole is not going to get the better of me."

Caroline laughed. "That's my girl. Crispin Calloway *is* an arsehole. But remember, he's a rich and influential arsehole, so don't give him any reason to sue you in return. Be extremely careful what you say about him in public."

"Point taken. I'll try not to score any own goals."

22. Home truths

During the next month Gina worked hard to minimise the impact of the *Monitor* exposé. Business dropped initially to a third of its previous level, the one exception being the weekend of the national rugby league grand final, always a busy time for brothels. Gradually, though, trade picked up, but not to the previous level.

The article wasn't the only thing affecting custom. Gina heard that rival brothels had taken delight in spreading the bad news to their customers.

The loss of business also affected the girls' earnings. Three left during the second week. They were good workers and she was loath to lose them, but at least their absence meant the others were less affected. Despite that, she saw their departures as a sign of failure. When she'd worked at the Austral Merchant Bank, staff retention had been a key measure for assessing her effectiveness as a manager.

She was now in complete control of the business. Her mother's chemotherapy wasn't expected to finish until early January, nearly three months away, and its debilitating side-effects were causing her to lose weight, while the constant nausea and fatigue made her so depressed she showed minimal interest in the goings-on at Casa Rosa. She'd begun to speak as though she would never return. This was so unlike her that Concetta, who spent a lot of time with Maria, told Gina she found excuses to be out of the house to avoid infection by Maria's dark mood.

Gina did what she could to raise her mother's spirits and keep her interested in the business, but to no avail. Finally, she insisted on being given full authority to run Casa Rosa the way she wanted. Maria quietly acquiesced. That had been a defining moment for Gina. Her ambivalence towards the caretaker role was replaced by a determination to turn the business around. She'd always thought of herself as an able administrator; now she was on a mission to prove she was a successful entrepreneur as well.

One of her first tasks was to install an extra phone line so she could use the Internet. It gave her the opportunity to consider developing a website for Casa Rosa to advertise the business on-line. All she needed now was a good (and inexpensive) website developer.

Once the business returned to profitability, she intended placing personal computers in reception, networked to her machine, so all the bookings and other records could be coordinated. As soon as that was in place, she would consign her mother's precious ledgers to the bottom of the filing cabinet.

She also bought mobile phones for Jock and Baz—who had returned from the States, his sister having recovered from her injuries sooner than expected—to give her better control over their whereabouts when they took the girls on outcalls. Jock had his own phone, an old one, which he had a habit of turning off "to save the battery". He would no longer have that excuse for being unavailable when she needed him.

She'd spoken to him about his attendance record after Chloe's attack, and he'd been quick to reassure her his timekeeping would improve. Though she tried keeping an eye on him since then, Simon and Liz still complained about his lateness.

Another talk was called for.

Lost in thought, she didn't realise someone was standing in her office doorway until she heard a throat being cleared. She looked up to see Simon staring at her.

"Can I have a quick word?"

She beckoned him in and he closed the door.

"Problem?" she asked in a neutral tone.

He sat skewed in the visitor's chair, as if ready to race off at the first sign of opposition to whatever he was about to say. She shoved her paperwork to one side and gave him her full attention.

He cleared his throat again. "Remember when I came for my interview and we discussed what my duties would be?"

"Yes." She was unsure where this might be leading.

"And you said I would be managing things once I got to know the ropes?"

"That's right, I did."

Simon pushed his spectacles above the bridge of his nose. "Well, I've been in that position for four weeks and you're still running things."

"Oh..." In all the recent turmoil she'd forgotten the real reason for taking him on. "I'm sorry, Simon. You're absolutely right—I did say that."

"So?"

So what did she want him to do? Did she still need him now that business had fallen off? Staff costs were her biggest single outgoing. On the other hand, if he left she'd have to do his job as well as her own. She didn't need an extra burden while fighting to keep the business afloat. Besides, if—no, when—business bounced back, she'd need to hire another receptionist.

"I'm afraid things turned out a lot different to what I planned, but you're right, I should give you more responsibility." He twisted in his chair so he was facing her full on. "I'm planning on buying more computers so we can all see what's going on with bookings and staff availability. Do you know anything about networking?"

He gave a scornful laugh. "Of course I do. I *am* studying IT at uni, remember?"

"Are you? Sorry, I'd forgotten."

"It's in my résumé."

"I'm sure it is." She couldn't remember seeing it, but computer skills hadn't been what she was looking for when she'd hired him. "Of course, I'd appreciate any help you can give me. We didn't cover that kind of stuff on my MBA course."

"I could write some software if you like. I've been thinking about it. A complete brothel management system—you know, bookings, accounts, health records, all that sort of stuff."

Mechanically she said, "Sounds interesting." She'd been thinking of using linked spreadsheets—the MBA's all-purpose tool.

He shrugged. "No worries. Just a thought."

Sensing she'd hurt his feelings, she asked, "Maybe there's something on the market we could buy?"

"No, I've looked."

"Are you sure you can do it?"

"I can if I have a computer to work with. Only when it's quiet, of course. I could even stay behind to work on it."

"Please, please don't go to a lot of trouble."

"No trouble, believe me."

"Okay. Well, as regards your responsibilities, I'll let you know what I can hand over after I've had time to think about it." She waited for him to leave, but he didn't move. "Something else on your mind?"

Removing his glasses, he leaned forward and gave her a resolute look. "I think you need to take more interest in your staff. They're not happy."

"Who? Liz? Jos? Baz and Jock?"

"Everybody."

Everybody? She found that hard to believe. Even so, it bothered her. "Isn't that to be expected after all the trouble we've been through? It's tough for everybody at the moment."

"No, it's not that, it's—" He paused as he struggled to find the right words. "They think you're standoffish."

"I'm not standoffish. Do *you* think I'm standoffish?"

Simon didn't reply; he continued to fiddle with his glasses as he waited for her to continue.

She thought over what he'd said. Her relations with the girls had been strained right from the start, that much was true. Because she'd seen herself as a temporary manager, she'd never made the effort to get to know them. Besides, she still didn't understand why they chose to work as prostitutes. Fair enough, if they were comfortable with what they did, that was their choice, but it was difficult for her to empathise with them.

When she didn't respond, Simon said, "And they think you take them for granted. The way they're talking, some of them won't stick around much longer." Before she could digest that remark, he added, "If I were in your shoes I'd do something about it."

Could that be why she'd lost three girls? No, they'd made it clear it was the drop in earnings. Two of them were single mothers who worked part-time.

She arched her eyebrows. "So, it's that bad?"

"Believe me, I hear the gossip."

"I do believe you," she said hurriedly, "but I'm surprised it's so sudden."

"Which is why you need to get closer to them. They feel a bit lost after what's happened lately. They miss your mother."

"Thanks for letting me know. I'll see what I can do about it."

He gave her a searching look that she found unsettling, and left the office without another word.

She thought over what his comments. Could he have a point? She had been, if not aloof, then certainly distant, she was well aware of that, but she'd been respectful and considerate of all the personnel. Admittedly, she rarely spoke to the girls. Often, when she walked into the kitchen, they stopped chatting or lowered their voices. She'd assumed it was because she was their employer. Now it seemed they regarded her as a pariah.

This new awareness surprised and disappointed her. Still, as her philosophy tutor used to say, perception is reality. If the staff thought a problem existed, she must deal with it. Her first step would be to make a determined effort to get to know them individually and see what she could do to motivate them.

She pulled out the staff register and perused the names. Sixteen girls were listed as regular escorts and twelve others who attended intermittently, mostly students or wives who worked when their husbands were away. The administrative staff comprised Simon,

Liz, Jos, and Heather, a part-timer, all on reception; Baz and Jock as drivers and gofers; and Mrs Danby, the cleaner.

Getting to know more than thirty people reasonably well would take some time. Her main challenge would be Juliette, the girl she'd ticked off when she found her smoking in the kitchen. She wasn't sure how to go about it—Juliette had hardly said a word to her in all the weeks Gina had been at Casa Rosa and the resentment was almost palpable. It might not be possible, but she had to give it a go.

She wished she knew why Juliette disliked her so much. On the other hand, if she were on side, it would make it easier to gain the respect of the others.

An opportunity presented itself the following afternoon. After spending half the day doing the laundry, Gina was exhausted. When she went into the kitchen to grab a coffee, she noticed Juliette sitting alone at the table reading a magazine.

"Hi!" She hoped her forced jollity wasn't too obvious.

Juliette responded with a grudging, "Hi," and carried on reading. Undeterred, Gina took her coffee to the table and sat facing her.

"How's it all going?"

Juliette looked up briefly. "Oh, the usual." She resumed reading.

Gina read the headline upside down of the article Juliette found so engrossing, but it was about a celebrity she'd never heard of.

"I can't remember the last time I read a magazine," she ventured.

At first, the comment yielded no response. Then, without ceremony, Juliette stood up, collected the magazine, and looked straight at her. "That would have been the *Wall Street Journal*." Her tone was sarcastic and dismissive.

Her ire rising, Gina said, "So what's your problem, Juliette?"

"You, of course."

She stalked off without a backwards glance.

"Hey! Come back here!" She leapt to her feet and ran after her, catching her as she entered the changing room. She followed her in and slammed the door behind them. Standing less than an arm's reach from Juliette, so close she smelled her musky perfume, she said, "All right, let's have it. What have I done to piss you off?"

Juliette faced her defiantly, lips pursed, eyes bright with indignation. "Your fucking attitude is what pisses me off, that's what. Poncing around here as if you're Queen Muck with bells on, thinking you're so much better than the rest of us. Well, you're not, so don't even think it. You're a fucking brothel worker like the rest of us." She paused to gauge Gina's reaction.

"Go on, anything else?"

The other woman's anger accentuated her broad English Midlands accent. "You couldn't even be bothered to introduce yourself to any of us when you started, could you? The first time you spoke to me was to give me a right bollocking."

"I didn't give you a bollocking, as you put it. I just reminded you of the house rules."

"It sounded like a bollocking to me and everyone else. How would you like to be bawled out?" She paused to catch her breath. "You think you can march around this place like you own it. Well, you don't. It's Maria's."

"Don't you think I know that? She's entrusted me to manage it until she gets back on her feet."

Juliette folded her arms across her chest. "And that's another thing. You've never once told us how Maria was getting on or asked if we might like to go and see her. No, if it hadn't been for Liz we wouldn't even know what bleeding hospital she was in."

Gina felt that barb more than the others. It was pointless denying the accusation. "Okay, I'm sorry about that. I didn't realise. I suppose I should have."

They fell silent, Gina struggling to understand the allegations and bring her emotions under control. After Simon's talk with her, she was well aware she was thought aloof, but did she really come across as a stuck-up bitch? And why hadn't she passed on the information about her mother?

She backed away and asked as calmly as she could, "Did you go to see her in hospital?"

Juliette unfolded her arms. "Most of us did at one time or another."

"That's good." Now what? Should she apologise for being aloof? No, damn it, she'd never been patronising.

"Look, I'm sorry if I come across as snobby, but it's not meant that way. Okay?" Juliette's gaze was uncompromising. "I've had a lot to put up with since I came home. This isn't what I expected to be doing, and my mother's illness has played on my mind quite a lot." Still no reaction. "And on top of all that...my boyfriend dumped me."

At last, Juliette laughed. "I'm not surprised. Probably had the same problem as us."

Gina told herself not to rise to the taunt. She waited, then Juliette said, "So why did he really dump you?"

"I didn't tell him about this place until we got serious."

"Ah... Couldn't have loved you very much then, could he?" It was said in a neutral tone and Gina studied her face for signs of malice. She found none, but the accusation had struck home. Could that have been the case? Had she deluded herself all along about his real feelings? The thought rekindled the memory of her distress and her eyes began to water.

"No, I guess he didn't." She turned to leave. "I'd better get back to work."

Juliette followed her out of the room. "Sorry...about your boyfriend."

"That's okay. I'm over it now."

23. Letter from America

"You have a letter," called Maria from the living room. "It's from America," she said.

"From America? Must be from the President." More likely it was from the Harvard Business School or one of her classmates she'd promised to keep in touch with. Gina dropped her bag and went into the entrance hall to collect the envelope from the bureau. The address was handwritten and the return addressee said Edith Chamberlain. Her pulse quickened. She slit open the envelope, unfolded the letter, and read it as she wandered into the living room.

Pinned to the letter was a photocopied newspaper article. She glanced at the attachment and was about to read the letter when she realised the clipping was George Chamberlain's obituary. He'd died from a heart attack while driving home on a Friday evening in late September. It went on to list his many business achievements and the work he'd done for charity. He was fifty-seven.

"It's from Edith, Morgan's mother. His father's died."

"Oh dear."

She scanned the letter quickly and then read it out loud.

"She says, *Dear Gina, As you will see from the attached, we lost our beloved George two months ago.*

He was travelling home when he suffered a massive heart attack and crashed his car. The doctors say he almost certainly died before the impact. We continue to thank the Lord that no-one else was killed or injured as that road is very busy on Friday evenings, as you know. We're also truly thankful that the twins were not travelling with him." Gina thought it was indeed a stroke of luck, as George often brought his twin daughters down for the weekend. *"You didn't know George that well, but he was a kind and generous man, a good, caring father, and my devoted husband and companion. His passing has left a huge gap in all our lives.*

Morgan, of course, was badly affected. I am not sure how long it will take for him to get over his grief— he is emotionally fragile, as you can imagine." Gina felt a twinge of guilt. He didn't deserve all this. *"Now, a belated thank you for your letter and for the return of the portrait. You need not have done so. It was freely given and yours to dispose of as you wished, but I understand and appreciate the gesture.*

I must say we were disappointed at the turn of events before you left, but that is water under the bridge now."

Maria said, "It sounds like she's softened."

"I don't think so. You never met them, Ma. They were seriously religious."

"If they're decent people why wouldn't they have accepted you for who you are?"

Hadn't Caroline said something similar? It was pointless arguing. Morgan's strong views on sexual morality would have prevented him marrying a brothel owner's daughter. And even if he could have brought himself to do it, his father would have cut him off without a cent.

She returned to the letter. *"I'm sorry to hear about your business problems and hope that your mother has a speedy recovery. I am certain you will sort things out and eventually succeed. You always struck me as a determined individual.*

As I say, I grew fond of you while you were here and, despite everything, you are still in my thoughts. If ever you return to America, please let me know. I would love to see you again. Kind regards, Edith."

Maria said, "She sounds like a nice lady."

"Poor Edith...and poor Morgan."

"When your Papa died I thought my life had come to an end. If it hadn't been for you, I'd have probably joined him. For all his faults, he was my one and only love."

Gina held her mother's hand. "I wish I'd known him better."

"Even when Nonno and Nonna died—and I adored them both—it didn't affect me as much as when Papa passed away. It wasn't just the way he died so suddenly—it was all the fun and excitement that died with him. My life's never been the same since."

"If only we realised how temporary our lives are," Gina said, "we wouldn't take people so much for granted. Here one minute, gone the next, and then we regret not enjoying them when we had the chance. You know"— she squeezed her mother's hand and leaned forward to kiss her cheek—"we could have lost you not so long ago."

Maria smiled. "Don't you worry, love, I'll be hanging around for a while yet."

~~~

Edith Chamberlain's letter brought back memories that Gina had largely blocked out since she returned home. Back, too, came the guilt and remorse that had persisted through the homeward journey, and which had been pushed into the background by the emotional upheaval she'd experienced since.

At Harvard she'd been socially active, dating widely, until she met Morgan. At first, she treated him as just another student who'd taken an interest in her, but he soon proved to be different. For a start, he was knowledgeable about the arts—books, film, music, galleries. He knew the best restaurants and always managed to get them a good table. His commanding personality captivated her, and she allowed herself to be swept along, not unlike being a passenger in his exclusive sports car.

She couldn't pinpoint when she fell in love with him, but she remembered her increasing anxiety as the time approached for her return to Australia, the time when decisions needed to be made and secrets revealed.

She'd agreed to stay on in America for two months after her June graduation. In early August they made what was to be her last visit to Martha's Vineyard before she flew home.

She had a premonition about this trip. In recent weeks Morgan had become more attentive, speaking about future events as if she'd be there when they occurred. Then there'd been the conversation with Edith a week or so before. She'd asked Gina to accompany her on a trip into Edgartown to buy art materials and they'd stopped at a café across from the bay for coffee and cake.

Edith said, "You and Morgan get along very well. I don't think I've seen him quite as happy with someone as he has been with you."

"That's nice to hear, though I'm not sure what he sees in me, to be honest."

"Really? I can. You're attractive, intelligent, something of a free spirit."

Gina laughed. "That will change as soon as I find a job."

"However, I've often wondered what it is you see in *him*..."

She gave it a few moments thought. "What's not to like? He's presentable, witty, *very* knowledgeable, good company—what more could I want?"

"But you're different in other ways..."

"True, we don't see eye to eye on politics and religion, but we respect each other's point of view." She chose not to add that because he was so firm in his convictions, he didn't get agitated when arguing his corner, which was why she kept her own emotions in check. "And we do have a lot of interests in common."

"Let's hope it stays that way," Edith said. "Tolerance can be short-lived." She changed the subject before Gina had time to absorb the significance of that remark.

Afterwards, she wondered if Morgan's mother had been alluding to some fundamental incompatibility between her and her son. She couldn't think what it was, and was about to dismiss the idea when it struck her. Edith had been sounding her out because he was on the verge of proposing. If that were so, she couldn't hold off much longer telling him the truth about herself.

On the last Saturday, Morgan's father, George, who stayed in Boston during the week to be close to his work, came down to the island to take the family out in his yacht. The twin sisters, who were studying at Harvard, were there as well. Although Morgan had given Gina a tour of the craft at its mooring, it was the first time she'd sailed in her.

The weather was warm and humid as the boat left the Edgartown marina, cutting across the wake of the Chappaquiddick ferry and out past Oak Bluffs into Nantucket Sound. In open waters the breeze remained light and they stayed on deck during the passage towards the Elizabeth Islands.

Engrossed in his navigation—taking care not to get tangled in lobster nets—George remained his usual taciturn self, but once they reached Buzzards Bay he relaxed and began to tell Gina stories about the area: how it had been settled by the Puritans from Plymouth and their struggle with the Wampanoag and Sippewisset Indians; the development and gradual decline of the prosperous whaling industry; the filming of *Jaws* at Mememsha, barely a stone's throw from his house; and how he loved to fish for striped bass, small tuna, and bluefish, which were prevalent during the summer months. While she listened to his father, Morgan stayed close by her side, his arm around her waist, occasionally pointing out an eagle or osprey riding high in the sky. She wasn't surprised that he knew the name and purpose of every lighthouse they passed.

They lunched aboard the boat. Afterwards, Morgan said he needed to discuss something privately with his father and the two men went into the wheelhouse. She remained with the women on the aft deck and couldn't fail to notice the meaningful looks that passed between his mother and her daughters.

When they returned to the island in the late afternoon, Morgan told his parents that he and Gina would stay in town for a while. The rest of the family made their way up-island in George's Mercedes.

They walked hand-in-hand down South Water Street and watched the boats on Katama Bay, their coloured sails caught by the warm evening sun. Gina said, "This is a great place for boating, isn't it?"

"Do you like it here?"

"Here in Edgartown or on the island?"

"Not just the island—America as well. The East Coast, at least. Do you think you could live here permanently?"

"I don't know...I'm not sure. In all honesty, I haven't given it serious thought. Why?"

Instead of answering, He led them to a low wall where they sat together and silently looked across the water towards the small island of Chappaquiddick. After a while, a light breeze came up. Morgan put his arm around her shoulder and said quietly, "So you're going back..."

She mused on this. "I miss my family, you know. We've always been close, and I haven't seen much of them in the past two years—just on flying visits."

Another silence. Was this the moment?

As she held her breath, he cleared his throat and turned to face her. "Gina, you know how much—"

She spoke quickly. "Morgan, don't say any more. There's something I need to tell you...and you're not going to like it."

Adopting a matter-of-fact tone, her eyes fixed on Chappaquiddick, she explained the nature of her mother's business to Morgan. She described the steps her mother had taken to insulate Gina from the business and how important it had been that she had a respectable career.

Apart from removing his arm from around her shoulders, he was surprisingly unresponsive. When she finished speaking she turned to face him and saw his agonised bewilderment.

"Your mother is a brothel keeper, living off immoral earnings?"

She tried to soften his judgement. "She calls it a bordello. It's up-market, not some sleazy establishment."

He got to his feet and glared down at her. "All these months you've led me to believe you came from a decent family. Why didn't you tell me this before? When you first knew I was serious about you? Why?"

"I wanted to... I was going to, but—"

Not waiting to hear her out, he strode off in the direction of the car.

She remained sitting on the wall, face wet with tears, more than aware she deserved his rejection, yet still surprised by it. But how else could he have reacted? Hadn't she known all along this would happen?

After a while, she heard the sound of a car pulling up sharply behind her and Morgan's voice calling out, "Get in the car. We're leaving."

Neither spoke on the journey to the house. When he stopped outside the garage and cut the engine, he said, "I still can't get my head around what you've just told me. It's surreal. You've no idea how much I cared for you...wanted to share my life with you."

She dabbed at her eyes with a tissue. "I'm sorry, Morgan, honestly I am. I'd give anything to turn the clock back. I never thought we'd be this close."

"It's too late now." He got out of the car and slammed the door shut. "What the hell am I going to tell my folks?"

He came round to open the passenger door. As he stepped back to allow her to climb out, she said, "I'm going back to Boston tomorrow. Let's keep what I've told you between us for the time being, okay?"

The following day, when it was time to leave, Morgan apologised for his mother's absence. "She had to go into town early."

He drove her back to Boston and they parted on civil but awkward terms. She wanted him to embrace her for the last time, an act of absolution perhaps, but he kept his distance, wishing her a safe journey home.

As she watched him drive down the road and out of her life, she realised she'd never made up her mind about a crucial issue: if he'd asked her to marry him, knowing what he now knew, what would she have answered?

24. More home truths

"Right, starting next Monday morning we're going to have a weekly meeting."

Gina waited for Simon's reaction.

"You mean, like a staff meeting? Are you serious?"

"Of course. One where I can let everybody know what's going on, and they can make suggestions and get things off their chest."

She'd given the matter a lot of thought since Simon's approach and her confrontation with Juliette. As far as she was concerned, a brothel was just another workplace. Staff needed to be consulted and kept informed. When she worked at the bank, a start-of-week meeting had been mandatory in all departments. Her staff had also expected her to give written feedback of their performance every six months and provide incentives to work more efficiently. She wasn't altogether sure how she'd achieve that at Casa Rosa.

He nodded sagely. "I'm sure it'll be very interesting."

"Right. I'll whack up a notice in the kitchen. In the meantime, perhaps you could spread the word around. I'd like as many people to be there as possible."

"You can't expect people to come in when they're not rostered on. They don't get paid for sitting around."

"Depends how useful they find it. Anyway, I'll provide minutes, and they can raise issues with me in advance."

"What about reception?"

"Bring Jos in early so you and Liz can attend the meeting."

"And the girls who are seeing clients?"

"I'll try to pick a quiet time."

~~~

The turnout for the first meeting proved disappointing. Gina had scheduled it for eleven o'clock so most people could be there, but only nine turned up. They assembled in the kitchen and sat around the long table.

She had a notebook in front of her. On the first page she'd written a rough agenda. On the second she made a note of who'd turned up: Simon and Liz, as expected, Chloe, Kellie, Holly, the spiky-redheaded punk, as well as Britney, another blonde, with an emerald stone in her nose, Amber, a short, slim Chinese girl, and Juliette, who had just arrived and was quietly chatting to Kellie.

Gina was surprised and a little apprehensive to see Juliette. Although she'd seemed mollified after their quarrel, she still had a resentful air about her when Gina was around. Perhaps she always acted that way. If so, she couldn't understand why her mother kept her on.

Baz, dressed in his customary Rabbitohs' red and green striped jersey, strolled in and was greeted warmly by the girls. He leaned against a bench and watched everyone with a benevolent expression. She liked Baz: he was dependable, uncomplaining, and unfailingly polite. She knew he never slept with the girls, even though some would have been happy to oblige. According to Liz, they'd once competed to seduce him. None had succeeded.

While she waited she deliberated whether to tell the meeting about the libel case. In the end she decided not to. The wisdom of bringing the case had played on her mind ever since Caroline raised serious doubts about it succeeding. Unless she got lucky, there was a distinct likelihood she'd have to withdraw the action, no matter how much of her ego was invested in it.

After allowing an extra five minutes for latecomers to appear—none did—Gina settled down to business.

"Before we start, I want to thank all of you for showing up. I must say I was hoping to see a few more here."

Kellie said, "It's not because we're not interested, only some of us have other responsibilities."

"Besides," Britney said, before Gina could speak, "we don't get paid for showing up. I'm only here because I'm rostered on at twelve anyway, but hey, what's an hour between friends?" She followed that with an unconvincing smile.

"Fair enough. I'll take that into account in future. I'll print minutes and leave copies here in the kitchen for anyone who's interested."

In her soft, high-pitched voice, Amber said, "Do we actually need meetings? Maria never had them. She just chatted to us."

"And she didn't stay cooped up in her office all day long, either," added Chloe, emboldened no doubt by the rising chorus.

"She was in and out of the kitchen all day long, and we were always chatting to her." This was Holly.

Gina put both hands up. "Okay, okay, I get the message. So you reckon I've been hiding from you, is that it?"

"You sure look like you'd rather not be here, especially with the likes of us," Holly said.

Kellie laughed. "Yeah, that's for sure!"

Gina was aware of Simon watching her, his slight smile clearly telegraphing, "I told you so." She sneaked a glance at Juliette. Her face remained impassive.

She breathed in deeply and slowly exhaled. She wasn't going to be drawn into an argument. "All right, let me be perfectly straight with you. You're right, I don't want to be here, but it's nothing personal. I came back from America expecting to start a corporate career. I never dreamt I'd end up here instead. Then I thought it would only be for a week, two at the most, but it's turned out to be a lot longer. Now, because of the bad publicity we've had, I'm going to find it more difficult to get the job I want. 'Brothel madam' won't look too good on my CV."

Holly said, "But you're not an escort, so why should it matter if you're running a brothel? It's just another job."

"It's not that simple. I wish it were. It's guilt by association. And you know better than me there's a stigma attached to sex work."

She paused to allow someone else to comment, but their eyes were focused on her.

"Anyway, that's water under the bridge. I accept I've been acting aloof—not intentionally—and now I'm trying to put things right."

She looked around the table for signs of hostility. None were obvious but she could see wariness in their faces. Juliette's face continued to remain inscrutable.

"Until a few days ago I was simply minding the business for my mother—it was a caretaker role as far as I was concerned. I was taking no more interest than was necessary. That's changed now. Because we don't know when she's be coming back to work, she's agreed I should manage this place the best way I think fit. That means you'll see a few changes."

Holly interrupted. "What sort of changes?"

"For a start, I'd like to try different ways to attract more custom. We need to get back to where we were before all the bad publicity. If I succeed, it'll mean more work for you."

That last statement seemed to please them.

"It's important we have meetings like this. Everybody gets to hear the same thing from one person and you also get to have your say. I'm not knocking the way my mother did things and if and when she comes back I expect she'll carry on like before. Meanwhile, we can give my way a go and see how it turns out. Okay?"

This was met with a murmur of approval. She was about to continue when she noticed Juliette looking confused. "Did you want to say something, Juliette?"

"You said 'if and when she comes back'. Does that mean she might not?"

"It's a possibility. There's no guarantee chemo will cure the cancer. We probably won't know until after Christmas. Could even be later than that."

Juliette looked unhappy but said nothing.

"Right, I have an agenda here. The first item is for me to report on the state of the business. Then I want to discuss some ideas I have for making the place a bit more efficient. Please feel free to add your own ideas. Finally, 'Any Other Business'—that's when you can talk about anything you like relevant to working here.

"Okay, let me tell you how the business is going…"

~~~

The meeting ran for three-quarters of an hour. Afterwards, back in her office, Gina asked Simon for his candid assessment.

"It went better than I expected. I thought you'd cop more flak than you did, especially from Juliette."

"We've already had a conversation. She seems worried about my mother, though."

"Most of the girls are. By all accounts she's been like a mother to them."

"I don't think I'm the mothering type."

"Still, you could show more interest. For example, what do you know about Tammi?"

She tried to recall the conversations she'd had with her. Nothing noteworthy was discussed as far as she could remember. "She's a sweet kid. Gets on well with everyone."

"Hobbies?"

"No idea."

"She makes teddy bears—good ones apparently—you can buy them in shops. Amber makes jewellery. Baz reads everything under the sun. Juliette has a bastard of a boyfriend. Kellie has a new boyfriend but he doesn't know she's an escort. Britney has twin boys and her mother looks after them. Her husband walked out on her. And so on. They're an interesting bunch when you get to know them."

"You obviously have. Okay, point taken." She knew he was right. However, it took time to get to know people.

Simon said, "By the way, we were surprised to hear you're suing the *Monitor*. Why didn't you tell us that before?"

"In all honesty, I didn't think they'd be interested. I only mentioned it because nobody wanted to say anything."

"It's good you told them. They seemed impressed."

"Anything else?"

"They don't understand what you meant by improving performance. I bet they think you'll be monitoring their on-the-job performance."

"Sorry, I should have given an example."

"Like what?"

"Like…customer satisfaction, for a start."

"And how do you measure that?"

"I don't know…questionnaires?"

Simon laughed. "I don't think our clients will hang around to fill out any forms."

"Of course not, but there has to be some objective way of measuring satisfaction. How many men visit just the once? Why don't they come back? Is it the girl or the amenities or the atmosphere or what? That's the kind of thing I'd like to find out. I can't go on guesswork."

"What did they do at that bank you worked for?"

"They had a market research company call our customers. Thankfully, mine were satisfied with the service they received."

"Pleased to hear it. So, are you proposing to give our non-existent client list to a market research outfit to conduct a phone survey?" He laughed at the thought. "You'd have Buckley's."

"Fair enough. How would you go about it?"

"Where I worked before, if a customer was happy, he'd renew his insurance; otherwise he'd go somewhere else. Each adviser was measured on how much new business and renewals they achieved."

She thought it over. "We could try something similar, I suppose."

"Maybe, but only for in-house business. The outcalls are mostly people visiting Sydney."

"There must be something else we can use. We can't measure some and not others."

"They already have their performance measured. You just have to check their earnings against the number of hours they put in. But that still won't tell you why customers don't return."

"I'll think of something."

~~~

Gina hadn't forgotten the confrontation with Juliette, and she raised the subject with her mother that evening. They shared the sofa in the lounge room, Gina nursing a glass of wine, Maria still in her dressing gown. She seemed in better spirits since handing over control of the business.

"She's a strange one," Maria said.

"But I don't understand why she feels so strongly about me."

"Maybe she resents you for being what she isn't, or for having more than she has."

"But that's hardly my fault, is it?"

"Julie's not been as lucky as you. Her father died when she was ten. Her mother married again and the stepfather used to interfere with her. Her mother wouldn't believe her, said she was trying to turn her against him. So of course he kept on doing it. One day she couldn't take it anymore and she left to live on the streets. She'd only be about fifteen then.

"She became a working girl so she could survive, but she stayed out of serious trouble. She also kept in touch with her mother by phone, and one day her stepfather answered and said her mother was in hospital. So she went to visit her mother and the doctor told her she had breast cancer and it had spread to her lymph glands. Anyway, her mother didn't live long after that."

"That's terrible."

"Oh, it gets worse. Everything in the will was left to the stepfather. Julie didn't get a brass razoo. You'd have thought her mother would have looked after her better than that, but she didn't. She never believed what Julie said about him, you see."

"No wonder she's resentful, if she's comparing the two of us. At least I never had a perverted stepfather."

"Since she came to Australia, she's been living with a no-hoper of a bloke called Victor. I wish she'd dump him and find someone else—he makes her life a misery. He deals drugs and steals stuff, and she can't stop him. He's on bail at the moment. She's worried he'll end up in prison this time."

So Victor was the 'bastard of a boyfriend' that Simon mentioned. "How can you be sure she's not on drugs if he's selling the stuff?"

"She's not. She's never used. Neither has he. He only deals."

"If she has that much sense, why doesn't she ditch him?"

"She must see something in him the rest of us can't. I'll say this for her—she's worked for me for three years and I can always rely on her. She's had less time off than anybody else. She often confides in me, too. I think I'm the mother she wishes she'd had."

Great, Gina thought, just what I need: pseudo-sibling rivalry.

"I just wish she'd stop looking so resentful."

Maria said, "She'd be the last girl I'd lay off if I had to cut back."

Gina sipped her wine. "I'm surprised. Chloe and some of the others do more business than Juliette."

"I know Julie can be moody, but she's versatile—doesn't care what she does if the client's prepared to pay for it. But I wouldn't want to lose Chloe, either. She's a lovely girl."

"What's this about cutting back, anyway?"

"Well, the way things have been going since I went into hospital..."

"Gee, thanks, Ma, for that vote of confidence!"

They sat quietly for a minute before Maria said, "How are you getting on with the others?"

Gina wondered how truthful she should be. She didn't want her mother thinking the staff were unhappy.

"They've been a bit unsettled recently, what with business being down and you not being well."

"I've heard rumours..."

"Oh...who's been talking?"

Her mother dismissed the question with a wave of her hand. "Doesn't matter."

"I've started holding staff meetings."

Maria made a face. "Meetings? You don't need meetings. They need to know you're out there helping them. You can't do that sitting in my office all day long."

"I know, I've already been given a lecture by Simon, thank you."

"I'm just saying..."

Gina saw that if she didn't get on top of this issue, her mother would lose confidence in her.

25. Death and life

Since the attempted rape, Chloe hadn't been comfortable working as an escort. However, one customer made her job bearable.

Given Mr Roberts's age, it was no surprise to either of them that often he couldn't manage an erection. Undeterred, he visited on average once a fortnight and Chloe enjoyed spending time with him, especially as on most occasions he ended up only chatting to her.

"I heard you weren't too well on Friday," she said. He'd cancelled at short notice.

"At my age, my love, there are days when it's a struggle to get out of bed in the mornings. I don't know what it was, but I did feel poorly. But I'm as fit as a Mallee bull today, so watch your step, young lady!"

She laughed. "So you reckon you're up for it today?"

"You bet! There's real lead in me pencil."

"Good for you. Come on, then, let's have a look at you."

He dropped his trousers and sat on the edge of the bed. Chloe sat next to him and put her hand on his semi-tumescent penis. "Yes, I think we can do something with that." She took a condom from the bedside cabinet but left the packet unopened. From experience she knew he was far more likely to go limp than otherwise.

As she fondled him, he said, "Did I ever tell you about the time I was in this brothel in Paris and the mirror fell off the wall?"

"No, I don't think so." He had, of course, and more than once, but knowing he liked to talk about his early sexual exploits she never discouraged him. She continued to squeeze and caress, feeling the firmness building as he recounted his bout of boisterous lovemaking.

"She was insatiable and so was I. All them months without a woman had made me randy as a goat. We were going at it hammer and tong and I was trying to hold back as long as I could, 'cause we were only allowed fifteen minutes they were that busy, and then I says to her, 'roll over, I want it doggy style now'. So she rolls over and grabs the bed head—it was one of them brass jobs—and I'm banging away again in next to no time."

His penis was now as stiff as it was likely to get. While continuing to laugh along with him, she knelt between his legs to fit the condom.

"Well, I couldn't help myself. I was going like a rabbit with his arse on fire and the bed's practically shaking to bits. She's going, 'ooh, aah, ooh, aah' and I'm shouting, "I'm coming!" And just as I came, the mirror on the wall above the bed comes crashing down! Right behind the bed head. We were both in shock and then we rolled about laughing. Next minute, the madam bursts into the room screaming at me in French, starts throwing my clothes at me, demands I pay for the mirror... Ah, you wouldn't believe the commotion."

Chloe joined in with his laughter. "You were a right larrikin, weren't you?"

"We had some good times, me and the lads."

She rolled on the condom, smoothed out the air bubbles, and took him in her mouth. He gasped and then the bed shook. Looking up, she realised he'd fallen backwards. She knelt over him. "Mr Roberts? You all right, Mr Roberts?" His eyes were closed. "Oh no!" She patted his face. "Please, Mr Roberts…" She grabbed him with both arms and shook him. He remained inert. She thought to feel his pulse but didn't know how. Then she remembered what she was supposed to do and raced downstairs.

"Liz!"

~~~

When Gina went into the kitchen to announce that Mr Roberts's body had been taken to the morgue, she found a small group gathered around Chloe, who sat at the table with a box of tissues in front of her. Juliette sat next to her with an arm around her shoulders.

No-one seemed to notice her presence so she went to the other side of the table and sat between Tammi and Geri, a slim, rather solemn brunette who was studying commerce at Sydney University. Chloe took a clean tissue and dabbed at her eyes. She gave Gina an apologetic smile. "He was such a sweet old man. I'm so going to miss him. I just wish we could have brought him back."

"Liz tried everything she knew."

"I'm sorry, I didn't mean to criticise Liz."

"Of course not. The doctor said it was probably a massive heart attack. He won't know for sure until they've done the autopsy. Did he have any family?"

"Two sons and a daughter. Grandkids too. Will they find out he was here when he died?"

"The police are handling it—I'm sure they'll be discreet."

Chloe blew her nose. "I never got any warning. One minute he was happy as Larry and the next he'd gone." She snapped her fingers. "Just like that."

Juliette said, "At least he went the way he'd have wanted."

"Not necessarily," said Tammi. "He might have preferred to have his family around him when he died."

"I don't think you get to choose who'll be around when you have a heart attack," Geri said. "And I'm sure he wouldn't have wanted his family around today!"

"I know I'd like to have my friends and family around me when I go. I'd hate to die alone or surrounded by strangers."

Gina said, "Chloe was his friend. I'm sure he died with a big smile on his face."

"Thanks, Gina." Chloe had ceased crying and was now searching through her bag for makeup.

Gina left the table and headed back to her office. As she walked down the hall she heard her name called. Looking round she spied Juliette following her.

"Can I ask you something?"

"Sure."

"Your mum, would she'd mind if I visited her at home?"

"I don't know. I could ask."

"Would you?"

"Of course. No worries."

The concern on Juliette's face was replaced with an appreciative smile.

"Thank you."

~~~

Gina knew that to increase profitability she needed to widen the gap between income and expenses, so she examined the previous years' accounts to identify major costs and sources of income. As expected, the biggest outgoing was labour. Other significant items were mortgage repayments, telephones, and electricity.

The mortgage wasn't something she could do anything about. If pushed, Maria could extend it, but that would cost more in the long run.

Gina confined her attention to telephones and electricity, before realising that phones were the business's lifelines. On the other hand, electricity usage was uncontrolled. She decided to focus on that.
The next area for scrutiny was income. The business relied on two sources: outcalls and in-house. The bad publicity had affected in-house revenue—hardly surprising with so many other brothels in the immediate vicinity—but outcalls remained buoyant.

She checked the invoices and found outcall advertising was carried by three newspapers and a couple of magazines. Shaking her head in disbelief, she went to the filing cabinet, opened the bottom drawer, and retrieved the *Daily Monitor* containing the despised exposé. She laid it face down on the desk. Working backwards from the sports pages, she soon found the classified advertisements. Under the heading of 'Adult Services' were listed two for Casa Rosa. Neither mentioned the bordello by name and each had its own phone number.

She slapped the desk so hard it stung her hand.

"You bastard! You absolute bastard!"

How could that holier-than-thou, self-righteous prick Calloway justify this contradiction in his own newspaper? She was staggered by his blatant double standards. How dare he parade himself as a moral guardian when he was profiting from the very businesses he campaigned against!

He needed to be told what a sanctimonious hypocrite he was. She found the *Monitor*'s phone number and was about to call when she remembered Caroline's instruction. She mustn't give him any excuse to counter-sue.

"You all right, Gina?"

She looked up to see Tammi standing in the doorway, a concerned look on her face.

"Sorry, Tammi. I didn't mean to alarm you. Something annoyed me, that's all."

Tammi nodded and left.

She sat back, deflated. How unfair it all seemed.

Well, if she'd been determined to chase him through the courts before, she was doubly so now. And there would be no compromises, either.

~~~

Mr Roberts's funeral took place the following Friday morning in Paddington. Chloe had been surprised when Gina volunteered to go with her. Gina never knew Mr Roberts, so the offer must have been for Chloe's benefit.

As neither woman was known to his family, they had agreed that, if approached, they'd were customers of the hotel where he used to drink.

The service was well attended and lasted for an hour. Chloe was in a melancholy mood afterwards. To cheer herself up, as they headed back to Casa Rosa in Gina's car, she told her a few of Mr Roberts's stories.

"I'm going to miss the old man. He was one of the few bright spots in this job."

Gina, waiting to turn right into Crown Street, looked at her in surprise. "I thought you liked working for us."

"Up to a point. I like the people I work with, but since that bastard tried raping me, I keep thinking the next punter could do the same. Except for Mr Roberts, of course, he was different." She took a tissue from her handbag as the memory of their last encounter made her teary again.

Gina said, "Liz said they do their best to keep the troublemakers out. That one looked like a regular punter."

"That's what bothers me—you can't always pick them. It's in the back of my mind all the time. Sooner or later another one's going to smack me around."

"Liz says we don't get many ugly mugs. Look at it this way, what are the chances of you getting the next one that comes along? Pretty low, I reckon."

She sighed. "I'm sorry, Gina, but I'm not sure I can do this job much longer."

"Give it more time. I don't want to lose you."

Her attitude surprised Chloe. According to Kellie, Gina couldn't understand why anyone chose to do the work they did.

"I thought you'd be pleased for me, you know, getting out of the business, starting a new life doing something more respectable."

Gina was slow in responding. "Yes and no. Of course you should get out of sex work, but..." Her voice trailed off.

"So what's the problem?"

"It's just that I need you right now. We're going through a bad patch and you're one of our best girls."

"I don't think it will make that much difference if I leave."

Gina didn't speak until she stopped the car on Tolley Street a few doors down from the bordello. After she turned off the engine, she said, "Well, please think it over carefully before you decide. Okay?"

But Chloe had already made up her mind.

26. Show us the money

At the second start-of-week meeting, Gina gave a brief account of Mr Roberts's funeral.

"His wife thanked us for the wreath we sent, although she had no idea who 'The Gang' was supposed to be until Chloe told her we were all his drinking mates."

Chloe said, "It turned out it to be the second wreath from his drinking mates."

This caused some amusement and then Gina got down to business.

"Last week our takings went up by three percent. That might not sound much, but it's better than the week before and the week before that. However, even at this rate, it will still take months to get back to where we were. So I'm going to spend some of the extra revenue on advertising. If anyone can come up with some better—and legal—ways we can spread the good word, please let me know. I need all the help I can get."

The group today was slightly larger than the previous week's. Two more girls—Miranda, a slim Filipino, and Geri, the commerce student—had turned up this time, but Jock was missing—though he'd been asked to attend—and it was Baz's day off. She'd hoped for a bigger turnout.

As nobody had any suggestions, she moved on.

"Cost cutting." A muffled groan. "I know, it usually means buying cheaper biscuits or something, but I'm focusing on cutting out unnecessary expenses. For example, I've been keeping an eye on the laundry recently and I noticed a lot of half-filled washes going through. When I tried to hold them back for a full wash, I was told we'd run out of clean sheets or towels. It's obvious we don't have enough, so I've ordered some more.

"I'm sure there are other areas where we could reduce costs. Any ideas?"

The question was met by a wall of blank faces. This wasn't unusual in her experience—managers were often left to answer their own questions. She was about to move on to the next item when Tammi spoke up.

"We could stop leaving the back door open. It makes the air conditioning work overtime."

"Good point, Tammi. I'll have an automatic closer fitted."

"And the TV," Amber said. "It shouldn't be left on when there's nobody around."

"Another good idea. Thanks, Amber." It was good to see two of them being constructive. She looked at the others. "Any more thoughts?" No-one spoke. "All right, let me know if you think of anything."

She went through some general housekeeping issues before addressing another idea she remembered from her days at the bank.

"As a business we need to have a clear idea of what we aspire to—what we believe sets us apart from the rest. In other words we need a mission statement."

"A mission statement?" echoed Kellie.

"Yes, a statement of our mission as a business. Why we exist, what we provide, what our core values are—that kind of stuff."

"You mean our missionary position?" Holly said.

Her question triggered a ripple of laughter.

Gina needed to keep them focused. She waited until she had their attention again. "The mission statement reflects what we see as important. It's what makes us different from the other houses."

"Do you have an example?" asked Kellie.

"I can give you one but it should be something we all come up with, so we each own it."

"Well, I won't know what you mean," Kellie said, "unless you tell us what one looks like."

"Okay, here's an example." She consulted her notebook. "'We continually strive to meet the needs of our clientele by offering a unique, value-based customer experience.'" She looked around the table to see how that registered with them. They mostly looked puzzled or confused, except Geri, who was shaking her head in disbelief.

"What's the matter, Geri?"

"That's gobbledygook. 'Unique, value-based customer experience'—gimme a break." She looked to the others for support and received murmurs of agreement. "It's corporate-speak, straight out of a management textbook."

"It's just an example." Trust Geri to challenge her. She probably covered management theory on her course. "I'm sure we can come up with something more specific than that." She wasn't going to mention she'd spent a half-an-hour that morning scouring the Internet for useful examples, and this was the best she could come up with. She was glad she'd lopped off 'to achieve enhanced outcomes'.

Needing them to take the concept seriously, she looked around for a sympathetic face.

"Tammi, how would you like your customers to describe their time spent with you?"

Tammi, normally bright and talkative, looked uneasy at finding herself the centre of attention. She considered her answer while the other girls made ribald remarks. When the banter died down, she said, "I'd rather they didn't talk about what we did."

Jock's arrival distracted Gina. He walked around the table to the counter and took a mug from the cupboard. The girls exchanged meaningful glances, while Britney stared hard at Jock's long back as if she'd gladly stick a knife in it. Gina wondered what he'd done to merit this resentment. She decided to ignore the interruption and move the discussion along.

"Sorry, Tam, I don't mean describing what actually took place. I mean how they feel after they've seen you."

"That they'd had a good time and wanted to come again?"

"And again and again," chipped in Holly. "Multiple orgasms guaranteed!"

Once more they tried to outdo each other with ribaldry. Gina struggled to keep her temper under control, made more difficult when Jock, having finished making coffee, picked up the day's newspaper and started reading it.

"Okay, quieten down a bit. I'm trying to be serious here. And, Jock, please pay attention now you're here." Jock put the paper down. "What Tammi has given us is a good advertising slogan. 'Our clients enjoy themselves so much they keep coming and coming.' What do you reckon?"

"Yeah, that's pretty good," Kellie said. "Can we have it as the missionary statement?"

"Mission statement," corrected Gina. "No, but we're on the right track. What I want is something that says why our business is special and how we go about doing it."

"Simple," Holly said. "To provide a public service and—"

"—shag customers for money. There you go." Juliette sat back, arms folded beneath her heaving breasts, seemingly satisfied she'd made a useful contribution to the discussion.

"Okay, in somewhat different words, that might describe what we do, but what is it that makes us stand out from the competition?"

"I dunno," Kellie said, "but what are you going to do with this statement once you have it?"

"Print it and hang it in reception and the waiting rooms. Maybe in here as well."

Kellie continued to look baffled. "Why?"

"So that everyone—you, me, the customers—all know what we're striving to achieve—the kind of business we believe we are. What it is that makes Casa Rosa better than the rest."

Geri said, "But, like Julie said, we only do it for the money. And I can't see our customers taking notice of your statement—they're glued to the porno while they're waiting. I've never seen anybody read the fire evacuation notice, so you have Buckley's of them reading gobbledygook about what we're supposed to believe in."

It was said so derisively that Gina knew further discussion was pointless. "Okay, we'll put that to one side for the time being. Anyone have any ideas for attracting customers?"

Holly said, "How about we give away a set of steak knives…?"

~~~

After the meeting, Gina held a post mortem with Simon in her office.

"That was a complete farce. They just sat there taking the piss."

Simon, leaning against the wall, arms folded, shook his head dolefully. "I'm surprised you tried pulling those corporate con tricks on them."

"They're not con tricks. They worked very well at the bank."

"These aren't bank employees." He sat down and gave her one of his grave looks. "If I were you, boss, I'd stick to increasing business. Do that and you'll have them eating out of your hand. At the moment they think you're in a parallel universe."

"I'm beginning to think they're right."

She considered his words. He was better placed than she was to know what was going on. Maybe she'd been focusing on the wrong issues. She changed the subject.

"We need to do something about Jock. He was late in again today. Did you see his attitude during the meeting? He made it quite plain he didn't want to be there."

"You want me to talk to him?"

"No. I'll…Yes, tell him he's on his last warning. If he can't toe the line, he's out."

~~~

"I thought I'd give you an update on how it's all going." It was Caroline calling. They hadn't spoken during the past fortnight.

"Any problems?"

"No. The other side's responded to our claim and rejected it outright, which is what we expected. The *Monitor* gets plenty of writs and they always say they'll contest them. I have to say it's the right strategy for them—they know most people can't afford to chase them."

"Did you tell them I don't give up that easily?"

"I sure did, darl."

"Good. They need to know I'm not a first round knockout."

"Remember, I told you the end could be a long way off."

"I know."

"Okay. How's business? Is it picking up yet?"

"Not much, but I'm working on it. I've increased our advertising and we're getting more outcalls."

"That's good to hear. Make a note of the measures you're taking to mitigate damages. It could prove important later on."

~~~

Gina now met with Simon before her weekly meetings, which gave her a chance to sound him out on her ideas before presenting them to the other staff—she didn't want a repeat of that second meeting, and she especially didn't want Geri ridiculing her again.

She'd also asked Simon to report on the previous week's business, which he was now doing.

"In the past week we've had a twelve percent increase. All due to the extra advertising, because it's mostly outcalls."

"Excellent. Maybe I should put ads in the suburban freebies as well?"

"If this continues, we'll need more girls. Why don't you ask the girls if they know of anyone who might be interested?"

"Okay. And I'll pay a spotter's fee as an incentive."

"That'll go down well."

She made a note on her pad. "While we're on the subject of staff, did you have that word with Jock?"

Simon grimaced. "He gave me some story about having trouble sleeping because of back pain. He said he'd definitely make an effort to be on time in future, but of course he's been late again."

She couldn't allow this to continue. His poor timekeeping meant they had to pay for taxis, and that affected profitability. She'd dragged her feet for too long.

"Let's find someone else. With the increased outcalls, we're even more dependent on our drivers."

"Okay." He waited while she wrote another note. "You know he's borrowed money off the girls and not paid it back, don't you?" She shook her head. "I thought they might have complained to you."

"How many?"

"Four to my knowledge. Two are out of pocket by five hundred dollars each. There have been some real blues over it."

"You should have told me earlier. They won't get their money back once he's gone, and I can't dock his pay."

"Sorry, I thought you knew."

From his tone it was clear he thought she should have known. She leaned back in her chair. "I know it's subjective, but apart from Jock and those girls, would you say morale is getting better?"

Simon gave a brisk nod. "Definitely. We were going through a bad patch when I spoke to you about it. I know some of the girls expected the place to close down after the bad publicity."

"Take it from me, we're staying in business. In fact, we're growing the business, as I'm sure they know." She looked to him for assurance. "They do know, don't they?"

"For sure. They all know you're a battler."

~~~

Since Mr Roberts's funeral, Chloe hadn't been at ease with herself. She wanted to move on from sex work and find something more meaningful, or at least more respectable, than placing her body at the disposal of strangers. What she didn't want was a return to the kind of work she'd done before, like waitressing and casual sales promotions.

Also since the funeral, Gina had been much friendlier. She seemed genuine, but Chloe couldn't help wondering if it had more to do with not wanting her to leave.

She was in the kitchen browsing the *Daily Courier* when Gina came in and sat next to her. The newspaper lay open at the Situations Vacant page and Gina casually asked if she'd seen any interesting jobs.

"I'm not qualified for anything apart from what I'm doing now, and I'm not sure I'm even suited to that."

"Of course you are, otherwise you wouldn't be so much in demand."

"I'd sooner be doing something else."

"Such as?"

"I don't know. Massage, maybe."

"You want to work in a massage parlour?"

"Hardly."

"You mean real massage?"

"So?"

"Nothing. I just wondered how different it would be. It's still all flesh and touching and... Okay, there's no sex, but there's no real money in it either, is there?"

Chloe folded the paper and shoved it towards the middle of the table. "All I need is enough to live on. Money isn't everything."

~~~

When Jock turned up at Casa Rosa the next day—predictably half-an-hour late—Liz immediately sent him to see Gina. Now he sat in front of her, arms folded, waiting for her to speak.

Try as she might, she couldn't bring herself to like him. Tall and lean, shaggy dark hair, long eyelashes and deep brown eyes—he was undeniably attractive, but his air of disdainful superiority—she might as well have been one of the escorts the way he sized her up—had always put her off.

"I'm told you've borrowed money from four of the girls and refusing to pay it back," she began.

He looked surprised at the accusation, and then laughed. "They didn't lend me a cent."

"So why do they claim you owe them money?"

He uncrossed his arms, folded them in his lap, and gave her a conspiratorial smile.

"What they mean is I haven't paid them for services rendered."

"What services?"

"What do you reckon?" He sat back and folded his arms again.

His smug look got under her skin but she tried to remain objective. She wasn't sure what to say. The house policy didn't prevent staff from using the girls' services, as long as it was outside work hours.

"Was this on the premises?" If so, the room should have been paid for up front.

"Of course not. I run the girls home, remember."

True, the girls were driven home at the end of their late shifts unless someone came to pick them up. As far as she could see, it wasn't a Casa Rosa problem if it was off the premises and after hours. The girls would have to sort it out themselves.

"Whatever, but that's not why I needed to see you."

She paused long enough to see a flicker of concern in his eyes.

"We've spoken to you numerous times about your timekeeping and it's still not good enough. We've given you every chance but you've shown no improvement, so I'm letting you go. You finish at the end of the week."

Though surprised by Gina's statement, he didn't react immediately. When he eventually spoke, his superior manner was no longer evident.

"You know I have a sleep disorder. You can't sack me for something that's not my fault."

"If you have health problems, you should see your doctor. I'm running a business here. I can't afford to have unreliable people working for me."

"Maria never complained. She knew I had a sleeping problem and she made allowances for it."

Gina tried to keep the irritation out of her voice, but it wasn't easy.

"Listen, I spoke to my mother and she said you'd been warned once before. The fact remains I need someone reliable, and you're not that person."

He jumped to his feet, face furious, and stared down at her. "In that case, you'd better find them quickly because I'm fucked if I'm staying here a minute longer than I have to."

He dashed out of her office before she could reply.

27. Public disgrace

Jos burst into Gina's office.

"Quick, quick, come and look at this."

Gina hurried after her into reception, where Jos parted the heavy curtains at the window. She peered out to see a group of demonstrators congregated on the pavement shouting slogans and carrying placards saying, "Brothels spread diseases", "Prostitution is rape", and "Protect family values". It took her a moment to realise they were targeting Casa Rosa.

"I'm not having this!"

She marched out of the building and approached the nearest demonstrator. The loud chanting made it difficult for her to get his attention and she was forced to raise her voice. "Would you please move away?"

When he ignored her, she shouted, "What's going on here?" He still took no notice.

She looked around for the leader and found him in the middle of the group—a short, red-haired man with a bushy moustache and beard. He was just about to use a loudhailer. She snatched it from his hands. As he tried to grab it back, she shouted, "What do you think you're doing?" She held it up as high as she could. "I asked you a question!"

His flailing arms couldn't reach. "Give it back!"

"Not until you tell me what the fuck you think you're doing."

"There's no need for that language." He squared his shoulders and stood so close to her that she smelled tobacco smoke on his clothing. He was forced to tip his head back to see her face. "We have every right to protest. Your brothel is spreading STDs in our community."

The flecks of spit that accompanied that statement forced her to step away and wipe her face with the back of her hand.

"Don't spit on me, you grub, and don't waste your preacher logic on me either. We're not spreading diseases. Now fuck off before I call the police."

A hint of a smile crossed his face. "Go ahead. It's a peaceful protest."

"In that case, you won't be needing this." Holding the loudhailer high above her head, she turned on her heel, and strode back into the building. She tried to slam the door behind her, forgetting that its hydraulic closer was designed to prevent just that. In the few seconds available to him, he pushed her against the door as he lunged at the instrument. Gina succeeded in holding on to it as she tried unsuccessfully to force the door closed. In frustration, and without thinking, she hurled the loudhailer over the man's head. When she heard it bounce off the roof of a parked car and land in the middle of the road, she realised she could easily have hit someone with it.

The man picked it up and after checking for damage retreated to his position on the pavement, where he again led the protesters through their chants.

Gina went back to the reception desk. "If they don't move soon, I'm going to kill that bearded dwarf out there. Call the police and tell them we're being threatened by an angry mob."

As the shouting continued outside, Gina remembered seeing an emblem on the placards and wondered what it represented. She signalled Jos to join her at the window. "What's that logo stand for?"

Jos studied it. "I think it's that political party. Can't remember their name—something to do with morals."

"Oh, great. That's all we need—attention from bloody moralisers. Why don't they go down to the casino and demonstrate there? Gambling's more harmful than prostitution."

"My hubby says the truly religious are too busy helping the poor and the sick to bother campaigning on moral issues. That lot out there are just a bunch of self-righteous pricks."

"Maybe, but they're not good for business."

~~~

When the police arrived they politely and firmly tried to move the demonstrators on. Gina and Jos watched from the front door as the ringleader insisted on his right to free assembly and refused to supply his name and address when asked by the police sergeant. When the officer ordered the group to move away, the ringleader insisted they stay exactly where they were. "We're upholding our democratic rights of protest," he shouted. When he refused a second time to give his details, he was grabbed by the arm and dragged away. Two constables then attempted to shepherd the others down the road.

As they shifted away, a demonstrator dropped his placard and bent to pick it up. Whether he stumbled or was pushed wasn't clear, but as he lay sprawled on the ground one of the officers stepped on him. A scuffle broke out and the three police found themselves struggling to maintain control. A moment later a paddy wagon pulled up sharply and three more officers jumped out and ran to help their comrades.

Only then did Gina notice the television and press cameramen recording the action.

"What the hell! How did they know this was going to happen?"

"I don't know, but we'd better get inside before they start filming us."

They retreated into the building and watched through the window as the police dispersed the demonstrators, all except for the ringleader, who'd worked free from the sergeant's grip and was heading back to Casa Rosa. He approached the front door and used his loudhailer to shout, "Whores! Prostitutes! Fornicators!" before the sergeant caught up with him again and grabbed him in a bear hug. He was half carried, half dragged to the paddy wagon and shoved inside.

When it became clear the protesters had left, Gina and Jos moved away from the window. "I hope they never come back," Jos said, as she returned to her desk. The phone rang and she took the call. Gina was on her way to her office when Jos called out, "It's for you."

She took the phone. "Hello."

"Am I speaking to Mrs Russo?"

The caller was female, which was unusual. Normally, women who phoned were either looking for a job or checking up on their partners.

"No, I'm her daughter. Who is it calling?"

"My name's Isobel Josephson. I'm a reporter. I've been watching the demonstration outside your building and wondered if you could tell me how you feel about the protest."

Gina was taken aback by the request. How did a reporter know who to ask for? And why were the media involved? She had a strong suspicion she was being set up.

"Who do you work for and how did you know about the protest?"

"I'm with the *Daily Monitor*. Miss Russo, we'd like to publish your reaction to the—"

"We want nothing to do with your rag. You've caused us enough trouble as it is." She was about to put the phone down when she heard Daniel's name mentioned. "What did you just say?"

"I said you don't have your sanctimonious boyfriend to protect you now."

"Daniel? He's not my boyfriend. Never was."

"Ah, so he's a client after all. Just as I thought."

"No, he is not!" She leaned over the desk and slammed the phone down before she heard any more. "The cheek of these people. They print lies about you and then have the nerve to call you up. Who the hell do they think they are?"

Jos said, "Parasites, Gina. Don't worry about them. They're not worth it."

But she did worry. Why had a moralistic political party chosen Casa Rosa—out of hundreds of brothels in Sydney—to demonstrate against prostitution? She could think of only one explanation: it was because Casa Rosa had been mentioned in the *Monitor* article. And the reporter who phoned was also from the *Monitor*. Coincidence? Hardly. There had been a television crew filming as well. Did the Monitor Group have interests in television? She had no idea. She knew someone who might know, but she had no intentions of calling him.

The phone rang again as she went into her office. She heard Jos say, "I'm sorry, but she's not taking any calls from the media. Thank you, goodbye."

~~~

Business dropped away during the afternoon. The receptionists grew tired of blocking calls from the media, which had tried every angle to extract at least a single sentence from Gina for their articles.

One intrepid reporter from a press agency even masqueraded as a client. When Liz showed him into a reception room, he owned up to his ruse and cheerfully asked to speak to the manager. Liz said, "I'm the manager. Now piss off!" and taking his arm marched him to the front door and pushed him into the street.

~~~

Later on, Gina was sitting in her office when Kellie raced in and shouted, "You're on the news!"

There more girls than usual in the kitchen and the two women had to crane their necks for a better view.

Holly pointed at the screen. "It's you, Gina."

She stared at the screen in horror. Her face was clearly visible as she wrested the loudhailer from the ringleader's grip. "Oh, my god," she murmured. Any last shred of anonymity had now disappeared—the entire world would now know she was a brothel madam. The screen showed her throwing the loudhailer over the man's head and into the street. The girls gasped and turned to look at her in wondrous approval.

As the camera showed the police struggling with the protesters, the newsreader said, "The Moral Australia Party said today that the police should have allowed the peaceful protest to continue." The red-haired ringleader was then shown being interviewed in the street. The newsreader continued, "Joshua Palmer, organiser of the event, spoke to our reporter, Adrian Murphy, immediately after the demonstration."

The camera closed in on Palmer's excited face. "We are exercising our democratic right to protest peacefully, and we'll carry on protesting until the government closes every brothel in this state. We can't allow this blight on our community to continue any longer."

The newsreader went on to say that the police had made no arrests despite one of its officers receiving a bloody nose. She moved on to a story about a large bushfire that had broken out in the north of the state.

Unable to stem her brimming tears, Gina got to her feet intending to dash to her office, but Kellie grabbed her hand before she could leave.

"Gina, I'm really sorry, love. I know how awful this must be for you, I honestly do."

Hearing this, Holly jumped up and placed her arm around Gina's shoulders. "We're all here for you, you know that."

Gina wiped her eyes with her sleeve. The other girls watched her, concern and curiosity on their faces. "Thanks, I really appreciate that." She snuffled and someone pushed a piece of paper towel into her hand. She blew her nose and saw the girls still watching her. She managed a weak smile. "Let's hope our clients don't watch TV."

Back in her office with the door closed, her tears resumed. She ran through the list of recent disasters in her mind and wondered if there would ever be an end to her catalogue of bad luck: her mother's illness, Morgan's rejection, the exposé, and now this very public outing of her situation. It wasn't fair, it wasn't her fault. Okay, she had no-one else to blame but herself for alienating Morgan, but her mother's illness was simply a cruel act of fate. Her other misfortunes, however, were imposed by an external force—the very force she'd been battling for weeks: the *Daily Monitor*.

Was Casa Rosa the target of a vendetta? What harm had they done to the newspaper? It was the other way around: the *Monitor* had damaged Casa Rosa's business. But the idea that a powerful newspaper like the *Monitor* would stoop to instigate a demonstration just because they'd been sued didn't seem plausible. In any event, how could that help their cause?

Another thought struck her. Perhaps Jock had put MAP up to it? She'd heard he was furious about being fired, making all sorts of dark threats against Gina and the business. A phone call was all it would take for him to tip off MAP. He could say he used to work at Casa Rosa, spin a story or two about how evil the place was, and let their indignation do the rest. That seemed more plausible than the *Monitor* theory, but she couldn't believe he was that well-informed politically.

Truth was, she had no idea what was going on. She was powerless and for the first time serious doubt crept into her mind. Did she have the inner fortitude to weather this storm? Was she able to hold everything together? Her MBA hadn't prepared her for this kind of crisis. All the knowledge and techniques she'd acquired never anticipated events like this. Maybe her mother was right—she was over-confident about her management skills.

Overcome by weariness, she closed her eyes, folded her arms on the desk, and lay down her head. If only she could go back in time and wake up in Martha's Vineyard walking along the beach, carefree and optimistic about her future. She missed Morgan. She missed his worldliness, his certainty. In particular, she missed how he treated her so respectfully. If only she'd known that lying to him and his family denied them the respect they too deserved. Why had she been so certain they would overlook her background? What if she'd—.

Someone was knocking on the door. Shaking herself into wakefulness, she went to open the door expecting to find one of her staff standing there. It was Jos. "Gina, someone's here to see you." Before she could wonder who it was, Caroline was standing there with a sympathetic smile, holding a bottle of wine in one hand and two glasses in the other.

"Hiya, darl. Soon as I saw the news, I said I'd better come over right away. I knew you'd be in desperate need of this."

"Only one bottle?" They embraced. "Just when I thought I didn't have a friend left in the world, up you pop."

"You know what they say about friends in need…"

"I know—they're a pain in the arse. I hope you brought a corkscrew as well."

28. Rapprochement

When his friend Kieran heard Daniel had quit his job at the *Monitor*, he suggested he should work in public relations. At first, he was reluctant to consider the idea. PR—ironically, he thought—had a poor public image. But Kieran, who had worked in PR for the previous three years, was persuasive, and eventually he accepted his assurance that for most of the time it was neither unethical nor simply a matter of putting out press releases and schmoozing media types. He went for an interview with Lemon Lassiter & Co, a small agency just finding its feet, and was taken on straight away.

Within a week he met Nikki, the marketing manager for a pharmaceutical company, his first account. In high heels, she was as tall as he was. Blonde, leggy, outgoing and friendly, with an artless laugh that carried across a crowded room, she couldn't avoid being the centre of attention.

Daniel's manager thought it would be a good idea for him to meet his client in convivial surroundings and gain an understanding of the kind of issues her company faced. When the waiter presented the dessert menu, his boss apologised and left to go to a meeting. Nikki and Daniel idled over dessert, getting to know each other better, and when he suggested a quiet lunch later in the week, she accepted.

Now he was looking forward to taking her to dinner, and afterwards, if she was agreeable, to a party given by his friend Rajit in Tamarama.

He collected his car keys from the bureau in the entrance hall and went to say goodbye to his mother, who was in the living room watching the seven o'clock news. "I've no idea when I'll be back. Don't wait up."

"Have fun," she replied.

He was on his way to the front door when he heard the newsreader mention Casa Rosa. He returned to the sitting room in time to see the incident where Gina struggled with the leader of the protesters. "Oh no," he groaned. "Oh, my god!" He watched the loudhailer sail over the head of the demonstrators to glance off the roof of a car parked nearby.

"What's the matter?" his mother asked, without taking her eyes away from the television. Joshua Palmer's face now filled the screen as he held forth on the evils of prostitution.

"You know who owns that place, don't you?"

"Her face looks familiar."

"Maria Russo. That's her daughter throwing the loudhailer."

"What's she doing there?"

"It's a long story. I'll tell you later. One thing's for sure, she'll be pig-sick seeing that."

He should call to offer sympathy. He should, but he'd not forgotten how she'd shunned him in the past. Even now she might be blaming him for this fiasco, thinking he was somehow involved.

His mother said, "Poor Maria! After all she's had to put up with. I must phone her and find out how she's getting on."

He changed his mind and rang Gina's number. What did he have to lose? She didn't answer. He left the house with the TV's image of an angry Gina imprinted on his mind. He considered going to find her to offer support, but that would mean standing Nikki up. He doubted she'd be sympathetic to Gina's problems.

~~~

After Gina and Caroline polished off the bottle of wine, they walked to the Trinity Bar on Crown Street. Though the place was busy, they arrived just as a couple were leaving and managed to grab their table. They ordered red wine and a bowl of beef nachos.

Caroline battled a background of loud music and raised voices to say, "If anyone asks me where I went tonight, I shall say I visited a high-class brothel and then clam up. I've always wanted to have an air of decadence about me."

"Stick with me and you'll succeed. So, any news?"

Caroline gave her thoughts on the libel action. "So, it's really a matter of how long you can go before you run out of money."

Gina experienced a touch of panic at the prospect. "Not long I suppose."

"We'll just wait to see how they react." She looked around at the enveloping throng. "Busy, busy. By the way, guess who I saw at the gym yesterday?" Before she could answer, Caroline said, "Your nemesis."

"Daniel? At the gym? He must have a new girlfriend."

"You're psychic. He met her through his new job."

"Oh... What new job?"

"He's in PR now. Jacked it in at the *Monitor* when they printed your story. Told his boss to stuff the job up his proverbial."

The nachos and wine arrived and Gina plunged a tortilla chip into the guacamole. As she raised it to her mouth, realisation dawned. Daniel's leaving the *Monitor* explained why that pushy reporter said Gina no longer had her sanctimonious boyfriend to protect her. The remark puzzled her at the time, but she quickly forgot about it. She'd had more pressing issues to think about.

Still holding the chip in front of her, she said, "Did he ask about me?"

Caroline regarded her over the brim of her glass and smiled knowingly. "I thought you said he was a scumbag, lower than a snake's willy?"

"Yes, but that was... Well, did he?"

"As a matter of fact, he did. I said you were doing it tough."

"That all?"

"More or less. You should call him."

"Why?"

"Because, you drongo, you wouldn't take his calls. You owe him an apology."

"I bet he thinks I'm a stuck-up, ungrateful bitch."

"He didn't say anything one way or the other."

Gina pushed the bowl of nachos closer to Caroline. "Here, you finish them. I'm not that hungry." She sipped her wine and reflected on recent events. "You know, if he hadn't seen me come out of Casa Rosa that time, none of this shit would've happened. I'd still be incognito instead of Sydney's best-known madam. I know I shouldn't blame him but I can't help it."

Caroline wiped a spot of guacamole from her lips with a napkin.

"You still owe him an apology."

~~~

When she arrived at Casa Rosa the following morning, Gina was surprised to see a large printed notice taking up half the width of the front door. It read:

> "Do not prostitute thy
> daughter,
> to cause her to be a whore;
> lest the land fall to whoredom,
> and the land become full of
> wickedness."
>
> Leviticus 19:29

The notice was pinned to the door with thumbtacks. Not wanting to risk her fingernails, Gina fished a pair of tweezers out of her handbag and prised the tacks off. She took the notice inside and seeing Liz behind the reception desk asked, "Was this on the door when you arrived?" She held up the sign.

Liz peered at the notice from where she sat. "No, I could hardly have missed it, could I? It must have gone up in the last hour. I never heard a thing."

Gina looked out of the window. The street had a peaceful Sunday morning look. No-one was near the premises.

"They must have been on camera while they did it. It's a pity it doesn't record."

"After yesterday's fiasco, I think we have a pretty good idea who's responsible."

"This is so unfair, Liz. What next? Firebombs? Will we have to post armed guards outside the building now?"

She carried the sign to her office and dropped it on top of the filing cabinet. Sitting at her desk, she pondered what to do if the persecution continued. She realised she'd embarked on a perilous journey of her own making and would have to contend with the consequences as best she could. She had no choice but to push on and hope it would soon come to a favourable end. Not doing so was unthinkable.

Even so, her powerlessness frustrated her. In her bones she knew the *Monitor* was in some way implicated. Jock didn't have enough substance or smarts to organise something like this. He couldn't even organise himself to get to work on time. Somehow the *Monitor* was responsible and they were determined to undermine her business.

She could take the story to the *Daily Courier*, the *Monitor*'s main rival, but she didn't have a skerrick of evidence to support her claim.

It was a pity Daniel no longer worked for the *Monitor*, otherwise he might have been able to help her. Thinking of Daniel, she recalled the previous night's conversation with Caroline. He'd asked after her, and not said anything derogatory. That meant he hadn't completely turned his back on her.

Caroline was right: it was time to make amends.

~~~

When the phone rang, Daniel was still in bed. He hadn't arrived home until one-thirty that morning and it wasn't yet nine o'clock. His head throbbed with pain; his throat was parched; his bladder demanded immediate relief. Despite all this, he needed more time before he faced the world. He nestled further under the sheets.

After a few minutes his bladder made it clear it could hold out no longer. Groaning, he hoisted himself out of bed and staggered into the en-suite. When he emerged, he heard his mother calling his name. She must have heard the toilet flush. He opened the bedroom door and saw her standing at the foot of the stairs.

"I thought I heard you up and about. You've just missed a call."

He yawned. "I might be up, but I'm not about. Who's calling me at this time on a Sunday morning?"

"Gina Russo."

"Gina? Really? I'll be..." He could hardly believe it. After all this time, Gina was calling him. Still in his pyjamas, he started down the stairs. "What did she say?"

"She left her number for you to call. She asked me to make sure you received the message."

"Amazing..."

"Would you like a coffee?" When he nodded, she said, "I'll going out for lunch later on—will you be all right on your own?"

"I'll be okay. I think I might go back to bed, though."

"Did you drink too much last night?"

"No, I couldn't. I was driving, so I had to behave myself. It's a migraine."

"I'll fetch you some pills."

The headache had started towards the end of the previous evening. A glass of wine with dinner and a couple of light beers at the party was all he'd allowed himself, knowing he'd be driving home.

He remembered being irritated by Rajit's constant attention to Nikki. Rajit had a penchant for long-legged blondes, especially outgoing ones like her. She lapped up the attention and Daniel questioned his wisdom in bringing her. Whether this triggered his headache he couldn't say—all he knew was that as it progressed, his mood became more morose, and despite her reluctance they left the party early. When they reached her apartment, she invited him in for a nightcap. He didn't stay long, saying he needed sleep to cure his headache. He would call her once his head was clear.

As for Gina... Daniel decided to hold off talking to her. She'd been so rude when he'd tried to speak to her before, no-one would blame him if he took his time getting back to her. If all she wanted was to apologise, it could wait another day or two. Perhaps appearing on the television news had disheartened her to the point where she desperately needed moral support.

In any event, she would have to wait until he was pain-free—no way could he deal with Gina without a clear head.

~~~

Gina looked through the previous night's receipts and wasn't surprised to learn that the house had serviced far fewer clients than usual for a Saturday. She also noticed that once again the outcall business was unaffected. This made sense, as she was now advertising the service under four different names. Maybe she ought to concentrate more on that side of the business if the picketing continued. Outcalls had low overheads, basically just phone and transport, and would be more profitable in the long run.

Would her mother agree to forgo the in-house trade? It had been the mainstay of the business and dropping it might prove too radical a change for her. She'd wait until her mother was feeling stronger before broaching the subject.

She checked her watch. It had been two hours since she left a message for Daniel to call. She remembered the previous night's conversation with Caroline, and an image of Daniel storming out of the *Monitor*'s offices came to mind. Had he done that because of her? The thought flattered her, until she remembered she'd alienated him to such an extent that he might no longer be prepared to speak to her. She hoped he was willing to forgive her, and not just because he was the only person she knew who could find out what was going on at the *Monitor*.

When he eventually called, she must make a grand gesture—something more substantial than, 'Sorry, Daniel. Can we be friends again?' He needed to know she was sincere.

But he would have to call first.

~~~

Daniel's migraine intensified, forcing him back to bed. By teatime, despite having slept solidly, he was groggy and nauseous. He went downstairs in search of his mother and found her working in her darkroom.

She looked up as he came in. "Feeling any better, dear?"

"Not really."

"I'll get you a coffee and a couple of tablets. Go and sit down."

A few minutes later, she brought him his drink and sat on the lounge next to him. "Do you think you can manage dinner tonight?"

"I don't think so. Sorry."

"In that case I won't bother. I ate at lunchtime. If you feel peckish later on, let me know and I'll make you a sandwich."

"Thanks. How was lunch?"

"The usual. I didn't stay long but I caught up with a few people I hadn't seen for a while. Crispin told me his wife's quite ill again. She's in and out of hospital all the time."

"Calloway?"

"Yes, your ex-boss. He wasn't pleased about you letting him down after doing me a big favour taking you on."

"He should learn to treat his staff with more respect, even if they are at the bottom of the ladder."

"I've known him a long time. He's my friend and nowhere near as bad as you make out."

This seemed a good opportunity for Daniel to broach a sensitive subject. "Frank McAllister reckons Calloway had a bit of a soft spot for you."

"Does he now? Well, Frank should stick to something he knows, like editing newspapers."

Daniel swallowed the two tablets with a sip of coffee.

"Were you always just good friends?"

"How do you mean?"

"Oh, you know..."

"No, I don't, and it's none of your business anyway."

"Sorry, I just wanted to put Frank right."

"Don't worry, nobody would believe you anyway. Rumours are indestructible."

~~~

Because his headache remained oppressive, Daniel chose not to call Nikki. Instead he sent her a text message saying he was too ill to phone. He thought of doing the same for Gina, then decided it wouldn't hurt for her to wait another day.

When he arrived at work the next morning he phoned Nikki straight away. He sensed reproof in her tone, which wasn't entirely unexpected. They agreed he should call her later in the week to arrange their next date.

By lunchtime his headache had receded sufficiently for him to call Gina. She recognised his voice and started speaking straight away.

"I wanted to tell you I'm truly sorry about what happened. Caroline told me. I seriously misjudged you and owe you a big apology."

Though a part of him wanted to give her a ticking off, he decided to go easy on her. "I suppose you were under a lot of pressure at the time."

"I should have trusted you."

She paused, waiting for him to comment. He could think of nothing else to say other than, "Well, yes, I suppose you should have."

"I'm sorry. I've been a complete idiot." Another pause, and then, "Daniel, would you let me take you out to dinner?"

"Yeah, okay, that'd be good. Call me when you're ready and we'll arrange something."

"I was thinking this week..."

He thought about Nikki and whether a dinner appointment might clash with their yet-to-be arranged date. "Can we make it lunch?"

"I'd prefer dinner, but if you can't manage it, lunch is fine."

In his line of work, finding free time for a non-business lunch was always hard to guarantee. If he agreed to meet her and then cancelled because of work commitments, she'd crucify him. Worse, it might be their last chance at reconciliation.

"No, dinner's fine. How about Wednesday?"

29. *A new direction*

Gina felt conspicuous sitting on her own in the restaurant. Other diners cast curious glances in her direction and the waiter approaching her table smiled sympathetically. She ordered a glass of Chardonnay and studied the menu, all the time keeping one eye on the door. The appointed time of eight o'clock came and went.

Why she was so nervous? They'd been friends for a long time before this recent misunderstanding, and he'd been pleasant on the phone when he finally called. Nonetheless, her unease grew as the minutes ticked past.

She took a mirror from her handbag and checked her face. Mascara and eyeliner were still intact, her hair remained glossy and in place. She touched up her lipstick and dropped the handbag between her feet.

By eight-fifteen the wine was lukewarm from being nursed for so long. She drained the glass and placed it on the table. A minute later her mobile phone gave a short ring to let her know she'd received a text message. He was running twenty minutes late. Her nervousness now gave way to irritation at being kept waiting. She rehearsed a few uncomplimentary greetings.

The maitre d', as plump as a turkey in his burgundy tuxedo, stopped by her table and commiserated with her.

"Sometimes the traffic is a problem. He won't be much longer. Can I get you another drink?" She wondered how many customers he'd seen waiting for dinner dates who never turned up.

At eight-thirty the street door swung open and Daniel strode in, looking mildly flustered as he scanned the restaurant. Her relief was palpable. Before he spotted her, the maitre d' approached him and with scarcely a word led him to her table.

She pre-empted his apology with a stern, "I was about to leave."

"I'm sorry, Gina. Honest, I couldn't help it." She didn't move when he leaned forward and kissed her on the cheek. "My mother lost her house keys. I had to dash home to let her in."

The sheen of perspiration on his face and the slight breathlessness of his speech gave credibility to his story and she grudgingly accepted his apologies. She noticed how much fitter he looked. It suited him—all that gym work must be paying off. She ought to follow suit before she turned into a middle-aged frump.

A waiter came and took their order for drinks. After he left she said to Daniel, "Any questions about the menu, don't bother the waiter, just ask me. I've read it front to back, back to front, upside down and inside out. I can even tell you where it was printed."

He laughed and then became serious. "I was worried you wouldn't stick around."

She winced. "Not noted for my patience, eh? Everybody was watching me thinking I'd been stood up. I bet the waiters were running a book on me."

He gave a rueful smile. "I should have called, but I was driving and only just managed a text message when I stopped at the lights."

He fell silent. It was her turn to apologise. "I know you've always tried to help me, and it wasn't your fault you saw me that day."

"If I'd known things would turn out like they did, I'd have kept my mouth shut, that's for sure."

"It's water under the bridge now." She toyed with her napkin. "So, spin doctoring..."

Daniel tipped his head to indicate a waiter who was standing a respectful distance away. "Can we order? I'm starving. You can use your photographic memory and tell me what I should have."

After their orders had been taken, Daniel gave her a rundown of his role at Lemon Lassiter. He spoke about his clients, the sort of problems they had, how he was expected to manage them, and touched on other, more prosaic aspects of his work. "Instead of reading press releases, I write them now. It's nowhere near as much fun as being a journo, although that has its downside, as I discovered."

The entrées arrived: carpaccio of trout for Gina; garlic prawn cutlets for Daniel.

As they ate, Gina said, "That was brave—walking out on principle."

"What else could I do?" He shook his head dolefully. "My dream job down the toilet."

"You never know how strong you are until being strong is your only choice."

"Very profound."

"Bob Marley."

"Makes a change from Nietzsche."

"Anyway, you could have shrugged it off. People put up with worse things to keep their jobs."

"I know, but I'd been betrayed. They didn't trust me. Okay, why should they? But getting me out of the way while they went to print, that really hurt. It was humiliating. And they treated you and your mum like shit."

She continued to encourage him to talk until the main course arrived—they'd both settled for rack of lamb—before steering the conversation round to her own problems.

"Do you think it's possible Calloway could have told MAP to demonstrate outside our premises?"

"Perhaps. He has a lot of influence."

"That's what I thought."

"But I doubt he did."

"No, I'm sure he's got something to do with it. I just need proof."

"That won't be easy. Besides, why pick on you?"

"The thing is, Dan, we have a lot to lose if he doesn't settle. If he keeps up this harassment, we'll be out of business and he'll have won."

He was so occupied with his plate she thought he wasn't going to answer. Then he looked up and said, "I'm surprised you're even bothering. A libel action can cost at least a quarter of a million dollars if they don't settle quickly." He waited for her reaction, but she couldn't think what to say. "It's a game for rich people. Do you have that kind of money to throw away?"

"No, of course not."

"Then why do it? You'll end up penniless and have nothing to show for it."

She smarted at his rebuke and for a moment said nothing. The truth in what he said wasn't lost on her, but so far she'd convinced herself the *Monitor* would settle in the face of her obstinacy. That was the image she'd tried to present. She'd not given any real thought to actually going to trial. Daniel's question reminded her how precarious her position was. Even so, his attitude struck her as negative.

"So what's my alternative? We can't sell the business, can we? We're only just keeping our heads above water."

Daniel rested his knife and fork on his plate and waited until he'd finished chewing before answering.

"I don't understand. By your own admission, you can't afford to chase Calloway through the courts, yet you're determined to do it. Sorry, but that makes no sense to me at all."

She tried to suppress her exasperation. "Look, you and I know I can't afford it. Calloway doesn't. Okay?"

"So you're bluffing..."

Leaning across the table, she said, "Don't you dare say that to anyone!"

"All right, back off! I won't say a word. But since when were you a poker player? Blink once and, bingo, you're out of the game."

"I don't intend blinking, but—" Her tone became more confidential, "—I do need your help."

"Oh..." He straightened up and studied her, before asking cautiously, "What kind of help?"

"I want to know if there's a relationship between Calloway and MAP. I'm sure there is one—I can feel it in my bones—but I don't have any evidence. Someone at the paper must know and I wondered if you might help me find out."

Daniel pondered her request as he continued to eat. When he'd finished, he said, "I sort of burnt my bridges when I left. There's one possibility, but only if he's willing to talk to me. That's my old boss, Frank McAllister. He takes a keen interest in MAP. I could try him, I suppose."

"If you could, that would be fantastic… but not if it's going to cause problems."

"I'll use my journalistic skills. By the way, your dinner's getting cold."

When she'd finished eating, she realised Daniel was watching her closely. She flashed him a smile. "Now, do you think you can manage dessert? Gianduja chocolate charlotte with mascarpone or ricotta cassata terrine with citrus salad or—" She realised he wasn't listening but staring at her intently. "What's up?"

"Was that why you wanted to see me? To get me to help you with Calloway?"

She held his gaze. "One reason, yes. But not the main one. In all honesty I did want to apologise and be friends again." She gave him a reassuring smile. "I really mean that."

He continued to look serious as he studied her face. Then he smiled. "Okay, I'll have the terrine."

~~~

How should he approach Frank? Given that his ex-boss had every reason to brush him off, it wasn't going to be easy, but contriving a convincing story was beyond him. In the end he decided to ask Frank straight out if he would meet him for a drink after work. To his surprise, Frank was pleased to receive his call and without hesitation agreed to see him at the Civic.

He arrived at the hotel to find it busy as usual. No table was free, so he stood near a doorway, middy of pale ale in hand, and idly watched the patrons come and go. Though the atmosphere was convivial he was apprehensive. He couldn't blame Frank if he didn't want to share any information.

Frank turned up on time, mobile phone glued to his ear, and whispered an apology as they shook hands. While he finished his call, Daniel fetched him a schooner of lager and they positioned themselves near one end of the bar.

Raising his glass, Frank said, "Cheers, Dan. It's good to see you again." He drank a good third of his beer in a single draught and licked his lips appreciatively. "I was ready for that. So, you've changed your mind and want to return to the fold."

Daniel smiled and shook his head.

"Pity. Andrea's still giving me the evil eye when she sees me."

Daniel had enjoyed working for Andrea but she wasn't someone you crossed without considering the consequences, and she could bear a grudge like no-one he'd ever met.

"I suppose I should have called her to explain things. Give her my regards—if she'll speak to you—and tell her it's not you I blame but Calloway."

"I'll try, but she'll not let me off the hook that easily. Anyway, mate, if you don't want your old job back, what's rattling your roof tiles?"

"I want to ask a favour." He gave Frank a moment to react, but he showed no objection. "Remember how you were investigating MAP, trying to find out who was footing their bills—did you ever get to the bottom of that?"

"Are you thinking of doing PR for them?"

Daniel told him about the demonstrations and Gina's suspicions.

Frank said, "Calloway's behind MAP, but you wouldn't know it. MAP is a respectable front for the Convinzi Trust, which most people have never heard of. It receives money from different sources, mostly evangelical churches. The Trust isn't under any legal obligation to reveal its donors, but there are still ways to find out who makes large payments."

"How?"

"Unless the money is in a brown paper bag and left on somebody's desk, there's usually a trail linking the payment back to the other party. It's a pity the Trust isn't a registered charity, because the gift would then be tax-deductible and the donor would lodge a claim. Being registered as a religious organisation, it avoids scrutiny and is exempt from taxation—which is why we have so many prosperous churches in Australia."

"How can you discover where their money comes from, then?"

"By nefarious means, I'm afraid. Like you, I suspected Calloway might be involved. He's been particularly interested in MAP during the past year. I know he's asked Larry to give them a favourable run, which doesn't please Larry, of course—he doesn't like the god squad any more than I do—but there's not much he can do about it."

He paused while he scanned the room. "See that bloke over there with his back to us?" He pointed to a grey-haired man in a dark suit sitting at a table with a small group. "Recognise him?"

"Sort of. He works for your mob, doesn't he?"

"He's our deputy financial controller—has been for the past twenty years. He'll never get the top job. A born deputy is our Jeff. He and I go back a long way. The other day, I asked him what charitable donations the

Monitor Group made. He mentioned a few, but not a cent went to MAP or Convinzi. So I said to him, 'Listen, mate, how come he isn't giving them money when we all know he won't have a bad word said against them?' and he said, 'He puts the donations through his private companies.'"

He sipped his drink before continuing. "I should've realised he'd have loads of companies and trusts set up to minimise tax. Jeff said those companies send in tax returns. So, to keep it short and protect the guilty, I'll just say he peeked at those accounts and, sure enough, there's a pattern of payments to the Convinzi Trust. And that's what makes Calloway a shadowy figure—he's donating to Convinzi and they fund MAP. He's bound to have some influence over MAP.

"However, having said that, I find it hard to believe he'd have a vendetta against your friend's brothel. It wouldn't show on his radar."

"Thanks, Frank, you've told me what I needed to know."

"Hold on a mo'. First, be extremely careful how you use this info. Only a few people know about it and you could drop someone in deep shit if you go shooting your mouth off. Second, you definitely never heard it from me, okay? And keep Jeff out of it, too."

"Okay, message received and understood. One thing I don't understand, though, is why you're so interested in all this."

"I'm a newspaperman. I love a good conspiracy, especially one involving politics and religion. Then there's Calloway himself. I respect him professionally—he's the best newspaper proprietor in the country—but he's a sanctimonious bastard and thick with the extreme Christian right. They have an agenda. If we're not careful, they're gonna take us back to the Dark Ages. Fundamentalists—and I don't care if they're Christians, Jews, Muslims, or Sixth Day Bicycle Riders—are so convinced of their infallibility they wouldn't give a shit about nuking the rest of us. If they're going to control the political agenda, I need to know who's pulling the strings. And it's not just Calloway and his cronies—there's foreign money involved as well."

"If you had independent proof of this, what would you do?"

"I dunno, Dan. Could be useful in salary negotiations..."

They both laughed.

Frank said, "I'll wait until that happy day before I make up my mind."

"Going back to what you said about being careful, how can I convince Calloway that I definitely know he's linked to MAP?"

"Dunno, mate. I'm afraid you'll have to use your PR skills."

~~~

Daniel called Gina as soon as he left the pub.

"Good news!"

"What did he say?"

Perhaps he was over cautious but discussing his conversation with Frank over the phone could be risky. There was an outside chance Calloway might be having Gina's phone calls monitored.

"Can we talk face-to-face? It's a bit sensitive."

"No problem. Tonight too late for you?"

"I can pick you up in fifteen minutes."

~~~

Daniel drove them to the Sir Stamford Hotel in Double Bay. Once they'd bought their drinks from the Lobby Bar, they went into the adjoining Library and settled into wingback chairs.

After he reported what Frank had told him, he said, "There's one big problem, though. You have to be extremely careful how you use this knowledge."

"Why?"

"Because if you accuse Calloway and he denies it, what are you going to do? What evidence can you present if he asks you to prove it? Nobody's going to back you up—it's more than their jobs are worth."

"Not even you?"

Would he be prepared to stick his neck out for her? Calloway might not employ him any longer, but someone that powerful had a lot of influence around town—there could be repercussions. "I don't know, but if I did, you'd still be faced with the same problem. I can't dob in Frank, and he won't dob in his informant either. Meanwhile, Calloway goes on the defensive and covers his tracks."

It was as well she wasn't holding her drink when she threw her arms up in exasperation. "Brilliant! I feel like I've won the lottery and not allowed to collect the prize."

"Hold on, it's not that bad. For one thing, you now know for sure he's Mr Big, so you know there's a reasonable chance he's behind the demos. Another thing is, he doesn't know you know, and you can use that to your advantage."

"How? I need him off my back, otherwise I'm sunk."

She picked up her drink and stared at it before taking a large swig. He watched her out of the corner of his eye. He'd not seen her looking this vulnerable before. Nor had he sat so close, so close he could detect her delicate, light fragrance, hinted with rose.

He placed his hand over hers and gave it a squeeze. "Let me have a think about it. Okay?"

Instead of pulling her hand away, she sighed and gave him a forlorn smile. "Thanks. I appreciate what you're doing, I really do."

He removed his hand.

In a subdued voice, she said, "What am I going to do, Dan? I've let Mama down big-time. I need to salvage something for her or I'll never be able to live with myself."

"I'm thinking about it." He had thought about it and had failed to come up with an answer. As he perceived it, no feasible options were open to them. Frank had told him all he knew and with Calloway keeping his activities hidden behind a legal wall, that line of enquiry was effectively closed. The MAP protesters were religious extremists and even if he were able to track one of them down he'd be unlikely to extract any information. They were stymied.

He was about to tell Gina he'd drawn a blank when she said, "Maybe I should go and see him."

"Calloway? You serious? That wouldn't be too smart."

She turned to face him. "Why not? Let's get it out in the open and be done with it. I can't carry on like this. I don't know what to expect next."

His gut feeling was that a confrontation between her and Calloway could only end one way. Subtlety wasn't her strongest suit.

"For a start, he won't see you, and if he does, he'll have his lawyer present. If you say one word out of turn, he'll have you on toast."

"In that case, I'll take my story to the *Courier*. I bet they'd love to take a shot at the *Monitor*."

"Same problem. Where's your evidence?"

"I know enough to be able to point them in the right direction. And don't forget, Casa Rosa has had plenty of publicity recently, so I have news interest."

He still didn't like the idea. If the *Courier* wasn't interested, she'd be left without a bargaining position.

"Not yet—too early."

"Time's not on my side, Dan."

He needed to do something and it needed to be under his control, otherwise as sure as sunrise she'd find herself in a deeper hole. He was reluctant to propose it, but only one plan of action seemed open to him.

"Let me see if I can arrange a meeting with Calloway. I won't tell him you're coming—that way he won't need his lawyer there."

"Why would he see you?"

"Because of my mum. She got me the job in the first place." He hoped he wasn't setting too much store by her association with Calloway. And, if pressed, what would he say was the reason for the meeting? To avoid a lie, he'd have to tell Renata, Calloway's secretary, it was personal.

"Okay, and then we hit him with what we know?"

Keeping her reined in was like playing Whac-a-Mole. "No, that won't work. He'll deny it. No, we're going to use PR skills. Instead of mentioning the defamation case upfront, we'll play on his sympathies—he must have some humanity in him—and tell him about your mum's cancer, how you and your mum stand to lose everything you own—that kind of thing. We'll say that a highly respected man in his position must have considerable influence and would be able to persuade the MAP guys from picketing your premises."

"Do you seriously think that'll work?"

"It stands a better chance than confrontation."

"And what if it doesn't work?"

"*Then* you go to the *Courier*."

30. Meeting of unlike minds

A fortnight passed and there was no movement on the defamation front. Gina was increasingly restless at the lack of action. To keep her spirits up, she needed regular evidence she was advancing towards her goal, but it wasn't forthcoming.

Then Daniel phoned her at Casa Rosa.

"It's on," he said.

"Calloway?"

"You bet."

With rising excitement, she said, "You're a genius. When do we see him?"

"Thursday morning. He thinks it's only me who will be there. I told his secretary it was personal. She was a bit reluctant until she remembered who I was."

"This is fantastic, Dan. I can't tell you how excited I am. He's going to get a big surprise when I turn up."

"Remember what I said before. No shooting from the hip. We're going there to win him over, appeal to his better nature, try to make him feel sorry for you. Okay? Don't pick a fight with him or you'll be dead meat."

There was no mistaking the reproof in Daniel's tone. A confrontation would have been more to her liking—at least she'd get to ventilate her frustration—but this was Daniel's show and she needed to keep him onside.

"All right, I'll try to be on my best behaviour."

"Better than your best behaviour. I mean it, Gina. This is your only chance. Don't blow it."

~~~

At work the following morning Gina received a call from her mother, whose shouting prevented Gina from comprehending what she was saying.

"Not so loud, I missed all that."

"It's over! No more chemo! I don't need to go again."

"Hey, that's marvellous, Mama! No further treatment?"

"Routine checks, that's all, just to make sure I'm still clear. I can't wait to get back to work."

Her spirits sank as she contemplated her mother taking back control. The business was still struggling. She couldn't hand it over in this state. "Take it easy, Ma, you're not fit enough yet. I bet the doctor didn't tell you to get straight back to work, did he?"

Her mother was slow to answer. "He said to give it a week or two."

"I thought so. Ease your way in when you're ready, okay? I'm managing, there's no hurry."

After the call was over, Gina thought about her future. Keeping her mother at home once she started feeling chipper wouldn't be easy. How long before she would be fit enough to take over completely? Two weeks? A month? This wasn't giving Gina much time to get Casa Rosa back on its feet. Whatever, once her mother was back in charge she could put it all behind her and strike out on her own. She'd move to the States, Canada, the UK—anywhere they spoke English and didn't know who she was.

However, one hurdle stood in her way: the lawsuit. Would Thursday's meeting prove to be the turning point? She wished she knew more about Calloway. All

Daniel would say was that on the surface he seemed a charming, old-fashioned gentleman. Below the surface, though, lurked a ruthless soul, according to the *Monitor*'s old hands. "He's a punisher and straightener."

She didn't much care for that description.

~~~

Seated in Calloway's office, Gina and Daniel faced the press baron across the polished expanse of his desk, populated by a set of three coloured phones and a memo pad with what she suspected was a Mont Blanc pen lying next to it. He wore a dark business suit, white shirt, and a navy blue silk tie with white and maroon stripes. His manicured hands held a pair of gold-framed spectacles. With his sweptback silver hair and sharp blue eyes, he had the look of a hawk eyeing its prey.

Her pulse raced. She'd tried to steady her nerves with some deep breathing before coming into the room, but now she was having difficulty suppressing her agitation. Seeing her enemy in the flesh and on his own turf had drained her confidence and she was no longer optimistic about the outcome.

Daniel had insisted on leading the discussion so he could exercise control—clearly not trusting her to show restraint. He'd warned her that Calloway would terminate the meeting immediately if she turned angry. She caught his eye and waited for him to begin.

Calloway, sensing Daniel's diffidence, spoke first.

"Well, Daniel, what brings you and this young lady to see me? My secretary said it was to be a private conversation. I assumed you would be on your own."

"I'm sorry, Mr Calloway. I should have mentioned I was bringing someone with me."

"I also assumed that you would wish to apologise in person for your abrupt departure."

"Again, all I can say is I'm sorry for what happened. I acted in the heat of the moment."

"You were very fortunate, Daniel, to secure a cadetship with the *Monitor*. If I didn't have such a high regard for your mother..." He paused to allow the message to sink in. Daniel looked suitably chastised but said nothing. "You'd better tell me what this meeting is about then."

Daniel cleared his throat. "Mr Calloway, this is Gina Russo." If the name meant anything to Calloway, it didn't show. Indeed, it must have seemed unfamiliar to him, for he wrote it on the memo pad in front of him. He turned his attention to Gina as Daniel said, "As you may know, her mother owns the Casa Rosa bordello, the one that was mentioned in a recent series you were running—"

Calloway turned back to Daniel, saying sharply, "*We* were running, Daniel."

"Yes, I know, but I wasn't responsible for mentioning Casa Rosa. In fact... never mind. Anyway, Mrs Russo's livelihood depends on her business operating smoothly, but since that article, and now with the Moral Australia Party staging protests outside the premises, her business has suffered very badly and if things carry on the way they are, she'll be forced to close down."

"I'm sure that's unfortunate for Mrs Russo," said Calloway, his smug expression belying his words, "but I'm sure she's raked in a lot of money over the years running her den of immorality."

Gina couldn't let this go unremarked. "My mother has cancer, Mr Calloway. She's also in debt because of my late father's gambling and if she loses the business she'll end up on the street without a penny to her name."

Calloway gave her an appraising look. "Why should I care if she married a wastrel? Poverty doesn't justify immorality. At least, not in my book."

He was deliberately provoking her. How dare he call her father a wastrel.

"My mother's business is no less legitimate than yours, Mr Calloway. How would you like it if people stopped you from publishing your newspapers?"

"My business doesn't encourage fornication. It doesn't tempt young women to sell themselves on the streets or bring illegal workers in from overseas, nor does it pay for drug habits or spread the clap."

What about those newspaper ads!

"That's ridiculous. Our business doesn't do any of those things either. You've fallen for your own propaganda!"

"Gina!"

She was rising out of her seat as Daniel spoke. He caught her arm to restrain her.

"Let it go. We're not here to debate the merits of prostitution. It's your mother's welfare at stake." He turned to Calloway. "I'm sorry, Mr Calloway, but it's important for you to understand that Mrs Russo runs her business to a high professional standard. Every regulation is met or exceeded—there are no issues about health and there are certainly no illegal migrants or underage girls. If all brothels were run like hers, the industry would be safe from the elements you're concerned about."

"But it would still be immoral, Daniel."

"That's your opinion, Mr Calloway. Other people see it differently."

"Perhaps they do, though I can't imagine why."

"The fact remains that as far as Mrs Russo's concerned, she's running a legal business."

"So am I, Daniel, and mine allows me to campaign against prostitution if I so wish. I obviously do and will continue to."

Gina saw that argument wasn't going to change Calloway's mind. "Mr Calloway, your newspaper is entitled to mount any campaign it wants, but why did you encourage MAP to demonstrate outside our building? We've done you no harm—why pick on us? Is it because we're suing you for defamation?"

"If your brothel featured in our pages, it would have been an editorial decision." He glanced at Daniel. "Maybe Daniel can tell you."

"I wouldn't know who made the decision—I was sent to Canberra to keep me out of the way." From his tone it was clear the memory still rankled.

"So," Gina said, "you're saying you have no influence over MAP?"

"Influence?" A smile flickered across his face. "Well, I'm sure they read the *Monitor*."

He got up from his seat to indicate the meeting was over. She decided not to hold back any longer. If she didn't play her trump card now, all was lost. "Despite the fact you're a major financial sponsor of both MAP and the Convinzi Trust?"

Calloway's eyes swivelled from her face to Daniel's and back again. He didn't speak until he returned to his seat. "Even if I am a financial sponsor as you put it, and I'm not saying that I am, I've not broken any law."

"Of course not, but why keep it a secret if it's no big deal? Maybe it's because it wouldn't look good if you were seen to be harassing someone who's suing you for libel?"

"My reasons are none of your business, Miss Russo."

A brief uneasy silence prevailed before Daniel, his tone much less respectful than before, said, "So let me get this crystal clear. Even though you have the power to prevent Mrs Russo's business from being victimised to the extent that she's going to lose everything she's ever worked for, you're still going to sit there and do nothing about it?"

Gina was surprised by Daniel's tone of suppressed anger. Calloway picked up on it too and shifted in his seat before replying.

"Mrs Russo has brought it upon herself. No-one forced her to keep a brothel. Now she has to live with the consequences."

"And you don't have enough Christian charity to back off and leave the poor woman alone?"

Calloway snapped. "I run a newspaper, Daniel, not a charity."

Daniel's face was hard as he leaned forward to address Calloway. "I'm sorry, but if you insist on that position I'm bound to tell you that we shall be going to the *Daily Courier* straight after this meeting."

"Ah! And what are you going to tell them? That I'm a Christian? That I think prostitution is sinful? I'm sure everyone in Sydney is well aware of that by now."

"About your links with a far right religious group with a shady background."

"And what evidence are you going to offer them? In fact, where did you hear that rubbish?"

"I'm not at liberty to say."

"Is that what you'll tell the *Courier*, you're not at liberty to say?" When Daniel didn't reply, he continued, "You'll be wasting your time, like you're wasting mine."

He got to his feet. "Now, if you'll excuse me, I have far more important matters to attend to."

Gina said, "Mr Calloway, I want you to know I'm not backing down. You've abused your power and you've nearly put us out of business, but I'm not giving up now."

He shepherded them towards the door.

"Oh, I would if I were you. We have much deeper pockets. You'll be bankrupt long before the court case is over."

~~~

They were seated in the restaurant on the upstairs terrace of the Rebellion Hotel sharing a seafood platter. It was Daniel's suggestion, as he'd forgotten to cancel the booking he'd made for lunch with Nikki.

Gina observed his introspective mood. He appeared more affected by the meeting than she was. On the way over from their meeting he'd barely said a word, apart from a bitter, "Well, that didn't exactly go to plan."

As she peeled a king prawn, she said, "So, we tried to bluff him and he's not fallen for it. He's in a completely different league to us, isn't he?"

He gesticulated in frustration. "Exactly! He gets me so angry with his smug arrogance. He knows he's powerful... all that influence... he can use his newspapers to pursue any agenda he wants, and what can we fight back with? Stuff all. We're left to play friggin' cat-and-mouse games to try to get some justice. It pisses me off."

"Remember what they say about playing cat-and-mouse games—always make sure you're the cat."

He gave her a baleful look. "Thanks, I'll bear that in mind."

"I couldn't believe it when you were brown-nosing him at the start."

"Me, neither. That was the hardest part of the meeting. God knows what my mother will say when she finds out I've totally pissed off Calloway."

She touched his hand. "I'm sorry... about your mum. I should never have dragged you into this. I was too wrapped up in... everything."

They ate in silence until Gina, hoping a change of subject would take his mind off the meeting, said, "You know, I never understood about your parents always being apart."

He wiped his mouth with his napkin. "Yeah, it is a bit odd. Mum and Dad are French, as you know. After they married, their careers separated them for long periods, they were often abroad at the same time—I had to have a nanny. Anyway, Mum says he was seeing someone else and if the ancient scutttlebutt at the *Monitor* is to be believed she may have been seeing Calloway too. I don't know all the ins and outs, but they finally went their separate ways but chose not to divorce. The funny thing is, they see each other quite a bit when she's over in Europe. I have this vision of them getting back together in their dotage and living in the south of France."

"Are you their only child?"

"I am now. I had a younger sister, Denise, but she died from leukaemia when I was ten and she was six. My dad took it badly—this was before they separated—but Mum got over it much sooner. I think she'd already reconciled herself to Denise's death and did most of her grieving before it happened. I also think it caused their separation, but Mum's adamant it would have happened anyway."

"So it's just been you and your mum all these years?"

"I've not been neglected. She taught me to stand up for myself and to stick to my principles. I hope she remembers that after she hears from Calloway."

Gina realised how little she knew about Daniel. He was so generally laid back it surprised her when he acted impulsively. Perhaps she should try a less stressful approach herself.

She caught his eye. "I'm dropping the lawsuit."

"What? Half-an-hour ago you said nothing but nothing would make you give up."

"Sooner or later I have to face reality. I'll struggle on until I get the business back on its feet." She moved her empty plate to one side and picked up her drink. "Dropping the lawsuit won't affect Mama. She went through worse things getting the business up and running."

"Don't make up your mind just yet. At least sleep on it. You don't want to kick yourself later for being too hasty."

A loud burst of laughter echoed around the room. Daniel swung his head round so fast Gina thought he must have heard his name being called. She followed his gaze and saw a blonde seated with two other women at a table on the opposite side of the room. "Oh, no!" He grabbed his napkin and wiped his mouth. "Excuse me." He walked over to the other table, napkin still clutched in his hand.

Daniel spoke to the woman, who introduced him to her companions. A moment later she made brief eye contact with Gina. The other two women did likewise, their expressions curious and mildly amused. She wondered who they were. Daniel had his back to her, so had no clue about the nature of the conversation.

When he came back, he said, "That's Nikki, my girlfriend. I was supposed to bring her to lunch here today but I cried off—told her I had an important business meeting." He shook his head in disbelief at his indiscretion. "We should have gone somewhere else."

"So how did you explain me?"

"I told her the truth. I said you were a close friend who needed my help with a serious business problem."

"I don't think she believes you. She keeps looking over this way. We'd better not play footsies under the table." She couldn't help smiling at the pained expression on his face. "Don't worry. I won't embarrass you."

"I knew it was her as soon as I heard that laugh. It's unmistakable."

"She sounds like a party girl."

"You bet."

Gina glanced across at Nikki's table and saw the three women were watching her again. The next time she looked they were huddled over the table with Nikki talking conspiratorially. A moment later the women burst into laughter.

She pushed her chair back and got to her feet. "I can't stay here any longer."

"Oh, sorry. Do you have to get back?"

"Let's just say I'd rather not be fodder for other people's amusement."

~~~

Outside the hotel, Daniel said, "I feel like I've made matters a lot worse today. For you, your mum, me..."

"You couldn't make matters worse for me. I got myself into this mess all by myself." She gave him an ironic smile. "But thanks for trying. It was a long shot anyway."

"I did my best. Are you in a hurry to go back?"

"No, things are fairly quiet at the moment. I told Simon to call me if it got busy."

"Good. How about a walk in the park?"

They strolled down Stanley Street towards Hyde Park. The day was too warm for a jacket. He took it off and threw it over his shoulder. As they walked, he explained how he'd met Nikki through his new job.

"I'm going to have to ask my boss to take me off her account—I could be accused of having a conflict of interest if we keep on seeing each other. And if we don't, it would make for a rather strained business relationship, wouldn't it?"

"Sounds as if you're not expecting it to last that long."

He shrugged. "I've only known her a few weeks, so I guess it's too early to say."

His answer annoyed her. What did he see in Nikki? She was hardly his type. Party girl was Gina's euphemism for a complete airhead, someone like Kellie, say. Limited ambition and too intent on having a good time. Daniel needed someone more focused, more mature in their outlook. No, Nikki wasn't his type.

She paused to look at the menu outside the Lord Roberts Hotel. "We should have come here. Better menu than the Rebellion."

Daniel said, "What about you? Any men in your life?"

She couldn't conceal her bitterness. "Fat chance I have of meeting anybody." She strode off down the street, forcing him to hurry to catch up.

"I think I touched a raw nerve. Sorry. I should mind my own business."

"Seriously, who the fuck am I likely to meet apart from punters, and I'm hardly likely to be interested in them, am I?"

~~~

As they continued down Stanley Street, despondency wrapped Gina like a cloak. The meeting with Calloway had served only to show her situation was completely hopeless. He wasn't fooled by her bluster. He knew he could easily put her out of business. She wouldn't be surprised if the demonstrations began again with a *Monitor* photographer close by.

Daniel had meant well with his tactics, but the idea that she could appeal to Calloway's better nature now seemed hopelessly naïve. People like him didn't get to be where they were by being compassionate.

As they reached the junction with Yurong Street, a long line of schoolgirls in green uniforms filed leisurely across the pedestrian crossing, chatting among themselves. A man on a motorbike folded his arms and waited for them to pass. "Take ya time, darlin's. No hurry. We have all day." His smile belied his sarcasm and the girls responded good-naturedly. Gina remembered when she was that age and how determined she'd been to make a success of her life, though at the time she had no idea how she'd do that. The memory embarrassed her and her spirits sank even lower.

On the steep uphill stretch approaching College Street, Daniel broke the silence by saying, "Here's my old school." He pointed to a sandstone building on their right.

"You went to Sydney Grammar? I never knew that."

They crossed to the southern section of Hyde Park and mounted the steps. Daniel said, "It's a long time since I came here. Even when I was at school, I hardly ever spent time here. Ever been inside the War Memorial?"

"Not that I remember. Maybe on a school trip."

"It's worth a look. Some other time perhaps."

He led Gina to a bench facing the Pool of Reflection fronting the memorial and they sat quietly for a few minutes, each lost in thought.

Her phone rang.

~~~

Daniel watched as Gina got to her feet, phone to her ear, and began pacing up and down in front of him. Judging by her gestures and agitated tone, she didn't like what she was hearing. When the call was over, instead of rejoining him on the bench, she walked to the pool's edge and stood with her back to him. He let a minute or two pass before picking up her handbag and walking over to her.

Her face was tight with suppressed anger. "That was Caroline."

"What happened?" he asked quietly.

"She chewed me up for seeing Calloway. Said I was too impetuous...or words to that effect. I should have told her beforehand."

"How did she find out?"

"Calloway's lawyers have been onto her father. They wanted to know if I'd instructed them to drop the case."

"Christ, they were quick off the mark. It's less than four hours ago. I must have really stuffed things up for you. I'm sorry."

She didn't answer. He studied the memorial's reflection on the tranquil surface of the pool and waited for her to calm down. When he sneaked a sideways glance, he saw tears coursing down her cheeks.

Instinctively he put a comforting arm around her. For a moment she remained motionless and he wondered if she might turn away from him; instead, she pressed her head against his chest and wept.

When her sobbing eased, he gave her the handbag and she took out a tissue to dry her tears. "Sorry, Dan. You must think I'm a complete idiot. It was bound to end in tears, wasn't it?"

He guided her back to the bench and they sat down. "What did you tell Caroline?"

She sighed. "I said I'd think about it, but in the meantime she was to let the other side know I'm still adamant about taking it all the way."

"But you're not, are you?"

She gave him a despairing look. "Daniel…"

For a short while they sat quietly. His shirt was damp but he didn't mind. Her vulnerability had been so unexpected. When she'd leaned against him, he'd had an overwhelming desire to keep holding her, pressing her close, shielding her.

In a resigned tone, she said, "What am I going to do? I've made a complete mess of my life. I lost my boyfriend because I lied about who I am. I'm running a brothel when I should be making a new career for myself. I've been seen on TV having a shouting match with a religious weirdo. I'll never get a decent job now. As soon as Mama's better, I'm off overseas where nobody knows me and I'll start all over again."

He didn't like the sound of that. He took her hand and squeezed it. "Give it a bit of time, okay? Things are never as bad as they seem. It'll all sort itself out eventually, you'll see."

"I wish." She gave another sigh. "I don't know why you put up with me."

"No?"

She was staring at the ground in front of her, still dejected, and made no reply.

"Well, I do," he said quietly. This time he caught her attention. "You're very special to me."

Her eyes searched his face for confirmation. "Really?"

His heart was thumping. "More than special…"

The anxiety melted from her face. She placed a hand on his shoulder and drew him towards her. They kissed and joy surged through his body as she placed her arms around his neck and clung to him.

After she broke away, her slender fingers continued to caress his face. She smiled. "Oh, Daniel, what a day…"

31. A plan

After they left the park, he and Gina walked hand-in-hand to the lockup where she parked her car. She gave him a lift home but declined his invitation to come in for a drink. Instead, she reached over and pulled him towards her, kissed him again, and thanked him for all his help.

"It's funny," she said, as she caressed his face, "all this time you were hiding in the open."

"I've always wanted you," he replied, "right from when I first saw you at uni."

She kissed him again. "Now go."

He watched as she drove away and then let himself into the house. Intoxicated by events he couldn't sit down for more than a few seconds. Out in the back yard he picked up a basketball and began tossing it into the basket attached to the wall. It was a calming therapy he used when restless.

As he played, his thoughts turned to Calloway. He couldn't imagine what made him think the man would take any notice of Gina's sob story. He'd never heard a single story of Calloway showing compassion and yet he'd seriously expected him to make an exception for a brothel owner, a representative of a group he clearly despised. He was at fault—he should never have suggested the possibility. Now he'd made matters worse for Gina.

And Calloway was right—she couldn't roll up to the *Courier* without credible evidence. She'd come across as someone bent on revenge. It would be like reporting a stolen garden gnome to the police—they'd promise to look into it and she'd never hear another word.

Something else made him feel uncomfortable: if she dropped the libel action straight away, she might regret it later. Stepping back from a conflict wasn't her style. And if she did regret it, he could end up copping at least part of the blame. Though it had been her suggestion to confront Calloway, it was he who'd facilitated the meeting, during which he'd failed to lead the conversation in the right direction. Knowing how helpless she was, Calloway had toyed with her. She'd let herself be riled too easily. He should have kept her on a tighter rein.

He wished there was some other way of getting at Calloway, of putting him under pressure, restricting his room for manoeuvre. They needed leverage.

He wondered about Calloway's private life. He'd been married for forty-odd years—something he was openly proud of—but there were no children. His wife was rumoured to be sickly. He recalled his mother saying Mary was always in and out of hospital.

Could he have a mistress? Men in his position often did, setting them up in their own apartments and visiting whenever they wished. If his wife was sick, marital sex might be out of the question. She could even turn a blind eye to his keeping a mistress, perhaps even encouraging him to have one. He'd read of wives who tacitly approved such arrangements. In one case, rather than have her husband use prostitutes, the wife asked her unmarried sister to provide what she was no longer able to, and the sister agreed.

Calloway frequently disappeared during the day, sometimes not reappearing until mid to late afternoon. Long lunches perhaps—to be expected of someone in his position—or business meetings... or visits to a mistress? And he was often in a better mood when he returned, as any man might be who'd recently spent time with his lover.

Daniel realised he was clutching at straws, but the more he thought about it, the more plausible it seemed that Calloway could have a mistress tucked away somewhere.

The problem, of course, was proving it, and he had no idea how to go about that.

~~~

Gina arrived at Casa Rosa the following day with mixed feelings. While she was feeling good about her changed relationship with Daniel, knowing that she must call Caroline to drop the lawsuit weighed heavily on her. She pushed that to the back of her mind and instead recalled the previous day's strange events. How unpredictable her life could be! Sometimes it was for the worse and sometimes, like now, for the good. Perhaps her luck was on the turn.

"Anything happen yesterday while I was out?" she asked Simon as she walked through the lobby.

"Nothing much. Fairly quiet in fact."

"Good. Glad I wasn't needed." She stuck her hand out for the bookings register. "Won't be long." She took it to her office.

As she posted the receipts into the spreadsheet, it became obvious that the previous evening had been busy, bordering on hectic. When she returned the register, she said, arching an eyebrow, "So, quiet last night, was it?"

"It was."

"But we took nearly twice as much as this time last week. You must have been run off your feet."

He took off his glasses and gave her a quizzical look. "Depends what you mean by quiet. There's an international convention on at Darling Harbour, but we've had busier days. Anyway, we managed... no dramas."

"I think you're telling me this place runs quite well when I'm not here."

He shrugged. "And why not?"

She ignored the implied criticism. "Everything got done that was supposed to be done? Laundry, supplies, and all that?"

"Yep."

"I'm impressed. You're doing a great job."

For the first time since she'd taken him on, he returned her smile without a hint of guile. "Thanks. By the way, can you spare me a few minutes when you're not busy?"

"Of course, let's do it now."

Simon left Jos to manage on her own and followed Gina into her office. He took a seat and when he had her attention said, "Go to your browser and type in 'localhost/casarosa'."

She looked at him suspiciously. "What have you been up to?"

He smiled but refused to answer. She followed his instructions and a moment later a web page appeared. Against a dusky pink background, 'Casa Rosa' was depicted in a deep gold cursive script across the top of the screen. Below the name was a montage of well-developed young women in scanty underwear. Nearer the bottom of the page, a warning stated that the site was sexually explicit, and beneath that a button labelled 'Enter' alongside the wording, 'I have read the terms and conditions below and certify that I am over 18 years old'.

He came round the desk and watched over her shoulder.

"Click 'Enter'."

A new page appeared, blank except for a button labelled 'Bookings'.

Simon said, "What I want to do here is to show images of the girls and list the services they provide. Outcalls only, of course."

"Mmm, I'm not sure about the photos. They won't want their faces shown."

"That's all right, they can be headless bodies."

"And we can take bookings?"

"Yes, but they must pay on-line, otherwise we'll get loads of crank reservations. Every time a booking's made, the details will be sent to whoever's looking after the desk."

She gave him an appraising look. "That's brilliant, Simon. You are a dark horse."

He smiled shyly and returned to his seat. "I've been thinking about it for a while. This is only a mock-up. When it's finished, you'll need to register a domain name so we can advertise it."

"I'm more than impressed. What do you need apart from photos?"

"A lawyer to cast an eye over the wordings so we're not exposed."

"No problem. I have a lawyer friend who I'm sure will help." Assuming she still have any credit left with Caroline after telling her to drop the case.

As Simon got up to leave, he said, "This could boost our business no end."

"Great. It's just what we need to turn things around."

~~~

Daniel called Gina mid-morning.

"Have you spoken to Caroline?"

"Not yet."

"Maybe you should wait another day or two?"

"Why? It's a lost cause."

"You're probably right, but another day won't make much difference. How long do you plan to stay at work today?"

"Depends on the alternative…"

"I'm off Nikki's account and they've not given me another one yet, so I'm at a loose end."

"Did you speak to her?"

"Yes. She mentioned she'd been seeing Rajit, a friend of mine I introduced her to at a party. So much for loyalty. Not that it matters—we weren't much of an item anyway."

"All's fair in love and war. Anyway, you have me now," she said, smiling and with a degree of smugness.

"Don't I know it. So, when can you leave?"

"I was told this morning my presence is no longer essential to the orderly running of this place, so I guess I can leave whenever I like."

"Right, I'll meet you in half-an-hour."

She'd call Caroline the next day.

~~~

They sat facing the harbour under a large shade tree in the Royal Botanic Gardens, having bought salad rolls and fruit juice from the kiosk. Gina listened in a skeptical frame of mind as Daniel outlined his theory.

When he finished, he said, "I know it's a stretch. The thing that worries me is that I'm being judgemental about his private life."

She laughed derisively. "Judgemental? All Calloway ever does is judge other people, like my mother for instance. It'd serve him right if he was caught with his pants down. It's wishful thinking, though."

"Maybe, but if he is up to something…" He bit into his roll and chewed quietly. "I'm still not sure about the ethics, though."

"Then why mention it?"

He took his time answering. "If he has a mistress tucked away somewhere, you could use the knowledge as a lever."

While the prospect was enticing, she had no idea how she was going to manage that. As for ethics, if Calloway didn't play by the rules, why should she?

"Okay, let's say you're right and he visits her in the daytime, how do I find that out without using a private investigator? They cost a motza and I have stuff-all for them to go on. It could take ages."

Daniel shrugged. "You're right. I should have thought it through more. Nice idea, though."

But the seed had been sown and the idea tantalised her.

"I need to be sure he's playing away from home. Could he be screwing his secretary?"

"Renata? You kidding? You've seen her—she's no spring chicken."

As best she could remember, Renata was about forty and, though average looking, carried herself well. Calloway was in his late sixties. He might take advantage of their close relationship, it often happened. "Did your old boss, Frank what's-his-name, ever say anything?"

"McAllister. He told me there'd been a rumour years ago about Calloway and my mum."

"You serious?"

He laughed. "I know. I asked her and she said that's all it was, nothing but a rumour."

"In Frank's job he must have heard lots of rumours. You could ask him."

"I dunno. He'll wonder what I'm up to."

"Aw, come on, the worst he can do is tell you to bugger off."

"All right, but wait until I've finished eating."

"It won't take a minute."

He shook his head in exasperation. "You'll never change, will you?" He put down the salad roll and took his phone out of his pocket. The conversation lasted less than five minutes and Daniel did most of the listening. As he put the phone back, he said, "I told him my mum denied having an affair with Calloway and did he know of any other rumours, like with Renata. He said Calloway gets suspected of everything you can think of but nothing's ever been proven, including having it off with Renata. He was seen dining with a woman a year or two ago but no-one knew who she was."

"Could've been his wife, or his daughter."

"He doesn't have any children. Mum says his wife had a hysterectomy just after they married. She's got long-term health problems, too. Doesn't travel far."

She offered him her last half roll. "I'm not hungry." He took it without reply, his mind clearly elsewhere. When he finished eating, she said, "Instead of being Casanova, he could turn out to be Mother Teresa in pants, dishing out food to the homeless."

"He's a hypocrite, not a saint."

"You said he heads up a charity."

"Okay, so he's not pure evil, but he still wields enormous power and god help you if you get in his way."

Her spirits were beginning to revive, even if Calloway's philandering was nothing more than conjecture.

"Okay, what have I to lose? If he's not seeing anybody, then it's just my time I've wasted."

And if it proved not to be a waste of time, she would be faced with another problem: how to use Calloway's infidelity to get her claim settled. But first...

"If you're sure he has a woman shacked up somewhere, there's a less expensive option."

"Such as?"

"I could tail him when he leaves at lunchtime..."

"You? Who d'you think you are—Miss Marple?"

"I'd ask you to help, but you have a job to go to."

"I'll do what I can."

She took his hand and squeezed it. "I know you will. But you're right—I don't have a clue how to go about it. It's a job for professionals."

From where they sat she could see the sun reflecting off one of the Opera House's white tiled roofs. She'd never been inside the building. That could be remedied. She suggested they walk over to pick up a programme. There might be something they would both like to see.

When they reached the foreshore walkway, Daniel said, "I could ask my boss for leave of absence. He hasn't found me a new account yet, so I'm just a gofer for everyone else."

She was surprised by his willingness to help. "You shouldn't, Dan. It's very kind of you but this could be a total waste of time." Seeing the look on his face, she added, "Okay, but don't put your job on the line."

"I could take next week off. I'm certain my boss won't mind."

"You really believe Calloway's up to something, don't you?"

"He's far too holier-than-thou. People like him always have a skeleton in their wardrobe. Just look at those TV evangelists who are always getting caught out. They're a bunch of self-serving hypocrites."

"So is this for me or for you?"

"For you, of course, but I have a score to settle as well. I'd love to see Calloway shown up for what he is—an absolute two-faced bastard."

32. Pursuit

The silver Mercedes emerged from the underground car park and eased into the George Street traffic heading south.

Gina, whose attention had wandered, spotted the car a couple of seconds later. "That's him! Quick, don't let him get too far in front."

Daniel turned off the radio, started the engine and waited to pull away from the kerb. He let three cars pass before taking off after Calloway. "I don't think we should get close in case he sees us."

He continued to hang back as they passed through Haymarket, but as they approached the traffic lights in Railway Square a bus asserted its right of way and veered across their path.

"Fuck!"

"Quick, change lanes!" Gina wished she was in the driver's seat.

"I can't just yet." He put his indicator on but nobody was willing to give way. By the time a gap appeared and he'd moved into the next lane, the lights were on red and the Mercedes had disappeared.

He pounded the steering wheel with his fist. "For fuck's sake!"

Gina said, "Hey, don't let it get to you. We'll try again tomorrow." The more time she spent with Daniel, the more she realised he wasn't as laid back as he appeared.

"I should have changed lanes earlier."

She patted him on the shoulder. "It's not your fault, Dan. Being a private dick isn't easy."

"Being a public dick isn't, either."

~~~

The next day was only slightly more successful. This time they managed to see Calloway take a right-hand turn into Mountain Street before being stymied by the changing traffic lights.

"Maybe tomorrow we should park down Mountain and wait for him to pass. What do you think?" Daniel asked, as he drove Gina back to Tolley Street.

She pursed her lips. "We're supposing he comes down here every day. For all we know, he might have a different engagement today. He's twenty minutes earlier than yesterday, so he could be going somewhere else. Or maybe he was going somewhere else yesterday. Or maybe he goes somewhere different every friggin' day!" She threw her hands in the air. "I must be mad. We're trying to shoot pigeons in the dark."

"But if we park outside his office, we'll probably get left behind again."

"The lights won't always be on red." Or could they? She only had three more days of Daniel's help. "Okay, I have a better idea. You park on George and I'll take my car and park on Mountain. We can keep in touch by mobile."

"Okay, that makes sense."

~~~

"Have you told Gina?" Holly asked.

"I told her I wasn't planning on sticking around much longer," Chloe said, as she watched Holly try on the new shoes she'd bought that morning. The two women were in the changing room getting ready for their afternoon shifts. "At first she tried to get me to stay and then she gave me a list of massage schools. Said she got them off the Internet."

"So which course are you doing?" Holly stood up, wobbling on the high heels. Chloe knew she much preferred flatties or boots, preferably Blundstones, but her Casa Rosa persona required she dress sexily and boots didn't fit the bill, unless she wanted to be a dominatrix, and Holly wasn't interested in sadomasochism. Nor was Chloe.

"Remedial massage."

"Sounds interesting. Does it pay well?"

"Enough to cover the mortgage payments—at least I'm hoping so." The truth was, she didn't know for sure if she'd find a position, which was why she still worked at Casa Rosa.

Holly said, "I wish I could find something that paid enough to pack this game in."

"I thought you enjoyed working here."

"Compared to working in a shoe shop for minimum wages, it's a breeze, but as a career it's rather limiting, don't you think? Let me know how you get on with the massage course. I might give it a go myself."

~~~

As Gina waited on Mountain Street, Calloway's vehicle slipped out of the car park and Daniel moved out to follow him at a discreet distance. However, instead of carrying straight on as before, the Mercedes turned left at the next intersection and continued in that direction until it reached Elizabeth Street, where it turned left again and headed north.

Daniel was too intent on sticking with Calloway to let Gina know what was happening. As he approached the lights at Market Street, they changed to red and he was separated from the Mercedes. His spirits sank; however, little traffic came in from the intersection and when the lights changed back to green he soon caught up again. He stayed close until his target reached Macquarie Street and headed down towards Circular Quay.

He wasn't surprised when the car turned into Albert Street. Odds-on he was dining locally, probably at the Royal Automobile Club, where Daniel's mother was a member. She'd taken him there twice for lunch.

He didn't follow Calloway—it would have been too obvious. Instead, he headed along the quay front back to George Street and at the next set of red lights gave Gina a call.

"This is proving harder than I expected," he said.

"If it were easy, private dicks would be out of work."

"So...tomorrow?"

"Same plan. If he goes for lunch again, we'll have to wait till Friday. I can't imagine him staying away for too long if that's where he gets his jollies."

~~~

Chloe, Kellie, and Juliette sat sipping cocktails in the Hilton's Marble Bar and discussed Victor, Juliette's less than law-abiding boyfriend.

She looked worried. "He's blown it this time. They've charged him with possession. With his record, he'll go inside."

"That should teach him a lesson," Chloe said.

Juliette studied her hands clasped in her lap. "I wish I knew what to do."

"You know what to do," Kellie said without sympathy. "He's nothing but trouble. You should've given him the flick years ago. He's a parasite."

"That's what Maria says. Last time he got off with a fine and promised me he'd stay out of trouble." Juliette gave a derisive laugh. "Guess who paid the fine?"

"Some people never change," Kellie said. "He's never going to behave himself while he's got you to prop him up."

Chloe knew Juliette wanted help in making a decision but Kellie's unsympathetic responses weren't making it easy. "What will you do if he goes inside?"

"I don't know. We've lived together for two years."

"Think about it," Kellie said. "Do you want another two years of the same thing, worrying about him all the time, not knowing when he's going to be in trouble again? Why chuck your life away on somebody who doesn't deserve it?"

Juliette considered the question for a minute before reaching into her handbag for a tissue. "Sorry, I didn't mean to lay this on you guys."

"Don't be silly. You know we're always here for you."

Chloe flashed a warning with her eyes and Kellie eased back into her seat. "Is there something stopping you from leaving him?"

Juliette shoved the wet tissue back in her bag. "Not really. The lease on the flat comes up for renewal in two months. I suppose I could move out, put his stuff in storage and send him the key."

Chloe said, "That's what I would do. It's time to move on. You can't shake off the past but you don't have to keep reliving it."

That set Chloe thinking about her own plans. She'd almost reached the end of the introductory massage course. The next stage, which would take twelve weeks, didn't start until well into the new year. If she was lucky, she might get a junior position on the strength of it.

"I'm looking forward to being a masseuse," she said, in an effort to change the conversation.

Kellie, who'd never been happy with Chloe's decision, said, "It seems a lot of hard work for little reward. Why stand on your feet all day when you can lie down on the job?"

"As long as I have a living wage, Kell, enough to cover my home loan, I'll be happy."

Kellie said airily, "I don't want to own property. Ties you down too much. I'm a free spirit."

Juliette said, "You're right, Chlo. All you need is your own place and a decent income."

"Listen to you two," said Kellie, "You're like a pair of old women! You'll be queuing for your pensions next."

Juliette sipped her cocktail. "We'll all be old one day. Better to think about it now before it's too late."

Kellie looked at them and shook her head. "You should hear yourselves. It's like being at a mothers' union meeting. Come on, liven up, or I'm going home."

That last remark convinced Chloe that something was wrong with Kellie, who wasn't normally grouchy. "What's eating you, Kell?"

"How do you mean?"

"You know what I mean. Is it Dave?"

Kellie gave her a defiant stare and then, deflated, waved her arm as if to say it was nothing of consequence.

"He's found out about you, hasn't he?"

Kellie nodded.

"How?"

"We were at this party and... he introduced me to some of his mates. You can guess the rest. One of them was a client. He must have told Dave afterwards."

Juliette placed her hand on Kellie's arm. "That's awful."

"Too right. After all this time, I thought he might be the one."

"I'm sorry, too," Chloe said.

Kellie gave her a bitter look. "Maybe I'll join you on that massage course." As Chloe was about to encourage the idea, Kellie added, "No, forget that. It's too much like hard work."

~~~

Thursday turned out to be interesting for Gina for two reasons. The first was that she managed to track Calloway to an address where his supposed mistress might live.

As agreed, she'd parked on Mountain Street and waited for Calloway's car to come past. She didn't have to wait long. A quick call from Daniel alerted her that Calloway was on his way. His car appeared a few minutes later in her rear view mirror. As he drove by she pulled out and stayed close behind. She wasn't worried about being recognised—her headscarf and sunglasses rendered her incognito.

She stuck with the Mercedes as it travelled down Mountain Street before turning right and then left into Harris Street. As they approached Pyrmont, she wondered if Calloway intended dining at the Fish Market. It might not be *cordon bleu* but the fish was guaranteed to be fresh. However, he continued westward. She'd never ventured this deep into Pyrmont before—fortunately, the traffic lights worked in her favour and she managed to keep the car in her sights.

The far end of Harris Street had a neglected air about it: a few shops, a café, some small businesses with shabby frontages. When she realised the road was about to terminate at the harbour, she knew he would have to turn off. Either that or his car had better be waterproofed.

Calloway turned left. She took the corner slowly so as not to draw attention to herself. Up ahead she glimpsed the Anzac Bridge's radiating cables, partially obscured by new apartment blocks, which, along with the modern and refurbished dwellings, revealed the area to be in an advanced process of gentrification.

The Mercedes turned left again, this time into a narrow street. She drove past the end of the street and glimpsed him pulling into the side of the road.

She turned at the next street and found a parking space close by. Quickly checking there were no traffic wardens around, she jumped out and scurried back to see Calloway feeding coins into a parking meter. He took the ticket back to his car and placed it inside the windscreen before locking the car and walking up to the porch of a house near the other end of the short street. He unlocked the door and disappeared inside.

She returned to her car and drove round the block so she could take a proper look at the house he'd entered.

Number 11 Lumley Street was a renovated sandstone terrace that looked well-maintained judging by its neat Federation green picket fence and ornate balustrade on the upper balcony. The windows were barred, but so were those of its neighbours—the price of living close to the city with its ever-present risk of burglary.

The challenge now was to find out who lived there. As an ex-journalist, Daniel ought to know how to do that.

She called him to let him know she'd successfully completed the mission—he'd once again lost touch while tailing Calloway and was waiting for her at Tolley Street—and drove back to Casa Rosa feeling pleased with her efforts.

~~~

The second interesting thing to happen that Thursday was the letter she received from Morgan Chamberlain announcing he would be in Sydney the next day for an important meeting. He would be staying at the Westin Hotel and leaving on Monday. If she could find the time, he'd be delighted to catch up with her over the weekend.

33. Closing in

Gina spent some time thinking about her next move. Daniel had called earlier to say he'd identified the owner of 11 Lumley Street. Crispin Calloway had bought the house two years before.

Gina thought it unlikely Calloway would have bought the house as a pied-à-terre. If that was what he needed, as a rich man he would have chosen a luxury apartment close to his office. In any event, Pyrmont wasn't much closer than Potts Point where he lived. It was difficult not to see the house as a hideaway for a mistress, but how to prove that?

Somehow she needed to create an opportunity to see the woman—would she be able to sneak a photo as well?—and confirm she was the sole occupant. A troubling thought: perhaps no-one lived there. Perhaps it was a lovers' tryst and his mistress travelled to the house each time they arranged an assignation.

If she was going to turn up on the doorstep, Gina needed a convincing story for being there. Furthermore, she'd have to make sure she arrived at the house while it was still occupied. That meant turning up not long after Calloway left; within half-an-hour, say.

She racked her brain for a solution. Why did people call unannounced? She cast her mind back to the visits she'd received at home from unexpected callers. Mostly it was Mormons or Jehovah's Witnesses. Once, a young man turned up hawking his paintings. Another time, children were collecting for a sponsored walk. She remembered a woman who had organised a petition to have a pedestrian crossing installed at the bottom of the road. Maybe that was the way to go—pretend to be someone collecting signatures for a petition.

She called Daniel and ran the idea past him.

He wasn't enthusiastic. "Why do you need a petition? Just rock up and pretend you're looking for someone you think lives there."

"And when she says they don't and closes the door, I'm no further forward. A petition will at least give me a chance to find out more about her."

"Okay, but what would be the subject of your petition? You're not a resident and you don't know the local issues. And if you did, who's to say she doesn't know more about them than you do? And you'd also need a fair few signatures to make it look credible. She'll be suspicious if she twigs she's the first one to sign."

"Thanks, Dan, that's raised my spirits like you wouldn't believe. Do you have a better idea?"

"You're on the right track. Maybe a survey or something."

The only times she'd been approached for a survey was in the street or a shopping centre. Still, why shouldn't you go door to door with a survey?

"Mmm…I could pretend to be checking on local amenities, what the residents think about them, that kind of thing."

"Like childcare facilities, parks, medical centres, libraries…"

"Great! I could make up a list and ask what she thinks about each one. I'll tell her I'm from the council. Which one is it, by the way?"

"Sydney."

"Okay, I'll start designing a survey form."

~~~

Daniel played cricket on Saturdays, so it was a good day for Gina to meet Morgan for lunch. She wondered if he had any purpose in mind other than renewing their acquaintance. They weren't on the warmest of terms when they parted in Boston. Still, much had happened since then and the passage of time often put things into perspective. Maybe he'd come to his senses and realised how much she meant to him. Maybe he'd ask her to go back to Boston with him. As if...

The Westin Hotel was part of the redeveloped General Post Office site and retained the original architecture. The lobby was high and expansive and it took a moment for her to locate Morgan, but he'd already seen her arrive.

He came towards her, smiling, and greeted her with a peck on the cheek.

"Sorry I'm late," she said breathlessly, stepping back a little.

"No worries—is that what you guys say?"

She laughed. "You're picking up the lingo."

"I've booked a table at the restaurant upstairs," he said, shepherding her towards the lifts. "You're looking *très chic*, by the way."

She gave him a grateful smile. "Thank you for noticing." She'd chosen to wear a white cotton summer dress randomly patterned in pale yellow and blue dots, caught at the waist with a blue sash. She'd not worn it for three years. She'd twirled around in front of the full-size mirror, delighted to find the dress not only fitted but flattered her figure as well. Then, like a teenager preparing for a first date, she cleaned her teeth a second time and redid her makeup.

The restaurant would have been al fresco had it not been for the glass roof. The nineteenth century clock tower loomed above. She'd not dined there before but she'd heard the food was excellent. It was also expensive.

When they were seated at their table and studying the menu, she said, "You'd better choose something substantial—you look as if you haven't eaten a lot lately." The loss of weight suited him, but she couldn't help wondering if he might have been ill.

"No, not at all, I've just been busy. I don't always find time to eat."

She studied him as he ran his eye up and down the menu. On the second finger of his right hand he wore a signet ring with the letters GC inscribed on it. She recognised it as the one his father had worn. His fingernails were as manicured as before; hair just the right length; shirt collar opened only as far as the first button. Still the same old Morgan.

Had it not been for the weight loss, he would have looked no different from the last time she'd seen him. He still had the same colour to his cheeks. Did he share his father's susceptibility to heart problems? She hoped not.

It was strange looking at him. After four months, during which time she'd often indulged herself in wishful thinking, visualising them being together again, the past a slate magically wiped clean, here he was sitting across from her as if they met like this all the time.

He looked up, met her gaze, and smiled. "It feels like old times, doesn't it?"

"That's what I was thinking. So, what are you going to have?"

"According to a restaurant review I read, the risotto here is a specialty. I love risottos."

She chose a salad. She was dining with Daniel later on.

"Would you like some wine?" he asked.

"A glass of Chardonnay, please."

"Okay, I'll join you."

After they'd ordered, he said, "I've missed you, Gina."

"I've missed you, too. I was sorry to hear about your father."

"Thanks. I'm still getting used to the idea of him not being around. I feel like a rudderless boat at times. I'm only now realising how much he influenced my life."

"It takes time."

"Remember the portrait of my dad that was on the stairs at home? Well, it's hanging in our offices now. That's where Mom had always wanted it. How's your mom, by the way?"

"She's finished chemo but is still resting up before she goes back to work."

"She's lucky to have you around."

She acknowledged the compliment with a shrug. "I was surprised to get your letter. I never expected to see you again."

"What you told me came as quite a shock. I maybe could have handled it better, not parted on such bad terms. Anyway, that's history now. I thought as I was here in Sydney I should at least look you up and say hello as one old friend to another. It wouldn't have felt right otherwise."

"I'm glad you did." She meant it. Regardless of her bruised feelings, it was good to see him, and she'd been curious to know how he was getting on.

"Mom told me things didn't quite work out the way you expected when you got back."

Gina gave him a rundown of what had happened since she started at Casa Rosa: the newspaper exposé; the demonstration and her appearance on television news; how she and Daniel confronted Calloway. Much of it was new to him and he seemed surprised by the turn of events. She was still talking when their meals arrived.

As she inspected her salad, Morgan said, "I can understand that Calloway guy wanting to close brothels but I can't figure out why he'd organise a demonstration outside your place of business."

"Maybe he didn't. Maybe we were the only ones the mob had heard of, given the publicity he gave us. But Calloway could call them off if he wanted to. He's conceded that. He's funding MAP—that's the Moral Australia Party."

"They a problem?"

"According to Daniel, they're the political arm of a group called the Convinzi Trust."

Morgan's face lit up. "Hey, Convinzi Corp used to be a client of ours."

"What do you know about them?"

"They're owned by a guy called Ted Salinski—a billionaire, very rightwing. They provide security personnel and equipment, do lots of work bodyguarding ambassadors, visiting dignitaries, that kind of stuff. Iraq, Afghanistan, Palestine, Pakistan, you name it, wherever there's political discontent and we—the US, that is—could be at risk, they'll be there. That's where the money is these days—security, it's a huge business."

"Who's Ted Salinski?"

"An interesting guy. He gives financial support to conservative Christian candidates at Federal and State level. He and Dad got on well for a while, then they had a difference of opinion and Salinski took his business elsewhere."

"Any idea what they argued about?"

"Salinski invited Dad to look over his spread in Virginia. Turned out to be a military camp. Nearly ten thousand acres, full of firing ranges and assault courses. Lots of armoured vehicles and helicopters, troop transporters, you name it. Dad was surprised because up until then he thought Convinzi was mainly a provider of security personnel, not a mercenary army. Still, that didn't faze him. It was only when Salinski hinted that he had enough men to take over Washington if the need arose that Dad began to wonder what his real agenda was. Salinski eventually confided in him that he was working with other groups to create a secret alliance to take over government if it became too liberal. My dad might have been a conservative but he believed in democracy."

"He never struck me as a fanatic."

"He wasn't. He told Salinski he was wrong to think he could take the law into his own hands. That's when they parted company."

"Is the Convinzi Trust in Australia part of his organisation?"

"I don't know. It's probably a joint operation with people who share his views, which means your Mr Calloway could be involved."

"Didn't your father report Salinski to the FBI?"

"What could he tell them? It was a private conversation. Anyway, they're probably keeping an eye on him already. Private armies don't go unnoticed." He ate another spoonful of food. "That review was right, you know, this risotto is great. So what are your plans?"

She wondered how much she should reveal, then realised he was unlikely to pass on anything he heard.

"We're hoping to establish Calloway has a mistress."

Morgan, surprised, said, "Then what?"

"We front up and tell him to settle my claim or we'll expose his hypocrisy in the *Courier*—that's a rival newspaper."

"*We* being you and Daniel, right?"

"Right."

He nodded knowingly. "So how's he helping you?"

She explained Daniel's involvement from his time at the *Monitor* up until their meeting with Calloway.

"Sounds like a cool guy," Morgan said. "However, it's not a smart move to blackmail Calloway."

Gina finished her meal and placed her knife and fork on the side of the plate. "Why not?"

Morgan continued eating without answering. When he'd cleared his plate, he said, "If I need a good reason to come back to Sydney, that would be it." He picked up his glass of wine and leaned back in his seat. "It was delicious." He met Gina's gaze. "If you threaten Calloway, it'll be, like I said, blackmail."

"No, it won't. All I'm asking is that he settles my claim."

"Or you'll ruin his life. That's blackmail."

"Oh, come on, Morgan. He never cared what happened to my mother when he printed that story. If she ends up begging on the streets it still won't bother him. He's a bully and a hypocrite. He doesn't approve of adultery any more than he condones brothels."

"Maybe, but two wrongs don't make a right."

She suppressed her irritation. For a while there she thought he'd softened, become less rigid in his views, but he was the same straight up and down moraliser of old. Nothing would be gained by arguing with him.

"I'll bear it in mind." She looked around at the other diners while she tried to get her thoughts in order. Her early expectations had evaporated, leaving her to wonder at her naiveté. She'd thought he'd at least apologise for the way he'd treated her, even suggesting they might pick up from before that dreadful moment in Edgartown, help assuage the guilt she'd felt since. That clearly wasn't on the cards.

After they finished lunch, she led Morgan on a walking tour of some of the city's attractions. Away from his home territory, he was just another visitor untutored in local custom and history and she enjoyed reversing their previous roles.

As they strolled past the State Library, he said, "Have you thought about what you're going to do once things settle down? It would be a shame to let your MBA go to waste."

"I'm not sure my MBA gives me much of an edge. I thought it would before I took over from Mama, but it hasn't helped much since. The girls don't want to be managed—all they want is more custom. I couldn't motivate them with the usual corporate stuff. In the end I met them on their terms."

Approaching the Opera House, he said, "It must have been a tough call taking over a brothel."

"The first few weeks were awful. I struggled not to hate my mother for putting me in that position or to look down on the girls. When the *Monitor* printed the exposé, I thought my life was over. Then slowly I changed. The more they tried to suppress me, the more I became part of the business. I got to know and like the girls and then, believe it or not, I began to rise to the challenge, almost relishing it."

"And Calloway?"

"One day he'll get his come-uppance."

"So you'll stay a madam?" He said it as if it were a foregone conclusion.

"Once Mama is ready to take over again, I'm pulling out. She's much better suited to it than I am."

"But if she has a relapse?"

She gave him a sideways look. "Thanks for that cheery thought, Morgan."

~~~

"So, are you flying to the US with your old flame?" Daniel asked with a wry smile as they drove to Double Bay for dinner.

"No, we couldn't get adjoining seats. I'll have to follow later."

She'd just finished telling him about her lunch with Morgan. Daniel had had a successful day at cricket and was in a chipper mood ("Batted at number four and not out on sixty-seven."). When he continued to smile, she pulled a face at him and said, "Bastard! You could at least pretend to be jealous."

He laughed. "From what you've told me, I can't imagine what you saw in him in the first place."

"He had charisma and I fell under his spell. He occupied a world I'd only ever glimpsed before. He's also very knowledgeable about the arts. I learned a lot from him. Looking back, I realise the only thing that stopped me from falling hopelessly in love with him was that we never got close enough. He was good company but I sensed him holding back. Deep down he wanted to be intimate but his morals prevented him and ... well, I suppose it was his way of keeping me at a distance."

On the other hand, his surface appearance could reflect how he was deep down.

Over dinner she told Daniel what Morgan had said about the Convinzi Corporation.

Daniel said, "If there's anything incriminating, I'm sure Frank would have found out by now, but I'll mention it if I see him again. We'll have to rely on the mistress strategy. If that fails, I can't see what else we can do."

She wished it weren't so, but her fate hinged on this last throw of the dice.

~~~

The next day, Daniel went to Gina's house. Working from her draft council survey they produced what they thought was a convincing document. Daniel acted out the part of Calloway's mistress in a dry run of the interview and it went well, Gina deftly responding to his petulant remarks.

"It's a pity we can't provide you with an accreditation badge," Daniel said.

"If she asks to see it, I'll pretend it must have dropped off in the car, which of course will be parked a distance away. I doubt she'll want to hang about on her doorstep waiting for me while I go and get it. Besides, it's not like I'm collecting money or trying to get into the house, is it?"

"The hardest part will be getting her to tell you her name. That's not something I'd expect to be asked in a council survey. They're usually anonymous."

"I won't ask, then."

"Okay, let's copy the form and fill a few of them out."

34. The quarry

With her clipboard resting against the steering wheel, Gina pretended to speak into her mobile phone as Calloway walked along the opposite pavement. He was almost level with her when he chose to cross the road. For a moment she thought he was heading straight for her. She didn't dare look, and held her breath until he'd safely passed behind her car.

She would give him ten minutes to clear the scene.

Before making her move, she took a deep breath. Here goes.

Calloway had been inside 11 Lumley Street for an hour-and-a-half and she'd been parked for half-an-hour before that. She would need to feed the parking meter again before setting off on her mission.

So far everything had gone reasonably well. She'd managed to find the only free parking space on the street, forcing Calloway to park around the corner. She'd watched him enter the building using his door key and then as he left saw him hugging someone she couldn't quite see. All the while, the street had remained peaceful with only minor traffic passing through.

She fed the meter and posted the new ticket in her car before crossing the road. Clipboard in hand, she walked purposefully towards the front door of number eleven.

A large, well-polished brass knocker graced the centre of a gloss painted door. Taking another deep breath, she grasped it and rapped three times in quick succession.

No sound came from within. She gave it a minute or so and knocked again, this time with more determination. After another minute or two, she concluded that whoever lived there either wasn't going to answer the door or had slipped out the back. As she turned to leave, the door opened quietly and a sleepy voice said, "Sorry..."

She turned around. A pale-faced man in a dressing gown stood barefoot on the threshold. His fair hair was tousled and he rubbed his eyes as if he'd only that minute tumbled out of bed. He looked to be in his late twenties or early thirties.

"I'm sorry," she said, "I didn't mean to wake you. I can come back later."

The man yawned. In a weary drawl he said, "I wasn't quite asleep. What do you want?"

"I'm from the council. We're conducting a survey on residents' attitudes towards local amenities. Would you have time to answer a few questions?"

He suppressed a yawn. "Just a couple of minutes."

"It won't take long, I promise." She looked at the clipboard. "First, Mister..." He didn't volunteer a name, so she continued, "How many people reside at this address?"

"One."

"One?" She shouldn't have sounded so surprised, but he didn't seem to notice.

"Yes, I live on my own."

She regained her composure and ploughed on. No, he didn't use the library or the park or the medical centre, and he had no need for a preschool or child-caring of any kind. Finally, she asked if he was satisfied with the availability of parking.

"I don't drive," he said.

She thanked him for his time and said goodbye. When she reached the pavement, she turned to see he was still standing in the doorway. To avoid suspicion, she went to the neighbouring house. As she was about to press the doorbell, he called out, "There's no-one in during the day."

"Thanks." She strolled to the next house and when she looked round again he was gone. Nevertheless, to maintain the charade, she pretended to press the doorbell at number fifteen, waited a minute, and then strode briskly to her car.

She couldn't wait to tell Daniel what she'd found out.

~~~

Daniel scoffed at the idea of Calloway being homosexual. "He's as straight as the proverbial arrow."

"How can you be so certain? They're not all camp, you know."

He waved a hand dismissively. "I just know." Frank would have mentioned it if there'd been any suspicion.

"Sorry, Dan, but gays don't wear badges saying they're queer. Look at the bloke who directed that play you were in at uni. Eric something-or-other."

"Anderson. Okay, we were surprised when he outed himself, but Calloway's different. He campaigns against homosexuality. Why would he do that if he was gay himself?"

"Because it doesn't matter to him. He's happy keeping it under wraps."

"It still doesn't make sense to me."

"Okay, so how do you explain the fact that he owns a house whose only occupant is a youngish bloke who looked like he'd just been shagged?"

He laughed at the image. "That's ridiculous, Gina. If you knew Calloway..."

"Well, he didn't go there for piano lessons, did he?"

Maybe she was right, but he still felt uneasy. Calloway was a long-time married man, a champion of conservative Christian values, a campaigner against what he regarded as sexual perversions. He might rationalise keeping a mistress but a male lover...

"Supposing he's family? A nephew, perhaps?"

She scoffed. "Do you visit your relations practically every day? I hardly ever see mine."

"I bet there's an innocent explanation."

"All the other possibilities are far less credible. I need to see Calloway again."

He groaned. "After last time, you won't even get into the building."

"But it has to be face-to-face. I want to see him try to wriggle out of this one. I want to watch his reaction when he knows I've finally got him on toast."

"If you pull that stunt with Calloway and it backfires, you'll be toast. I think you should hold off until we're certain about the relationship."

"Dan, what do you think we've been doing this past week? Playing Where's Wally? This is as good as it's going to get."

"I'm just worried for your sake."

"Don't be. And remind me again who said Calloway's 'smug arrogance' made him so angry the other day..."

He still felt the same way, but if they let emotion guide their actions, the hole they were in could get much, much deeper.

She was waiting for him to say something. Reluctantly he saw that regardless of the consequences she would press ahead. If he refused to help, their relationship would suffer—he would be the reason she didn't triumph over Calloway. If only he could be certain she was right about the gay lover angle.

"Let me sleep on it."

She was about to say something in response, and then let it go.

~~~

Try as he might, Daniel could think of no way to verify Gina's suspicions. He had nothing to go on: no name, no photographs, nothing in writing, just her description of someone she seemed to have got out of bed still half asleep.

He did sleep on it, and in the morning he realised he had no choice. The problem was Gina's; he was only acting as a facilitator. Whether or not she was successful confronting Calloway, at least he'd stuck by her.

As expected, he came up against a brick wall trying to organise the meeting. Renata said Calloway wouldn't see anyone without knowing the subject to be discussed, something he had no intention of revealing ahead of time. Perhaps, she said, he could put something in writing and she would make sure Mr Calloway saw it. When Daniel insisted that the matter had to be discussed face-to-face, she said it was out of her hands—she was simply following her boss's orders.

He struggled to come up with a different strategy. He knew they couldn't barge in to see Calloway. Unless their visit was authorised, they'd never get past the reception desk in the lobby.

He thought about and then dismissed the idea of ambushing Calloway as he left the building, as that could lead to unpleasant consequences. The last thing they needed was a restraining order placed on them.

There seemed to be only one avenue left open to him: to ask someone to intercede on their behalf, someone Calloway would listen to and trust, someone who would listen to Daniel and trust him...

~~~

Two weeks passed before the meeting was arranged. Renata phoned Daniel and suggested a date and time, which he accepted.

He was still uneasy about Gina confronting Calloway with her accusations. While he reluctantly agreed with her assertion that Calloway could be a closet gay, he wasn't happy for her to use it as a bargaining chip. He wished he shared her certainty, but she had form when it came to reaching hasty conclusions.

It had been difficult persuading his mother to use her friendship with Calloway to arrange the meeting. She wanted to know what it was about and was annoyed when he wouldn't tell her.

"So what am I supposed to say, then?"

"Tell him it's something that could become seriously embarrassing for him if he doesn't talk to us."

After a long and at times heated discussion, she agreed, while still having reservations, to see what she could arrange, though when she first spoke to Calloway he flat out refused. It took two more attempts before he relented. However, she imposed a condition on Daniel: he must respect her friendship with Calloway; he was not, repeat not, to get involved in the discussions—Gina would have to fend for herself.

~~~

The night before the meeting, Gina lay awake running through various scenarios in her head, each one concluded with an embarrassed and humbled Calloway pleading for her not to reveal his secret. She slept well but woke early the next morning and immediately other, far less attractive scenarios invaded her thoughts.

The one that disturbed her most was where she was challenged to take her story to the *Courier* while he quietly moved his lover out of the house. What evidence would she have to back up her story? After all, she didn't even know the man's name. She was back to playing poker again. Last time, Calloway had called her bluff and she'd left with her tail between her legs.

Her stomach soured as the realisation grew that she was about to be humiliated again. She could still back out, of course, but she knew she'd regret it later. She must go through with the meeting. What was it Shakespeare said? A coward dies a thousand deaths, a hero only one. The least she could hope for was not to end up mortally wounded.

35. Head to head

They approached the security desk at the Monitor building, gave their names to the guard, and waited while he contacted Renata. Gina was a jangle of nerves—she would have much preferred to be sent straight to the ninth floor where Calloway had his office.

"Well, look who's here."

She swung round to see a tall blonde striding towards them, handbag swinging from her shoulder, eyes trained on Daniel, who said, with manufactured enthusiasm, "Hi, Isobel. How are you?"

Isobel looked pointedly at Gina and then at Daniel. "Returning to the scene of the crime or hoping to get your old job back?"

"Isobel," Daniel said, "this is Gina." To Gina he said, "Isobel and I once worked together."

She didn't need reminding. "We've already spoken on the phone."

"Aha, of course, you're the brothel woman, aren't you?" Isobel's face broke into a knowing smile.

Gina bristled at the description but held her tongue. Daniel said, "Gina's a close friend of mine, Isobel, so if you don't mind…"

Isobel addressed Daniel while continuing to glance at Gina, "I said all along you were involved with that brothel, didn't I?"

"I wasn't, but so what? It's water under the bridge now."

Gina moved to catch Isobel's attention. Perhaps it was because she was so wound up that she couldn't hold back.

"Don't you ever feel ashamed of how you victimise people? Why don't you get a real job instead of spreading dirt around?"

Isobel stepped back and pointed her finger at her. "That's good coming from you. You're the one who works in the dirt business. Really, you're no better than one of your prostitutes."

Before she could respond, Daniel had raised his arm between the two women. "Okay, that's enough, Isobel. Haven't you got a meeting or something to go to?"

She smiled. "Whatever, at least it will be with decent people." She started to walk away. "Bye," she said with a cheery wave.

With difficulty, Gina fought the urge to hurl abuse at the retreating figure. If she didn't keep her emotions under control, she's be in no fit state for the meeting with Calloway. But it wasn't easy—she knew she'd been trumped by Isobel.

The security guard slapped two passes on the counter. "Level 9, you can go up now."

~~~

In the lift, she said, "What an absolute cow! How could you have worked with her?"

"By keeping my cool. I thought for a minute you were going to strangle her."

"It crossed my mind. No, I just wanted to get in her face."

"It didn't look that way. You need to be a lot calmer with Calloway. C'mon, take a couple of deep breaths and relax."

Gina barely managed one intake of breath before the lift stopped and the doors opened. Renata was waiting for them and led them into a small meeting room overlooking Sussex Street.

"Mr Calloway will be with you in a minute." She smiled a farewell and closed the door quietly behind her.

Gina was distinctly nervous at confronting Calloway and still smarting from the encounter with Isobel. A part of her was already preparing to apologise for wasting everyone's time. Another part, bolstered by Daniel's presence, told her she hadn't come all this way without giving it one last shot. As each part vied for supremacy, Calloway walked in, looking tanned and confident, followed by a heavy, dark-haired man carrying a bulging and well-worn leather briefcase.

Calloway said, without smiling, "So we meet again, Miss Russo, Daniel." He paused as they mutely acknowledged his greeting before introducing the other man. "This is Vern Richardson, my legal counsel." Richardson gave the pair a brief nod. Calloway said, "Please take a seat."

As the other man pulled a legal pad from his case, Calloway turned to Daniel and said briskly, "I've agreed to meet you under sufferance and I hope this won't be another waste of my time. What did you want to see me about?"

"It's not me who wants to see you. I was simply asked to facilitate the meeting. I'm here as Gina's friend."

Gina cleared her throat, ready to speak. She wished the other man wasn't there. She hadn't expected that. His large physical presence was intimidating.

She focused her attention on Calloway with as much determination as she could muster.

"I'll come straight to the point, Mr Calloway. In the past few weeks I've been following you around at lunchtime when you leave your office."

Calloway looked surprised and turned to Richardson. "Isn't that called stalking?" Richardson nodded and made a note.

"And it seems that most days you visit number eleven Lumley Street..."

Calloway's demeanour changed immediately, a hard look replacing the smug authority that had taunted her since he'd entered the room. He flashed a look at Richardson before saying, "Go on."

She clasped her hands to keep them from shaking and tried to maintain an even tone. "That house belongs to you. A young man lives there on his own."

She paused briefly as she watched Calloway's face begin to redden.

Emboldened, she said, "I believe he's your lover."

For a moment he seemed stunned. Then he shot from his seat with such force that the table shifted towards her. Richardson reared back in alarm, as did Daniel. Calloway's face was livid.

"You stupid, stupid woman!"

He was breathing with difficulty, clenching and unclenching his fists, the veins standing out on his neck. She shoved her chair back to stay out of reach, conscious of Daniel now crouching forward in his seat ready to intervene.

Calloway's furious eyes bore into her. When he next spoke, his voice was an intense hiss. "How dare you suggest that I'm involved in such a vile practice. How dare you even think that I would do anything as disgusting as that!"

She wasn't going to let him browbeat her. She'd plainly touched a raw nerve. Leaning across the table, she stabbed her finger at him. "I saw you hugging him. I saw him after you left. Close up. In his dressing gown, sleepy-eyed, just out of bed. I saw him! He looked gay enough to me. Of course he's your lover. How can you deny it?"

She barely had chance to right herself before he roared back, "How dare you accuse my son of being a homosexual!"

What he said didn't register straightaway, and when it did she sank slowly back into her seat, a feeling of dread seeping through her body. Calloway, still on his feet, still breathing heavily, watched her in silence. He appeared to be as shocked as she was by his declaration. He slowly shook his head before dropping into his chair.

No-one spoke. For a moment the only sound was Richardson's busy scribbling. Daniel gazed unbelievingly at Calloway; Calloway continued to stare with loathing at Gina; Gina tried not to look cowed.

Finally, in a tired voice, Calloway said, "You see what an absolute fool you've made of yourself? You've not only admitted to stalking me, you've now accused both me and my son of being homosexual, in front of witnesses, which constitutes—"

He turned to Richardson, who supplied the correct legal term without looking up. "—slander."

"So, Miss Russo, now it's your turn to be sued for defamation."

He got to his feet and walked slowly towards the door. With his hand resting on the door handle, he turned to Richardson and said, "I'll leave you with Miss

Russo, Vern. I'm sure you'll explain the gravity of the situation to her."

As he opened the door, Gina broke her silence.

"One minute, Mr Calloway..."

He glared at her. "Are you going to make more slanderous accusations?"

She kept him waiting for a second or two before saying, "You think you've got away with this, don't you? But you've overlooked one thing. You don't have any children, do you?"

Calloway hesitated, clearly unsure whether to continue on his way or reply to her assertion. He looked at Richardson. Some non-verbal signal must have passed between them because he closed the door and came back to the table.

The mocking demeanour had gone. When he spoke, his tone was matter-of-fact, verging on the confidential, as he addressed Gina.

"I'm afraid you've been misinformed. I do have a son. His name is Ian and he has serious mental health problems requiring daily medication. I try to visit him every day, either at lunchtime—as you're aware—or in the evening on my way home. I cook him a meal and make sure he takes his pills. They're powerful drugs and they make him sleepy, which is why you saw him in his dressing gown looking tired."

That didn't ring true. "But surely you'd have a nurse looking after him? And why isn't he in a clinic if he's so sick? A man in your position could easily afford the best treatment in the country."

"I don't have to explain any of this to you. However... He's been in and out of hospital most of his adult life. He hates being institutionalised. He's also had excellent nursing care at home. Unfortunately, he can be violent and unpredictable. Fortunately, he's never attacked me. Does that answer your question?"

"What happens when you can't visit him? You can't look after him all the time."

"I have a couple of people who go in to clean and do his laundry once or twice a week. They're able to manage in my absence. He's learning to trust them."

He sounded convincing and she couldn't think of anything to say that would shake his story. It was certainly conceivable that he wouldn't want to draw attention to a son who was mentally ill and violent. People were not understanding about that kind of thing.

Her spirits sank as she nodded agreement and wondered how deep a hole she'd dug for herself. Whether she liked it or not, he deserved an apology, and she needed to say it quickly. She cleared her throat and flashed Daniel an apologetic look. In that instant she glimpsed something in his expression that caused her to hesitate.

"You say he's your son?"

"Of course. Are you doubting me?"

She shook her head. "No, not at all." She paused, but her eyes never left Calloway's face. "It's only that I'm told your wife could never have children."

Calloway switched his attention to Daniel, who returned his gaze without flinching. For half a minute no-one spoke. Even Richardson put down his pen and watched the two men with keen interest. Then, abruptly, Calloway turned to mutter a few words in Richardson's ear. Both men rose to their feet.

Richardson said, "Please excuse us while we discuss something." He collected his pad and pen, dropped them into his briefcase, and followed Calloway out of the room.

After they'd left, Gina drew a deep breath and let it out in a long sigh.

"Wooo, that was scary." She stood and stretched out her arms to release the tension. Her chest and back were damp with sweat. "So you were right about him having a mistress all along."

"Yes, except I was about thirty years out."

"He nearly got away with it, didn't he?" She'd nearly apologised. If Daniel hadn't been with her, she'd be lapping at her wounds now. "Would you have said something if I'd not remembered about his wife?"

"Mum made it clear that I wasn't to say anything, but he knew I'd told you. I think I'm in for a tongue lashing when she finds out."

She was finding it hard not to feel guilty over exposing Calloway's deceit. After all, he'd taken care of his invalid son by himself. Despite his wealth, he'd been prepared to invest his own time in Ian's care. That involved sacrifice, which in turn required a dedication that could only have been fuelled by love.

A thought came to her. "Do you think his wife knows?"

"It's likely, but the *Monitor*'s readership certainly doesn't."

"What do you think they're talking about?"

"Damage control."

36. Revelation

Daniel was standing by the window when he heard the door open. He looked over his shoulder to see Vern Richardson entering the meeting room on his own. As Daniel returned to his seat, Richardson said, "Mr Calloway would like to see you in his office."

Daniel looked at Gina, wondering if she'd be happy left alone with Richardson. She seemed surprised but said nothing.

When he arrived at Calloway's outer office, Renata said, "Mr Calloway's on the phone. Please take a seat and I'll let you know when the call is over."

He wondered if he'd been dragged away so Richardson could get Gina to agree to something he'd have counselled her against. Calloway had been caught out. Having a mistress, no matter how long ago, would considerably damage his reputation, particularly with a grown-up son as evidence of the relationship. Calloway would have told Richardson to plug any possible leak. Would he do that by threats and intimidation? It seemed likely. Calloway was highly influential. A word in the right ear and Gina could be fitted up with a criminal charge that would be difficult to fight. Drugs supposedly found on Casa Rosa's premises, for example, would be a clincher.

He wished he was back in the meeting room with her.

Renata said, "Mr Calloway's free now. Please go in."

~~~

Vern Richardson shuffled sheets of paper around without any obvious purpose. Twice he took out his pen and made a quick notation, before recapping it and returning it to his pocket. Gina waited for him to speak, unsure of what to expect. She was just about to ask when he shoved the papers back into his briefcase and extracted the familiar yellow pad.

"Right…" He looked up and flashed a quick apologetic smile before resuming his usual sober demeanour. "Mr Calloway has asked me to bring matters to a satisfactory conclusion for all parties."

He looked to her for approval before continuing. She gave a slight nod, though she had no idea what she was agreeing to.

"We are prepared to meet your claim for damages arising from the perceived libel against yourself and your business. However, it is contingent upon your acceptance of certain warranties in the deed of settlement."

Gina was listening to his words so carefully that it took a moment for her to absorb the meaning of what he'd said.

"You want to settle subject to certain conditions?" she said, trying to keep her voice even. "All right, but shouldn't I have my lawyer here?"

"Once we have agreement in principle, we can leave them to handle the details."

"I'd be far happier if she were here with me."

"Let me just run through the main points with you first. Then you can call her and she can advise you."

"Okay, what are the conditions?"

"The first is that in order for Mr Calloway to settle the action you must drop your claim against the *Monitor* and warrant that you won't bring the same claim against the *Monitor* in the future. The second, as you probably realise, is that you do not communicate in any way to any other party the knowledge you have gained regarding Mr Calloway's son."

"What about Daniel? I can't stop him speaking about it. Not that he would, I'm sure."

He smiled. "I think you'll find that Mr Calloway is taking care of that right now."

~~~

Calloway met Daniel at the door and, unexpectedly, directed him away from his desk towards a low table in a corner of the office. He invited him to sit in one of three armchairs before returning to the door and calling Renata. She trotted in, notebook and pen at the ready.

Calloway said to Daniel, "Would you like tea or coffee, or a soft drink perhaps?"

The solicitous request took Daniel by surprise. He was being treated as an equal. Had Calloway finally realised he was no longer a cadet reporter? "A glass of water would be fine, thanks."

Renata left the office and Calloway came over and sat in the chair next to Daniel, close enough for Daniel to smell the other man's deodorant.

Calloway looked to be weighing up what to say. To break the silence, Daniel said, "That was an unpleasant meeting, Mr Calloway. I'm sorry it got out of hand."

Calloway said, "Yes, it was most unpleasant. Did Yvonne—your mother—know what was going to be discussed?"

"No, I wouldn't tell her."

"I wish you had."

"Would you still have agreed to see us?"

"Maybe. How well do you know your friend?"

"Gina? Very well, why."

"Do you trust her?"

"Of course. I know she can be hot-headed but she's discreet."

Calloway fell silent. Daniel watched him carefully, unsure of where the conversation might be leading. When Calloway resumed speaking, his tone was confidential.

"What I'm about to tell you must remain in this room. I need your assurance that you will treat it in strictest confidence."

"Of course." What else could he say?

Renata came in that moment with a tray bearing Daniel's glass of water and a cup of coffee. After she'd left, Calloway leaned towards him and said, "I spoke to your mother a few minutes ago. I thought it necessary under the circumstances."

Daniel remembered what his mother had told him: not to get involved as it would compromise her friendship with Calloway. He would get it in the neck when he got home. He wished Calloway hadn't spoken to her first.

"Why did you do that? She had no idea what Gina was going to say to you."

"No, she didn't. But she knows about Ian."

"She's never mentioned him."

"She's had her reasons not to." Calloway looked down at his hands, clasped as if in prayer, and up again. "There's something you should know, Daniel."

As Calloway's sharp blue eyes fixed upon him, Daniel realised what he was about to say.

"Ian's your half-brother."

Daniel was conscious of Calloway watching him, waiting for his reaction, but he was too stunned by the revelation to take it all in.

Calloway sat back and said, "This must come as a great shock to you."

Daniel gave a brief nod. His mind was in turmoil. So many questions jostled for answers that he didn't know which to ask first. "I'm struggling to take it in."

"I'm sorry you had to learn it from me."

"But why wasn't I told before? I don't understand." He'd been betrayed. All these years his mother had kept from him something he had a right to know. Couldn't she trust him? Was she so ashamed she daren't risk him knowing? What other reason could she have? It didn't make any sense.

Calloway spoke quietly. "It's rather complicated."

Daniel nodded. "I guessed it would be."

"When your mother joined the *Monitor*, I was editor-in-chief. I didn't take over from my father until he was forced to retire a few years later." He pointed to the wall behind Daniel. "That's the old man up there."

Daniel turned his head to look at the portrait. The family resemblance was unmistakable, especially the striking blue eyes.

Calloway continued, "He was known to everyone in the company—including me—as the Old Man. He was strict. He didn't tolerate poor attendance, untidiness, sloppy dress, any kind of bad behaviour. He demanded the best from people and he usually got it.

"From the moment I first met your mother I was infatuated. She was attractive, talented, her French accent sounded exotic to my ears. Of course, I was married and any sensible person in my position would have made sure not to get involved with her, but I was young, younger than you, and couldn't see the risk. Like a demented moth, I flitted around her, taking more interest in her work than it merited. We began seeing each other outside of work and one thing led to another. Then the Old Man found out."

Calloway paused, as if he couldn't bring himself to continue describing what must have been a painful and embarrassing experience.

"I was summoned to this office. He was furious, as you might expect. I won't go into details, but he pointed out the disgrace to the family, to my wife, to the company, to my faith. He told me to examine my conscience and do the right thing."

Daniel felt uneasy listening to this confession, particularly as it involved his mother and it was from someone who less than an hour earlier he'd regarded as an enemy.

Calloway continued. "I didn't need to think about it for long. It was obvious for the sake of my marriage, for Mary's sake, that I had no choice but to stop seeing Yvonne. When I told the Old Man of my decision, he said he would dismiss Yvonne, albeit with a generous termination payment. I asked him to let me do that and he reluctantly agreed. The Old Man lacked subtlety when it came to handling people."

He sat back and fixed his gaze on the portrait of the Old Man. "Things were never the same between us after that."

Daniel could imagine the younger Calloway having more concern for his own reputation than anyone else's. He would have worried that Daniel's mother might tell everyone about their affair.

"My mother, did you sack her?"

"I had no need to. As soon as I passed on what the Old Man had said, she resigned. She left the same day."

That didn't surprise Daniel. What did surprise him was that she'd allowed her emotions to get the better of her with Calloway, though what she'd found desirable in him escaped Daniel. It must have been his status in the organisation.

"I guess that wasn't the end of it, was it?"

"Yvonne got in touch with me four months later to say she was pregnant. My first reaction was to suggest she give up the child for adoption, but I was also delighted that I was about to become a father. I've always wanted children, but Mary had a hysterectomy shortly after we were married and she's never been well enough for us to consider adoption.

"I was with your mother when Ian was born in the Mater Hospital. I've never felt happier than when I held him that first time." He paused as if to savour the moment again, and Daniel couldn't help but be moved by the vision of Calloway cradling his new-born son— Daniel's half-brother—in his arms.

"You could have turned your back on everything and started a new life with Ian and my mother."

"Believe me, I thought about it long and often, but I wasn't strong enough. The truth is, I knew the Old Man was right. Your mother sensed it too. She never once suggested I leave my wife or break with my family.

"After Ian was born, your mother changed. It might have been post-natal depression or it could have been the realisation we had no future together. Either way, although Ian remained a bond, things were no longer the same between us.

"She asked me to arrange for Ian to be adopted. I know I'd thought about adoption before Ian's birth but now I was devastated at the thought. Your mother was insistent—not because she didn't love him but because she was in no position to care for him properly. Nowadays, her depression would have been treated but at the time it was considered temporary, if in fact it was recognised at all. Nevertheless, it continued and I had no option but to agree. I arranged for a private adoption agency to find suitable parents for him and I set up a trust fund to provide for his education."

Daniel said, "Did my mother know you'd be watching over Ian?"

"No. I felt she wouldn't have appreciated knowing. A year later she married your father. I don't know if she told him about Ian. I never asked, but she knew I didn't dare risk the Old Man finding out, let alone Mary.

"For eighteen years all went well with Ian. I received unofficial, periodic reports about him and his adoptive family. I was happy knowing he was growing up like any normal boy."

He paused before continuing, his tone now tinged with sadness. "One day I received a report to say he'd been in trouble. He was in his final year at high school and had started to play up. His behaviour was unpredictable. He could be pleasant and reasonable one day, violent and abusive the next. Matters came to a head when he was arrested for stealing a car and ran it off the road, completely writing it off. While he was in the remand centre he was diagnosed as schizophrenic. He was bound over for good behaviour and required to undergo treatment."

Daniel said, "Was that when you became involved?"

"Not then. I thought if he was receiving proper treatment, there would be no need for me to step in. But it got worse. Not long after that incident, he set fire to the school gym. This time he was sentenced, but instead of imprisonment he was diverted to a mental hospital. I arranged for him to be transferred to a private clinic, which is where he stayed for the next two years."

"Did that help him?"

Calloway shook his head. "Schizophrenia is difficult to treat."

"Why didn't you leave him in the clinic?"

"He was very unhappy there. I didn't want to see him suffer any more than he had to, so I bought him a place to live where I could keep a close eye on him and allow him a degree of independence. The rest of the story you know."

"So you met him and told him you were his father. How did he react to that?"

"Better than I expected. He knew he was adopted. While he was in hospital his adoptive parents separated and neither was keen to take him back."

"So my mother still doesn't know about him?"

"She does now. In the circumstances it was only fair I tell her before you did."

"You spoke to her just now?"

"Yes. She was shocked, to say the least. I tried to explain but I don't think she quite understood."

Daniel could imagine his mother sitting at home wondering what the hell was going on. A child whom she'd given up all those years ago unexpectedly reappears in her life, damaged, cared for only by Calloway, and he, Daniel, a significant factor in bringing about this disclosure.

"Does she want to see him?"

Calloway gave a slight shrug. "I don't know. I said I'd phone her again after I'd spoken to you."

Daniel thought it more than likely his mother would want to meet her son, but her long friendship with Calloway might now be ruptured by the deception.

"And your wife? Does she know?"

"I didn't know about Ian when I told her about the affair. After he was born, I thought, because of her liver disease, she had enough to put up with, so I didn't tell her."

Calloway became silent. Daniel took the opportunity to say what had been on his mind throughout their conversation.

"Don't you think you've been a bit of a hypocrite, taking the moral high ground in your newspapers while keeping your own behaviour out of sight?"

Calloway smiled apologetically. "I'm sorry if that's how it seems. I'm a born-again Christian, well aware I'm a sinner. What I did was offensive to God, I agree. However, you'll find I discriminate in what I campaign against. I focus on social issues like prostitution and gambling, not personal ones like adultery."

What was that about people in glasshouses and stone throwing? Daniel chose not to pursue the point.

37. Resolution

Daniel waited for Gina in the expansive foyer. He sat and stared sightlessly at the marble columns that rose to the high ceiling, turning over in his mind the implications of what Calloway had just told him.

He had a half-brother, someone other than himself who could call his mother his own. He was her first-born, a position Daniel had mistakenly assumed had been his for the past twenty-seven years. Didn't mothers have a special place in their hearts for first-borns?

He wondered if he should pay Ian a visit. Did Ian even know about him? He'd forgotten to ask Calloway that.

He remembered asking his mother if she'd had an affair with Calloway. She'd sidestepped the issue. He was uncomfortable with her deception, though now he understood why. Nevertheless, it rankled. She'd excluded him.

"You look like you've seen a ghost."

He hadn't seen Gina approach. "Sorry, I'm trying to come to grips with the news."

"I know, it's amazing, isn't it? I still can't believe he's settled."

"I mean, my news."

"Uh-oh." She sat down next to him while he summarised what Calloway had told him.

"Oh my god, Dan, that's incredible. You poor boy, you must feel your life has turned upside down." She clasped his hand in both of hers. "To think if it hadn't been for me you would never have known. This is so weird."

"I guess I'll have to get used to the idea. I wish she'd told me though, before all this. It's not how I'd have wanted to find out."

"Tricky one. I'm not sure what I would do in her situation. After all, she never expected you to learn the truth."

"I don't know what to think. It's taking a bit of getting used to." He wasn't looking forward to seeing his mother. There were bound to be recriminations, he was sure of it. He'd added a complication to her life, one she no doubt could do without. Nevertheless, like him, she'd have to get used to it. "Looking on the bright side, she's still my mother, isn't she?"

She squeezed his hand. "Yes, nothing's changed there. By the way, one of the settlement conditions is that I keep my mouth shut about your half-brother. I wouldn't have told anyone anyway, but they've bought my silence." She kissed him on the cheek. "Come on, let's go back to my place and tell Mama about the settlement."

~~~

Although she mentioned it in confidence to Simon, Gina held off announcing the news about the settlement until the next staff meeting.

She was impressed with Caroline, who not only continued to be supportive but also proved highly efficient, phoning her with regular updates on progress, the latest being that Caroline's father had received the draft agreement and pronounced it satisfactory. Gina needed to show her appreciation somehow. She'd make a start by sending her a beautiful and extravagant floral display. Caroline loved flowers.

As she prepared her notes for the meeting, it occurred to Gina that a small celebration was in order.

~~~

Daniel felt obliged to update Frank on Gina's battle with Calloway. Frank may not have been directly instrumental in helping her uncover Calloway's indiscretion but his willingness to provide background information had been the catalyst for instigating the first meeting with the media magnate.

Once again the two men met at the Civic Hotel for a lunchtime drink.

Frank was finishing his sandwich as he arrived. "Now, Danny boy, 'what good tidings comes with you?'"

When Daniel gave him a quizzical look, Frank added, "Ignore the grammar, it's Shakespeare. So what's up?"

Faced with the dilemma of protecting Calloway's confidences, not to mention his mother's role in the affair, and yet wanting to be open with him, he decided to economise with the truth.

"My mother spoke to Calloway and he must have thought it was a small price to pay to keep her on side."

It was Frank's turn to look quizzical. "I didn't realise she had that much influence."

If only he knew how much. "They still meet socially."

"I hope the settlement was a good one."

"Gina seems pleased with it."

"Lucky girl. There's not many who can say that."

Feeling guilty about withholding the full story, Daniel tossed the only nugget of information he had to Frank.

"By the way, Gina found out something about Convinza from an ex-boyfriend in the States."

Frank showed immediate interest and listened intently as he summarised what Gina had told him, including the sinister nature of Ted Salinski's operations. When he finished, Frank said, "I knew about the US connection."

"I thought you would."

"I know something else as well. The Trust is importing weapons into Australia."

"You serious?"

"Very."

"How did you find that out?"

"You know I've been investigating the Trust and MAP for some time now. It seems my researches were causing concern. The FBI tipped off our mob and I got a call from a mate of mine who works for ASIO, more or less telling me to lay off. Our blokes are very interested in Convinza."

"But why would Convinza be importing weapons?"

"That's what ASIO wants to know. From what you've told me, it looks as if they could be planning to create a private army here as well."

"Would Calloway know this?"

"Why wouldn't he?"

"Shit, Frank, he could be heading for real trouble."

"Do you care?"

Did he? He knew Calloway was a ruthless bastard but he'd stuck by Ian all those years. "I don't know, Frank. He can't be completely bad."

Frank studied Daniel carefully before saying, "Let me know when you find his good side. In all the time I've worked for him I've yet to see it." He finished his beer. "Fancy another?"

Madam, MBA

~~~

Attendance at the staff meetings had gradually increased but Gina was surprised at today's turnout. The new driver, Mickey, turned up with Baz, as did the usual complement of Kellie, Chloe, Tammi, Holly, Amber, Geri, and Juliette. Simon and Liz from Reception were there, together with Bella, who'd been taken on that week. Britney and Miranda, who normally started later in the afternoon, were also present, so there weren't enough seats for the latecomers. Gina had no idea why the number had swelled.

After going to her office to fetch a chair, she went through her notes and told the group that business was picking up faster than expected. Outcalls in particular had grown strongly as a result of the increased advertising.

When she finished speaking, she noticed Chloe trying to catch her eye. "Yes, Chloe?"

"I want to make an announcement." Everyone turned to look at her and for a moment she looked as if she'd changed her mind. "You know I've been training as a masseuse? Well, I'm still training but I've been offered a position at a fitness centre in North Sydney."

Gina looked on as everyone congratulated Chloe. One of her best girls was leaving. She'd been given fair warning it would happen and she'd even encouraged her to find a suitable course, but now she couldn't help feeling it reflected on her competence as a manager. Her mother wouldn't be pleased either.

She said, "I hope it works out well for you. When do you start?"

"In the New Year."

The mention of New Year reminded Gina that Christmas was almost upon them.

"How does everyone feel about a Christmas party?"

"When?" asked Geri.

"Let's say the middle of next week. Wednesday? We could close the doors at six. What do you think?"

Holly said, "Should we invite our best customers?"

Who were their best clients? Gina had no idea. She threw the question back to the group.

Juliette said the clients might not be happy meeting each other.

"That's a good point, Julie."

Holly said, "I suppose some of them would still want to mix business with pleasure."

"In that case," Gina said, "it's strictly staff only. We all need a night off."

"I'm going to dress up as one of Santa's elves," Tammi said.

Kellie replied, "Yeah, and I'll come as the Christmas fairy."

"As long as you don't try sitting on top of the tree," said Geri.

After they'd spent a few minutes discussing the party format, Gina decided to make her announcement.

"One more thing before we close the meeting." She got up from her chair and went to the fridge. She removed two magnums of Veuve Cliquot and placed them on the table.

"Is it your birthday?" Tammi asked.

She shook her head. While Simon went searching in the cupboards for glasses, she said, "It's something much better than my birthday. You'll be pleased to hear that the *Monitor* has come to its senses and settled our claim. So I think it calls for a little celebration, don't you?"

Without waiting for an answer, she grabbed the first bottle and eased off the cork, which exploded into the ceiling before bouncing back onto the table. The girls reared back, squealing in surprise.

"Oops, maybe I should have taken it outside."

While she poured out the champagne, she tried to deal with the questions being fired at her.

"How much was the settlement?"

"Enough to cover expenses and lost profits." That was all they needed to know. In fact, the settlement had been far more generous than she'd expected.

"Will they print an apology?"

"Yes, but it'll be buried in the middle of the paper where no-one will see it. I intend photocopying it and making sure it's left in our waiting rooms."

"What did you have to do to get them to settle?"

"I had some help in high places, but all along we had a strong case."

When the glasses were filled, Simon proposed a toast. "To Gina, for being a true Aussie battler and keeping us all in business."

They raised their glasses. "To Gina!"

A wave of satisfaction washed over her. Not only had she beaten Calloway and saved the business, she'd also won approval from her staff, and that meant more to her than she'd realised.

She found herself wondering if she should stay on and insist her mother take more time to recover. Who knew what another six months could achieve with everyone pulling together? No, that wasn't going to happen. She was becoming sentimental. Anyway, it was her mother's business, and she was the better manager.

It was time to focus on her own future.

38. Career move

Gina and Daniel were travelling out of the city along Broadway and onto Parramatta Road, passing the University of Technology on their right and Sydney University on the left. "I always wondered where they were," said Daniel, half to himself.

Gina looked across and smiled. She was driving, while he sat alongside, arm stretched across the back of her seat, waiting for an explanation for the unexpected journey. She'd called the previous day to invite him to go with her to see something 'very interesting', but it was on the understanding that he didn't ask what it was beforehand. She didn't want him to have any preconceptions.

Five minutes later, she turned left into a side street and stopped the car.

He looked around at the nondescript surroundings. "Okay, so where are we?"

"Camperdown."

"Never heard of it."

"It's only a few miles from where you grew up and you've never heard of it?"

"Uh-uh."

"You're definitely a boy from the Eastern Suburbs."

They got out of the car and walked back to Parramatta Road. It was an unusually warm day for

April and despite her eagerness she tried not to walk quickly.

"This had better be good," said Daniel, as he strode along beside her.

When they reached the corner, she took his hand and they crossed at the lights. She guided him down the road for fifty metres before coming to a halt. "Right, here we are."

A variety of businesses, apartment blocks, car yards, and a petrol station surrounded them. Heavy traffic rumbled past in an unbroken procession.

"Impressive, Gina. You've brought me all this way so I can experience the busiest road in Sydney at close quarters."

"Look over there." She let go of his hand and pointed to a rundown backpackers' hostel on the opposite side of the road.

Daniel stared at the building and then back at Gina, clearly puzzled by her intentions. "You're not seriously—"

"—thinking of buying it? Why not? That place could be a goldmine in the right hands. It's on the market and it's a steal at the price."

"Why would you want to own a dosshouse like that? Or were you thinking of turning it into another brothel?"

"Mama is the brothel expert, not me." She grabbed his arm. "Look at where it is, Dan. It's such a great location—close to public transport, on a main road, only a few minutes away from two universities and two major hospitals—think of the out-of-town visitors they must get—and it's not that far from the city centre."

"True, but—"

"Now, try to imagine it looking elegant with the word 'Hotel' on a board outside."

He gazed across the road before answering. "You want to turn that shambles into an up-market, boutique hotel?"

"Of course. Four stars at least."

"Aren't you forgetting something? You don't know anything about hotel management."

She'd expected that. "It's the hospitality industry and I know something about that. Don't forget—I managed to keep Casa Rosa running at short notice while my mum was sick. Anyway, I can learn. And I can hire people who know the business."

She took his hand again and led him back to the traffic lights. As they waited to cross, she said, "I've already been to see it, and I've asked the agent to let us look around on our own. The manager knows we're coming."

~~~

Seeing it for the second time, Gina was apprehensive. Daniel would be wondering if she'd taken leave of her senses. Could he, like her, see past the shabby décor and imagine how it might be transformed? She had him agree that the building appeared to be solidly constructed. She pointed out the sprinkler system and the rudimentary lift—the type that needed both doors closed manually before it could be operated—which they took on a slow journey to the top floor.

Gina asked the manager to leave them to find their own way down.

"I'd have to replace the lift, it's simply not big enough, and a barrow load of money needs spending on conversions. The plumbing looks like the Romans put it in, so that'll need replacing. The only air conditioning is in the manager's office. In some ways, all I'm buying is a shell."

Daniel looked at her thoughtfully. "Are you sure you want to do this? What happened to those lofty ideas you had of being a high-powered executive?"

"Running Casa Rosa has helped me to see things differently. It proved more challenging than I expected, but it was also far more satisfying. I was doing it for me and Mama, not for some large, faceless corporation. Now I have the bug. I love the idea of creating a successful business from scratch."

"Great, but I don't see how you can stump up the money to buy and renovate this place. It won't be cheap."

"I know, but I now have some capital to invest. Mama says I can use the settlement to start my own business if I want to."

"I thought she needed it to pay off her debts."

"She says she was paying off the loans before I took over and she'll carry on paying them off now she's back."

"Even so, the settlement can't be enough to buy this place."

"You're right. I've spoken to the bank. They're willing to help, but... The thing is, they would rather I had a co-investor. They think they'd be too exposed if it were just me." She waited until she had his complete attention. "I was wondering, suppose we bought it together?"

It took him a moment to recover from his surprise at the suggestion. "You mean, become business partners?"

"Why not? Forget being a corporate warrior and become an entrepreneur instead. It's a bigger challenge and you never know where it might lead."

"You want me to give up my job and work with you?"

Perhaps it was too much to expect him to share her enthusiasm. "Is that such a bad thing?"

"I don't know. Working together could be the kiss of death for our relationship."

She turned to look out of the dusty window. The view was of rooftops and backyards. "I've been thinking about that. If we focused on what we're each good at—me managing the day-to-day business, you doing all the marketing and publicity—it would minimise any friction."

He joined her at the window and studied her face. "How much thought have you put into this?"

"I came here last week with the agent. We spent nearly an hour going over it and I asked him a hundred questions. Afterwards, I drafted a business plan. I know it's loaded with ballpark figures and assumptions, but it showed a decent return on investment. Of course, I wouldn't commit to anything until I had real estimates."

"What about council approval?"

"The agent said it would be a breeze."

"It'll be a lot of money, Gina."

"Too much?"

"I suppose I could break into the money Grandma Bouvier left me." He looked again at the shabby surroundings. "Mmm...I need to have a long, hard think about this."

"Don't do it just for me, will you? It has to be a business arrangement—you need to be sure you really want to do it."

~~~

They worked their way back down the building. On each floor they rechecked areas of concern, speculating on the cost and feasibility of improvements until they reached the lobby. Gina thanked the manager for allowing them to look around and they stepped out into bright sunshine.

Daniel stood on the pavement edge and looked up at the unimposing façade. "We'll need to get professional estimates for all the work before we even think of making an offer."

He was right. They couldn't go off half-cocked on such a project. They needed sound cost estimates or the business would be in strife before it got off the ground. The issue of how long it would take to finish the conversions had to be addressed as well—that time represented lost income.

Daniel said, "The car park at the back needs covering over and making secure."

"At least it's a decent size," she said.

This second viewing had brought home to her how big an undertaking it would be. She was having second thoughts about asking him to be her partner. Would he do it mainly to please her? And did they have the business nous to turn a rundown hostel into a chic boutique hotel? It was a big step up from running a small bordello.

She went to stand next to him, half closed her eyes and tried to imagine how the building might look with rendered brickwork, new windows, an imposing entrance, and an elegant sign with a classy name. "The Ritz"? Perhaps not.

She cast a sideways glance at Daniel. He looked as serious as she'd ever seen him.

Maybe with hard work they could make it so successful that after three or four years they'd open a second, and then a third—eventually a chain of hotels all around Australia. Why not? She didn't get to be a Harvard MBA without having some talent. And Daniel was well-connected. He'd be able to publicise the hotel by word-of-mouth as well as by more conventional means.

Her thoughts were disturbed by Daniel suddenly throwing his arms around her. "Okay, sweetheart. If you're game then I'm interested in taking it to the next stage."

She grinned and hugged him back. "I knew you couldn't resist a challenge."

He kissed her. "You're right. You're irresistible" He pulled her closer and they kissed again, this time a longer, lingering embrace.

Oblivious to the honking of car horns and truck drivers' ribald calls, she closed her eyes and imagined herself on the *Daily Monitor*'s front page—Gina Russo, Australian Businesswoman of the Year.

Well, maybe not the *Daily Monitor*.

THE END

Acknowledgements

Never having visited a brothel or hired the services of a prostitute, I was dependent on other sources for authenticity. Here are the main ones.

Studies

Working girls: prostitutes, their life and social control

Published in 1991, this is the most extensive study on the subject of prostitution carried out in Australia. Dr Roberta Perkins conducted the survey on behalf of the Australian Institute of Criminology. It disposes of many misconceptions about the lives and motivations of sex workers.

Books

In My Skin

A powerful and extremely well-written memoir by Kate Holden, a former escort, whose drug addiction led her into prostitution.

There's a Bear in There (and he wants Swedish)

Merridy Eastman was a *Play School* presenter whose acting career stalled. Needing to work, she became a night receptionist in a Sydney brothel. Her account of brothel life is both entertaining and informative.

Red Velvet: Memoirs of a Working Girl

After hearing a radio interview with Lisa Lou, I bought this book (which came bound with a red satin garter). My copy was in serious need of good editing, but it provided further background.

Conversations in a Brothel: Men Tell Why They Do it

I bought this book by Jacquelynne Bailey after seeing a TV documentary *Why Men Pay For it* that it had inspired. It's a fascinating read.

Callgirl: Confessions of a Double Life

This book by Jeannette Angell was sent to me by a friend who knew I was researching the subject. Angell has a PhD in social anthropology. She became a Boston (Mass) callgirl when, destitute, she answered a newspaper ad for an escort. For three years she led a double life, lecturing in the evenings while seeing clients during the day.

Other Sources

Conversation Hour: Inside a Brothel...

Richard Fidler spoke with three brothel owners in this radio interview. I remember sitting in a supermarket carpark jotting down notes as the interview progressed. I found it very educational.

Australian Federal Police

The PR people were very responsive to my questions on illegal immigration and sexual servitude.

Newspapers

I received considerable help on how newspapers really operate from ex-journalists, especially the late Neil Marr.

Internet

For a brief period, I helped administer an escorts' website, through which I was able to chat to some of the women and gain first-hand accounts of the business.

...and finally

To my wife, Janis, for her proofreading and prolonged support, our daughter, Abigail, for proofreading and vetting the legal stuff, and to both Abigail and son Matthew for providing general encouragement.

About the Author

Perry Gretton lives high on a hill on the beautiful Central Coast of New South Wales, Australia, overlooking Tuggerah Lakes and the Pacific Ocean.

Apart from writing fiction, he produces technical documents and videos, carries out proofreading, editing, and the occasional manuscript appraisal, and designs and develops websites.

Perry is married with two children and a cat.

Website: www.perrygretton.com

www.ingramcontent.com/pod-product-compliance
Lightning Source LLC
Chambersburg PA
CBHW071854290426
44110CB00013B/1145